# STILL KILLING

## Landmines in Southern Africa

**Human Rights Watch Arms Project**

**Human Rights Watch**
**New York · Washington · London · Brussels**

ISBN: 1-56432-206-8
Library of Congress Catalog Card Number: 97-77862

*Human Rights Watch Arms Project*
The Human Rights Watch Arms Project was established in 1992 to monitor and prevent arms transfers to governments or organizations that commit gross violations of internationally recognized human rights and the rules of war and promote freedom of information regarding arms transfers worldwide.  Joost R. Hiltermann is the director; Stephen D. Goose is the program director; Alex Vines is the research associate; Zahabia Adamaly, Andrew Cooper, and Ernst Jan Hogendoorn are research assistants; Rebecca Bell is the associate;  William M. Arkin, Kathi L. Austin,  Monica Schurtman, and Frank Smyth are consultants.

Addresses for Human Rights Watch
485 Fifth Avenue, New York, NY  10017-6104
Tel: (212) 972-8400, Fax: (212) 972-0905, E-mail: hrwnyc@hrw.org

1522 K Street, N.W., #910, Washington, DC  20005-1202
Tel: (202) 371-6592, Fax: (202) 371-0124, E-mail: hrwdc@hrw.org

33 Islington High Street, N1 9LH London, UK
Tel: (171) 713-1995, Fax: (171) 713-1800, E-mail: hrwatchuk@gn.apc.org

15 Rue Van Campenhout, 1000 Brussels, Belgium
Tel: (2) 732-2009, Fax: (2) 732-0471, E-mail: hrwatcheu@gn.apc.org

Web Site Address: http://www.hrw.org
Gopher Address://gopher.humanrights.org:5000/11/int/hrw
Listserv address: To subscribe to the list, send an e-mail message to majordomo@igc.apc.org with "subscribe hrw-news" in the body of the message (leave the subject line blank).

# HUMAN RIGHTS WATCH

Human Rights Watch conducts regular, systematic investigations of human rights abuses in some seventy countries around the world. Our reputation for timely, reliable disclosures has made us an essential source of information for those concerned with human rights. We address the human rights practices of governments of all political stripes, of all geopolitical alignments, and of all ethnic and religious persuasions. Human Rights Watch defends freedom of thought and expression, due process and equal protection of the law, and a vigorous civil society; we document and denounce murders, disappearances, torture, arbitrary imprisonment, discrimination, and other abuses of internationally recognized human rights. Our goal is to hold governments accountable if they transgress the rights of their people.

Human Rights Watch began in 1978 with the founding of its Helsinki division. Today, it includes five divisions covering Africa, the Americas, Asia, the Middle East, as well as the signatories of the Helsinki accords. It also includes three collaborative projects on arms transfers, children's rights, and women's rights. It maintains offices in New York, Washington, Los Angeles, London, Brussels, Moscow, Dushanbe, Rio de Janeiro, and Hong Kong. Human Rights Watch is an independent, nongovernmental organization, supported by contributions from private individuals and foundations worldwide. It accepts no government funds, directly or indirectly.

The staff includes Kenneth Roth, executive director; Michele Alexander, development director; Cynthia Brown, program director; Barbara Guglielmo, finance and administration director; Robert Kimzey, publications director; Jeri Laber, special advisor; Lotte Leicht, Brussels office director; Susan Osnos, communications director; Jemera Rone, counsel; Wilder Tayler, general counsel; and Joanna Weschler, United Nations representative.

The regional directors of Human Rights Watch are Peter Takirambudde, Africa; José Miguel Vivanco, Americas; Sidney Jones, Asia; Holly Cartner, Helsinki; and Eric Goldstein, Middle East (acting). The project directors are Joost R. Hiltermann, Arms Project; Lois Whitman, Children's Rights Project; and Dorothy Q. Thomas, Women's Rights Project.

The members of the board of directors are Robert L. Bernstein, chair; Adrian W. DeWind, vice chair; Roland Algrant, Lisa Anderson, William Carmichael, Dorothy Cullman, Gina Despres, Irene Diamond, Fiona Druckenmiller, Edith Everett, Jonathan Fanton, James C. Goodale, Jack Greenberg, Vartan Gregorian, Alice H. Henkin, Stephen L. Kass, Marina Pinto Kaufman, Bruce Klatsky, Harold Hongju Koh, Alexander MacGregor, Josh Mailman, Samuel K. Murumba, Andrew Nathan, Jane Olson, Peter Osnos, Kathleen Peratis, Bruce Rabb, Sigrid Rausing, Anita Roddick, Orville Schell, Sid Sheinberg, Gary G. Sick, Malcolm Smith, Domna Stanton, Nahid Toubia, Maureen White, Rosalind C. Whitehead, and Maya Wiley.

# CONTENTS

# ACKNOWLEDGMENTS

This report was researched and written by Alex Vines, research associate for the Human Rights Watch Arms Project and Human Rights Watch/Africa. It is based primarily on his fieldwork in southern Africa from September 1992 to April 1997. The report also draws upon material from previous Human Rights Watch reports on Angola, Mozambique, Namibia and Zimbabwe. Stephen Goose, program director of the Arms Project, edited the report and wrote Chapter XII.

Information was helpfully provided by: the United Nations Coordination Unit in Luanda; João Paulo Borges Coelho, Department of History, Eduardo Mondlane University, Maputo; João Honwana at the Centre for Conflict Resolution, University of Cape Town; and, Lt. Col. Martin Rupiah (Ret.) Director of the Centre for Defence Studies, Department of History, University of Zimbabwe.

Field research was assisted by grants from Oxfam (UK/Ireland) in 1993 and Oxfam (America) in 1994. The Arms Project gratefully acknowledges funding from the Rockefeller Foundation and the Ploughshares Fund.

# ABBREVIATIONS

ANC          African National Congress, the South African ruling party.

CCW         1980 Convention on Conventional Weapons.

CMAO        Central Mine Action Office, the U.N. liaison office for mine clearance in Angola.

CND         Comissão Nacional de Desminagem (National Demining Commission), the coordinating body for mine clearance in Mozambique.

COREMO    Comité Revolucionário Moçambicana (Mozambique Revolutionary Committee), a pre-independence Mozambican nationalist group.

DHA         U.N. Department of Humanitarian Affairs.

DPKO        U.N. Department of Peacekeeping Operations.

FAA         Forças Armadas Angolanas (Angolan Armed Forces), the new, post-1992 election military of the Angolan government.

FAM        Forças Armadas Moçambicanas (Mozambican Armed Forces), the pre-election government army.

FALA       Forças Armadas de Libertação de Angola, UNITA's army.

FAPLA     Forças Armadas para a Libertação de Angola, the Angolan government's old, pre-election armed forces.

FLEC       Frente Nacional de Libertação de Cabinda, Cabinda separatist groups.

FNLA      Frente Nacional de Libertação de Angola, one of the three nationalist groups that fought for independence in Angola.

FRELIMO    Frente de Libertação de Moçambique (Mozambique Liberation Front), the ruling party in Mozambique.

| | |
|---|---|
| ICRC | International Committee of the Red Cross. |
| INAROEE | Instituto Nacional de Remoção dos Engenhos Explosivos (Angolan National Institute for the Removal of Explosive Ordnance), the official coordinating body for mine clearance in Angola. |
| MK | Umkhonto we Sizwe, the ANC's military wing during the Apartheid years. |
| MPLA | Movimento Popular de Libertação de Angola (Popular Movement for the Liberation of Angola), the MPLA is now the governing party of the government of Angola. |
| NAMPOL | Namibian Police Force. |
| NDF | Namibian Defence Force, the post-independence army. |
| NGO | Nongovernmental organization. |
| OAU | Organization of African Unity. |
| ONUMOZ | U.N. Operation in Mozambique, the U.N. mission in Mozambique 1992-1995. |
| PLAN | People's Liberation Army of Namibia, the military wing of SWAPO during its nationalist struggle. |
| PVs | Protected Villages. |
| RENAMO | Resistência Nacional Moçambicana (Mozambique National Resistance), the former rebel force in Mozambique. |
| SADC | Southern Africa Development Community: Angola, Botswana, Lesotho, Malawi, Mauritius, Mozambique, Namibia, South Africa, Swaziland, Tanzania, Zambia and Zimbabwe. |

| | |
|---|---|
| SADF | South African Defense Forces, the apartheid South African army. |
| SANDF | South African National Defence Force, the post-apartheid military. |
| SAWDF | South West Africa Defence Force, the pro-apartheid Namibian unit. |
| SPLA | Southern People's Liberation Army (SPLA). |
| SWAPO | South West Africa People's Organization. |
| UCAH | U.N. Humanitarian Assistance Coordination Unit. |
| UN/ADP | U.N. Accelerated Demining Program, in Mozambique from 1995. |
| UNAVEM | United Nations Angola Verification Mission. |
| UNDP | United Nations Development Program. |
| UNHCR | U.N. High Commissioner for Refugees. |
| UNICEF | U.N. Children's Fund. |
| UNITA | União Nacional para a Independência Total de Angola (National Union for the Total Independence of Angola), the opposition guerrilla force in Angola. |
| UNOHAC | U.N. Humanitarian Assistance Coordination Office in Mozambique until UNOMOZ withdrawal. |
| UNTAG | U.N. Transition Assistance Group in Namibia in 1989. |
| UPA | Union of the Angola Peoples. |
| WFP | U.N. World Food Program. |
| ZDF | Zambia Defence Forces, the Zambian army. |

| | |
|---|---|
| ZANLA | Zimbabwe African National Liberation Army, the armed wing of ZANU during the Zimbabwean nationalist struggle. |
| ZAPU | Zimbabwe African People's Union, the second largest party in Zimbabwe and headed by Joshua Nkomo. |
| ZANU | Zimbabwe African National Union, the main ruling party in Zimbabwe and headed by President Mugabe. |
| ZIPRA | Zimbabwe People's Revolutionary Army, the armed wing of ZAPU during the nationalist struggle. |
| ZNA | Zimbabwe National Army, the post-independence army. |

# I. SUMMARY AND RECOMMENDATIONS

Southern Africa is the most mine-affected region in the world. For over thirty years landmines have been killing and maiming civilians throughout the region. The first known mine casualty occurred in northern Angola in 1961. By 1997 ten of the twelve countries in the Southern Africa Development Community (SADC) had recorded landmine incidents.

A conservative estimate is that southern Africa has today some twenty million mines in its soil. Mines have claimed over 250,000 victims since 1961. The experience of southern Africa demonstrates graphically that the only solution to the global landmines crisis is a comprehensive ban on the use, production, stockpiling and export of antipersonnel mines, combined with greatly expanded programs for mine clearance and victim assistance.

The use of antipersonnel landmines has been widespread in the colonial and post-colonial wars that have plagued much of southern Africa for the last three decades. During this period many millions of landmines were imported into southern Africa, while a smaller number were manufactured there.

Sixty-seven types of antipersonnel mines from twenty-one countries have been found in southern Africa. These countries are: Austria; Belgium; China; Cuba; former Czechoslovakia; France; former East Germany; former West Germany; Hungary; Israel; Italy; Portugal; Romania; former Soviet Union; South Africa; Spain; Sweden; United Kingdom; United States; former Yugoslavia; and Zimbabwe.

Only some 400,000 mines have been removed since serious clearance operations began in 1991. Despite international clearance efforts in Angola landmines continue to be planted by both the National Union for the Total Independence of Angola (União Nacional para a Independência Total de Angola, UNITA) and government forces. In recent years landmines have also been used in criminal acts in Angola and Mozambique. Criminal groups linked to drugs and gun-running have laid landmines in central Mozambique in order to stop the restoration of state control in remote areas. Some of these mines have been found on access roads to the Cahora Bassa hydroelectric power line rehabilitation project, thereby threatening the viability of this multinational, multi-million dollar commercial project. In 1996 landmines were available in Angola, Mozambique, Namibia and Zambia in exchange for food or second-hand clothing. Mines can be bought in South Africa for as little as U.S.$25.

Not all landmines have reached southern Africa through open, legal channels. In the case of former Rhodesia and apartheid South Africa landmines were purchased in contravention of U.N. sanctions. South Africa also used stocks of landmines captured in its invasions of Angola in the 1980s to supply insurgent

1

forces in Angola, Mozambique and Zimbabwe, as well as the illegal Rhodesian regime. The U.S. supplied landmines to UNITA rebels in Angola until 1991. More recently, in 1993 and 1994, UNITA rebels in Angola purchased weapons, including landmines, in contravention of U.N. sanctions.

The provenance of landmines transferred to southern Africa can be complex. For example, in the 1970s French landmines removed from the ground in Algeria were later sold to Mozambique. Today, mines removed from the ground in Mozambique by both the government and the Mozambique National Resistance (Resistência Nacional Moçambicana, Renamo) are sometimes preserved for re-use or sale.

At least two countries in southern Africa have produced and exported antipersonnel landmines—South Africa and Zimbabwe. In 1997, both nations pledged no further production or export. Namibia may also have been a producer, according to U.S. military assessments.

**Limited Military Utility**

A close look at southern Africa's landmine legacy over the last thirty years reveals few, if any, examples where antipersonnel mines have provided significant or lasting military advantages. Government minefields in Mozambique were quickly breached by Renamo rebels during the 1977-1992 war. In Angola, government mine belts around the main towns did not stop UNITA from capturing several of them. In the 1960s and 1970s, saboteurs simply shoveled their way across the minefield protecting the Kariba power station in Rhodesia, did their damage and left. In 1988 South Africa scrapped plans to build a thirty-kilometer-long minefield along Namibia's northern border in part because it determined that such a barrier would only delay any potential invasion by some thirty minutes.

The use of antipersonnel mines has provided short-term military advantages in some cases, but often at tremendous cost to civilians and often in contravention of humanitarian law. This was the case in Mozambique for the Mozambique Liberation Front (Frente de Libertação de Moçambique, Frelimo) during 1972-73 in its Tete offensive against the *aldeamentos* (protected villages) during its nationalist struggle against Portuguese colonialism. UNITA, both in the 1976-1992 war and in the 1992-1994 war used landmines to deny food production and access to water sources in certain areas of Angola, resulting in horrendous civilian suffering.

Soldiers and guerrillas alike fear and dislike landmines. In Mozambique, Renamo had to offer special privileges to its forces to clear and use them. An Angolan sapper (mine specialist) from the Angolan Armed Forces (Forças Armadas Angolanas, FAA), admitted in October 1996 that, "I hate mines. They destroy the lives of Angolans on a daily basis and make our country poorer. They are the worst sort of environmental pollution you can find."

## Human, Social, Economic and Environmental Costs

Landmines are blind weapons that cannot distinguish between the footfall of a soldier and that of an old woman gathering firewood. They are inherently indiscriminate weapons. Landmines recognize no cease-fire and, long after the fighting has stopped, they can maim or kill the children and grandchildren of the soldiers who laid them. An old man who planted a landmine in northern Angola in 1965 recently returned to help find it. The mine was still operational, still waiting after thirty years to claim a victim.

The ongoing threat created by live landmines can prevent civilians from living in their homes and using their fields, and can seriously threaten the ability of an entire country to re-build long after the war has ended. Simple fear of landmines, whether they are present or not, denies land and homes to people.

In Mozambique's Maputo province, the village of Mapulenge, which had been the center of a community of 10,000 people, was deserted for four years because local people had been told it was badly mined. A three-month mine clearance operation in the village in 1994 uncovered only four mines. These, and the spreading of rumors, had been sufficient to depopulate the area for four years. Four antipersonnel mines costing U.S.$40 resulted in years of fear and tens of thousands of dollars spent, before the community felt safe to return. Also in Mozambique, the U.N. concluded a contract for the clearance of 2,010 kilometers of roads in 1994. Many of these roads had been closed for years. Yet clearance produced only twenty-eight mines, although other pieces of unexploded ordnance were also uncovered.

In Namibia, on December 22, 1995, a twelve-year-old boy named Absalom Luuwa lost his left leg when he stepped on a South African R2M2 antipersonnel mine in a minefield the South Africans laid around Ruacana before Namibian independence in 1990. Absolom's family was devastated. He could no longer walk to school and was sent eighty miles away to a hostel. His family cannot afford to pay for his medical treatment. The whole community is frightened by the threat of landmines and has moved the local school several miles away, making children lose more study time. The councillor of Ruacana, Absolom's uncle, explained in April 1996: "This minefield has been cleared twice, by the South Africans and now by the Namibian Defense Force with U.S. military help. But these mines still kill and maim. We don't trust anybody now about these mines — Americans, South Africans and our government. The solution is to ban these mines, and those who make these killers should pay for their legacy. Ruacana cries because of mines. Our families want them eradicated. If you can do it for small-pox, you can do it for landmines."

Antipersonnel mines are also notable for the particularly egregious nature of the injuries they cause. The majority of landmine explosions that do not cause death result in traumatic or surgical amputation. In Angola there are some 70,000 victims seriously maimed by landmine injuries. As reported in the *British Medical Journal* in 1991:

> Landmines...have ruinous effects on the human body: they drive dirt, bacteria, clothing and metal and plastic fragments into the tissue causing secondary infections. The shock wave from an exploding mine can destroy blood vessels well up the leg, causing surgeons to amputate much higher than the site of the primary wound.

The result for the individual is not one but, typically, a series of painful operations, often followed by a life at the margins of a society heavily dependent on manual labor. In Zambia, Sylvia Maphosa, a pregnant Lusaka housewife, stepped on a landmine in 1991 laid over fifteen years before, while collecting firewood outside Lusaka. She cannot walk and speaks with difficulty. She sustained severe head wounds and had her right limbs shattered in the explosion.

The landmine legacy in southern Africa has serious environmental consequences. In Zimbabwe, the border minefields have become a haven for tsetse fly. Wildlife also suffer. Mines used by poachers in Angola's Mupa National Park have decimated elephant stocks. In Zimbabwe since 1980, more than 9,000 cattle have been reported killed in minefields. The Hwange and Gonarezhou national game parks have also reported mine incidents involving wildlife. There have been several cases of buffalo wounded by landmines attacking people living near the game parks.

## Mine Clearance

Angola and Mozambique have been major targets of international assistance in mine clearance. Yet, only some U.S.$45 million has been invested in mine clearance in southern Africa since May 1991, resulting in less than 400,000 mines being cleared, the majority of these from large defensive minefields.

Clearance efforts have been surrounded with controversy. In Mozambique, the U.N. mine clearance program became victim to inter-agency competition for control over funds and bureaucratic delays. It was also thrown into disrepute when a U.S.$7.5 million contract for clearance of priority roads went to a consortium of the British weapons manufacturer, Royal Ordnance, Lonrho de Moçambique and Mechem of South Africa. Both Royal Ordnance and Mechem are companies which have produced or designed landmines in the past, some of which in all likelihood have been found in Mozambique. Mechem in mid-1995 received a multi-million U.N. contract for clearance of priority roads in Angola and in 1996 another contract for Mozambique.

The record in southern Africa shows that, in and of itself, mine clearance cannot effectively deal with the landmine crisis. It is often too little, too late. When undertaken at all, efforts are often badly funded and poorly coordinated. Even if demining were given top priority, it would not be a solution. Mines are being laid worldwide far faster than they are being removed. Moreover, while the average mine costs between U.S.$10 and $20, the average direct and indirect costs of removal range from U.S. $300 to $1,000 a mine—a ratio frightening in its implications for a region with roughly twenty million uncleared mines and new ones still being planted.

## Country Summaries

### Angola

Angola is the most mine-affected country in southern Africa, with U.N. and U.S. estimates as high as nine to fifteen million mines. Globally, only Afghanistan is thought to be more heavily mined. Angola also has one of the highest rates of landmine injuries per capita in the world. Out of a population of about nine million, it has over 70,000 amputees, one in 470 people. Even with renewed peace, the millions of mines present a hazard not only to civilians who might step on them, but also to the reconstruction of the war-devastated economy and the rebuilding of society.

Mines were used extensively by both government and rebel forces during the near continuous fighting between 1961 and 1994. Mine warfare intensified during the "third war" from late 1992 to late 1994, with thousands of new mines being laid by both sides to obstruct roads and bridges, to despoil agricultural land and to encircle besieged towns with mine belts up to three kilometers wide.

Landmines continued to be laid after the signing of—and in violation of—the Lusaka peace accord of November 1994, as part of the continuation of sporadic hostilities, as a barrier to freedom of movement, and in order to mark frontiers in contested zones. In 1997, Human Rights Watch continued to receive reports of limited planting of new landmines by government and UNITA forces, Cabindan factions, as well as bandits and criminal elements.

As many as fifty-one different types of antipersonnel mines from eighteen countries have been identified in Angola. Existing records on the locations of mines are extremely scanty. There is still no comprehensive mine survey for Angola. According to various estimates, only some 80,000 mines have been cleared since 1992, and some 150 square kilometers of land returned to the population. The United Nations, the government, UNITA, commercial firms and nongovernmental organizations are all involved in mine clearance activities in Angola.

The government of Angola first publicly stated its support for a total prohibition on antipersonnel mines in May 1996. However, the government has done little to demonstrate its commitment to that objective, while showing a reluctance to begin significant destruction of its stockpile of mines.

## Botswana

Rhodesian forces planted landmines in northern Botswana in the late 1970s. All the mines reportedly have been cleared. The Botswana Defense Force maintains a stockpile of mines. The government of Botswana has been largely silent on the mine ban issue, but encouragingly attended the February 1997 international conference in Austria aimed at developing a total ban treaty.

## Malawi

In the late 1980s and early 1990s, Malawian troops used landmines to protect the Nacala railway corridor from Renamo attack. Many of the mines were supplied by the United States. Malawi also has a problem with mines along the Mozambique border, where mine-laying strayed inside Malawi, though landmine incidents are infrequent. The government of Malawi had not been active in international efforts to control or ban antipersonnel mines. However at the 4th International NGO Conference on Landmines, held in Maputo, Mozambique in February 1997, a Malawi official stated that Malawi "condemn(s) the manufacture, export, import, use and stockpiling of any type of mines." He indicated Malawi's support for the Ottawa process aimed at the signing of a total ban treaty in December 1997, and said, "Malawi is now working on draft legislation to join the world community to ban landmines subject to approval by Parliament; and Civil Society is committed to campaign for the ban and eradication of landmines in the world."

## Mozambique

As in Angola, landmines were used extensively by all sides in the decades-long fighting in Mozambique. Mines have claimed some 10,000 victims and continue to do so on a daily basis. More than 1,000 people have been injured by mines since the October 1992 peace accord. Landmines constitute one of the most immediate obstacles to postwar redevelopment, and hinder delivery of relief aid, resettlement, and agricultural and commercial reconstruction.

Human Rights Watch believes that the frequently cited U.N. estimate of two million mines in Mozambique is too high, with the real total in the hundreds, or even tens, of thousands. But the number of mines is not the measure of the problem. Mozambique clearly has a serious problem that threatens civilians daily and is curtailing economic reconstruction.

A limited number of mines have continued to be planted since the peace accord, by both government and Renamo forces, in some cases simply to wage local vendettas. Bandit groups, criminals, and poachers have also used mines.

Nearly forty types of antipersonnel mines from more than one dozen nations have been reported in Mozambique. As noted above, mine clearance efforts in Mozambique have been plagued with delays and controversy.

President Chissano announced in October 1995 that Mozambique was prepared to head an international campaign against antipersonnel mines, but little concrete action was taken for the next year and one-half as the Mozambican military wanted to retain the option of using landmines. However, as the 4th International NGO Conference on Landmines (held in Maputo February 25-28, 1997) approached, greatly increased attention to the issue domestically, regionally and internationally spurred a policy decision. On February 26, Mozambique's foreign minister addressed the NGO Conference and announced an immediate ban on the use, production, import and export of antipersonnel mines. Destruction of Mozambique's stockpile was not addressed.

## Namibia

The South African Defense Force (SADF) used mines in northern Namibia during its occupation of Namibia, primarily in fenced and marked areas around military encampments and installations, but also around power lines. The landmines that the SADF planted in northern Namibia were not properly cleared when South African forces withdrew just prior to independence in 1990. These mines continue to injure people and livestock and to disrupt civilian life. A limited number of mines have been planted in Namibia since independence, perhaps most notably by poachers.

A U.S. Department of Defense database indicates that Namibia has produced wooden PMD-6 mines, but Namibian officials deny the claim. Twenty-seven types of antipersonnel mines from nine other countries have been reported in Namibia. The condition of some of Namibia's stockpile of mines is suspect; Human Rights Watch has obtained copies of two confidential documents indicating that the arsenal at Grootfontein Military Base is poorly maintained and contains explosives and weapons, including several mine types, that are unstable and very hazardous.

While putting increased emphasis on the need for mine clearance in the past two years, the government of Namibia has shown little interest in the international effort to ban antipersonnel mines. Namibia did, however, vote for the December 10, 1996 U.N. General Assembly resolution recognizing the need for the conclusion of a comprehensive ban treaty "as soon as possible." More importantly, in March 1997 the Namibian government made its first statement in support of a ban, when Foreign Affairs Minister Theo-Ben Gurirab told the National Assembly that Namibia had joined the worldwide crusade for an immediate and total ban on antipersonnel landmines.

### South Africa

On February 20, 1997, South Africa demonstrated bold leadership by announcing, effective immediately, a comprehensive ban on use, production, and trade of antipersonnel mines, as well as its intention to destroy existing stocks, except for "a very limited and verifiable number...solely for training specific military personnel in demining techniques and for research into assisting the demining process."

While South Africa has no problem with mines on its own soil, it had been the largest producer and exporter of mines in all of Africa. It used mines in or supplied mines to many other African nations. South Africa produced a number of antipersonnel mines: the M2A2; the R2M2; the No.69 MK.1; Shrapnel Mine No.2; SA Non-Metallic AP and the MIM MS-803. South Africa's mines have been found in Angola, Mozambique, Namibia, Zambia and Zimbabwe and exported further afield to Cambodia, Rwanda and Somalia. As recently as November 1996 South African citizens were offered landmines to protect their houses from crime through the classified columns of a national daily newspaper.

In 1996 the minister of defense stated that South Africa had 261,423 antipersonnel mines in its stockpile, along with 49,756 antitank mines. In addition to its own mines, South Africa is believed to have stocks of more than twenty other types of mines from six other nations.

South Africa's ban announcement was preceded by other important steps. In March 1994, South Africa announced a formal moratorium on antipersonnel mine exports. The moratorium was turned into a permanent ban in May 1996, when South Africa also announced that it was suspending all use of antipersonnel mines. South Africa is now emerging as a leader in the field of mine clearance equipment. South Africa has also played a prominent role in supporting the Canadian-led initiative aimed at the signing of a total ban treaty in December 1997. South Africa will host an important OAU conference on landmines in Johannesburg May 19-21, 1997.

### Swaziland

Swaziland has a very limited mine problem. Several Swazi citizens have been killed or maimed by mines along the Mozambique border, including army officers patrolling the border and Ministry of Agriculture officials rehabilitating the fence which controls the spread of foot-and-mouth disease.

The government of Swaziland had been largely silent on the issue of an international ban on antipersonnel mines until the February 1997 4th International NGO Conference on Landmines, held in Maputo, Mozambique. At that conference, a Swazi official called for a ban "with immediate effect" and stated the government's support for the signing of a ban treaty in December 1997. Although the Umbutfo Swaziland Defence Force is believed to maintain a small stockpile of landmines, the official said, "Swaziland does not use, buy or manufacture landmines."

### Tanzania

Tanzania experienced a limited number of landmine incidents in the 1960s, blaming Portuguese forces, which denied laying the mines. Tanzanian armed forces used mines in Uganda in 1979 and in Mozambique in 1986-88. The Tanzanian government has said little about the international effort to ban antipersonnel mines. However, in a November 1996 letter to the NGO ban campaigns in Zimbabwe, Mozambique and South Africa, Minister for Foreign Affairs Jakaya M. Kikwete wrote: "We...have no hesitation in supporting your proposals...to develop greater cooperation and coordination among NGOs, IOs [international organizations] and governments aimed at a comprehensive antipersonnel mine ban...[and to] urge other SADC members to sign a protocol prohibiting the use, production, trade and stockpiling of antipersonnel landmines."

### Zambia

Zambia has minefields along its Angolan border and its Namibian border. Zambians continue to be victims of mines laid over fifteen years ago. Public awareness of the problem is poor.

In 1994, Zambian defense ministry spokesperson, Major General Jack Mubanga, said, "There are a lot of landmines in Southern and Western provinces, but it is too costly for the government to embark on an exercise to have them removed. It is very expensive to carry out such an assignment."

Zambia continues to maintain a stockpile of antipersonnel mines. Nearly thirty types of antipersonnel mines from ten nations have been found in Zambia. Zambian police are concerned about the weapons trade from Angola into western Zambia, which has included landmines.

Zambia had been generally quiet on the landmines issue, saying it was not a priority, until it issued a statement on October 24, 1996 at the 51st session of the U.N. General Assembly expressing support for an international ban.

### Zimbabwe

The government of Zimbabwe estimates that there are one to three million mines planted along its borders with Zambia and Mozambique. Zimbabwe inherited the lengthy border minefields from the Rhodesian government, which the Rhodesians boasted constituted the second largest man-made barrier in the world, after the Great Wall of China. Initially the minefields were demarcated on both sides by security fencing with prominent warning signs. By 1977 the Rhodesians stopped demarcating the minefields on the hostile side and stopped maintaining them. As a result mine laying became uncontrolled and unrecorded and booby trapping flourished. The minefields remain lethal today, claiming new victims. Clearance of the minefields will be dangerous, costly and time consuming.

On February 12, 1997, at an international landmines conference in Austria, Zimbabwe's representative said, "My delegation would like to take this opportunity to state clearly and categorically that Zimbabwe does not [nor] intends to produce or manufacture any antipersonnel mines, nor does it export or sell such weapons." Human Rights Watch warmly welcomes this as a commitment by the government of Zimbabwe not to produce or export antipersonnel mines in the future. Human Rights Watch is also greatly heartened by his statement that "Zimbabwe subscribes to the...contents of the Austrian draft convention on the banning of antipersonnel landmines. Zimbabwe is fully behind all efforts to ban the manufacture, stockpiling, transportation, and the use of antipersonnel mines."

Human Rights Watch is dismayed, however, at the claim made at the same time that while Rhodesia made three types of mines, it stopped production in 1977, and "at independence in 1980, Zimbabwe did not adopt the programme to manufacture the antipersonnel mines." In March 1995, a senior government official acknowledged to Human Rights Watch that Zimbabwe had produced ZAP PloughShear ("Claymore" type) mines until October 1992, but said a decision had been recently made not to produce any more antipersonnel mines. Zimbabwe Defense Industries (ZDI) has acknowledged manufacturing the PloughShears, while maintaining "a claymore mine is not a land mine." ZDI has stated that the government ordered a stop to production in 1992 and that "as a result ZDI was forced to destroy all claymore mines on its stocks."

However, PloughShears were offered for sale in 1994 at the Bulawayo International Trade Fair and in 1996 the London-based Centre for Defense Studies reported that Zimbabwean-manufactured antipersonnel mines had been exported to Sudan's Southern People's Liberation Army (SPLA). Zimbabwe's mines have also been found in Namibia and Mozambique, though the date and method of transfer is uncertain.

In addition to the Rhodesian and Zimbabwean made mines, at least seven other antipersonnel mine types from four other countries have been used in Zimbabwe.

**Efforts to Control Mine Use**

The Landmines Protocol of the 1980 Convention on Conventional Weapons (CCW), an international treaty intended to diminish the impact of landmine use on civilians, has proved utterly ineffective in stemming the landmines crisis in southern Africa or elsewhere.  South Africa became the first and only southern African nation to ratify the CCW in September 1995.

Complex rules, discretionary language, and broad exceptions and qualifications have undermined the utility of the Landmines Protocol. Moreover, even its limited rules have been rarely followed.  Government armies and rebel groups have both regularly used mines deliberately against noncombatants and failed to take even minimal precautions to safeguard against collateral harm to civilians.

In southern Africa, in every war since 1961, every group has used landmines in contravention of international humanitarian law.  The Portuguese colonial military forces, minority rule South African units, Rhodesian forces, Popular Movement for the Liberation of Angola (Movimento Popular de Libertação de Angola--MPLA), National Front for the Liberation of Angola (Frente Nacional de Libertação de Angola--FNLA) and National Union for the Total Independence of Angola (UNITA) in Angola, People's Liberation Army of Namibia (PLAN),   Umkhonto we Sizwe (MK) in South Africa, Comité Revolucionário Moçambicana (Coremo) and Mozambique Liberation Front (Frelimo) in Mozambique and the Zimbabwe African National Liberation Army (ZANLA) and Zimbabwe People's Revolutionary Army (ZIPRA) in the Rhodesian war are all guilty of this. The same is true in the post-colonial wars in Angola and Mozambique, where the two governments, supporting forces (such as Cubans, Tanzanians, and Zimbabweans), and rebel groups (such as UNITA, Renamo and

Angola's Frente Nacional de Libertação de Cabinda) have used landmines in a manner in which civilians were the greatest victims.

The Landmines Protocol was amended in a more than two year review process ending in Geneva in May 1996. South Africa took part as a State Party, while Angola, Mozambique, Zambia and Zimbabwe attended the negotiating sessions as observers. The revised protocol that emerged continued to be weak, the result of the lowest common denominator being agreed upon in the search for consensus. Military considerations dominated the discussion to the almost complete exclusion of humanitarian concerns. Nations concentrated on negotiating loopholes to restrictions on use, while giving no attention to negotiating the elimination of the weapon. Rather than stigmatizing the use of antipersonnel mines as an indiscriminate killer of civilians, the protocol encourages nations to use a certain kind of mine that is promoted as having less impact on civilian populations: those that self-destruct and self-deactivate, and are detectable—"smart mines" as they are often called.

But the "smart mine" technological answer to the problem is no lasting solution. The southern Africa experience shows that landmines are rarely used responsibly, and that even just one mine accident can terrorize a community for years. Smart mines too are indiscriminate, will have a failure rate, and will cause civilian casualties. Moreover, given the magnitude of the crisis, the only way to significantly deter use is to attach to antipersonnel landmines the same stigma attached to chemical and biological weapons, and such a stigma cannot come about if some mines are legal and others illegal.

**Momentum for a Ban**

Internationally, the move toward a total ban on antipersonnel mines has clearly overtaken the limited CCW approach to controlling mines. Nongovernmental organizations (NGOs) created the International Campaign to Ban Landmines (ICBL) in 1991 and it has grown into one of the most diverse and successful coalitions ever. The ICBL now consists of more than 900 NGOs in more than fifty nations.

In southern Africa, various coalitions of NGOs or concerned people have formed national campaigns to ban landmines as part of the ICBL. The oldest is the South African Campaign to Ban Landmines, which began in July 1995. In November 1995 the Mozambique Campaign to Ban Landmines was formally launched. Four new campaigns were stimulated by the planning for the ICBL's 4th NGO Conference on Landmines in Maputo in February 1997: in Zambia in September 1996, in Zimbabwe in October 1996, in Angola in November 1996, and in Somalia in February 1997.

The movement has rapidly spread beyond just NGOs and has been endorsed by the International Committee of the Red Cross (ICRC), UNICEF, United Nations High Commissioner for Refugees (UNHCR), United Nations Department of Humanitarian Affairs (DHA), the U.N. secretary-general, the most influential media sources, and—increasingly—governments around the world.

The U.N. General Assembly passed a resolution on December 10, 1996 by a vote of 156-0, with ten abstentions, urging nations to "pursue vigorously" an international ban and to conclude a ban agreement "as soon as possible." Clearly, a new international norm is emerging. No southern African states were among the abstentions.

Admittedly, for many of these pro-ban nations, their actions have not matched their rhetoric. Some southern African states are finding their militaries reluctant to deny themselves the option of using antipersonnel mines in the future, despite clear evidence that these mines have little utility, and that they are disliked by those soldiers who have experience in using and facing them.

Some thirty nations have already unilaterally suspended or banned use of antipersonnel mines, including South Africa, Mozambique, Swaziland, Germany, France, Canada, Australia, Belgium, Norway, Portugal, and the Philippines. More than twenty nations have prohibited the production of antipersonnel mines, including South Africa, Zimbabwe, Germany, France, Italy and Portugal. More than fifty governments have prohibited export of antipersonnel mines, including South Africa and Zimbabwe, the only two southern African nations known to have exported mines. U.S. military sources indicate that there have been no significant antipersonnel mine exports globally in over two years.

The Organization of African Unity (OAU) has endorsed a total ban, first with the Resolution of the 62nd Council of Ministers in June 1995 and again in 1996. The Organization of American States adopted a resolution in June 1996 calling for the establishment of a hemispheric mine free zone. The six Central American states declared themselves the first mine free zone in September 1996, and the CARICOM (Caribbean)states followed suit in December.

A key event was the Canadian government-sponsored conference held in Ottawa from October 3 to 5, 1996 which brought together fifty pro-ban governments, as well as twenty-four observer states, dozens of nongovernmental organizations with the ICBL, the International Committee of the Red Cross and other international groups. Angola, Mozambique, South Africa, and Zimbabwe were among the states participating.

In Ottawa, states agreed to a Final Declaration calling for a comprehensive ban and, more importantly, a Chairman's Agenda for Action, which laid out concrete steps for achieving a ban rapidly. And in a dramatic announcement at the end of the conference, Canada's Foreign Minister Lloyd Axworthy stated that Canada would host a ban treaty signing conference in December 1997. The conference also featured perhaps unprecedented cooperation between governments and NGOs, which has continued in the wake of the Ottawa conference.

There has been great enthusiasm for what is now called the Ottawa process. Austria hosted a preparatory meeting from February 12 to 14, 1997 to begin discussions of the elements of a ban treaty. One hundred and eleven governments participated, though many of them were not prepared to commit to a December 1997 time frame. Present in Vienna were Angola, Botswana, Mozambique, Namibia, South Africa, and Zimbabwe. South Africa, the first nation to speak, made a particularly strong statement in support of the Ottawa process. Zimbabwe also made a statement of support. Belgium will host an international meeting to further develop the ban treaty in June 1997, followed by treaty negotiating sessions in Norway in September, culminating in a treaty signing in Ottawa in December.

A region-wide ban on use, production, stockpiling, and transfer of antipersonnel mines in southern Africa is an achievable goal. Angola, Malawi, Mozambique, Namibia, South Africa, Swaziland, Tanzania, Zambia, and Zimbabwe have all publicly stated their support for an immediate and total ban. South Africa and Mozambique have already unilaterally banned use of antipersonnel mines, and those two nations, as well as Malawi and Swaziland have indicated their willingness to sign a ban treaty in December 1997. Lesotho and Mauritius have declared that they have no stockpiles of antipersonnel mines.

At an ICRC seminar held in Harare April 21 to 23, 1997, military and foreign affairs officials from all twelve SADC nations called on southern African governments to establish a regional antipersonnel mine free zone, to immediately end all new deployments of antipersonnel mines, and to enact comprehensive national bans on the weapon. Participants also called upon governments to announce their commitment to sign a ban treaty in December 1997. The meeting was held in cooperation with the OAU and the government of Zimbabwe.

The ICBL is committed to extensive follow-up work to its February 1997 Conference in Mozambique to move the region toward a total ban. There will be an OAU meeting hosted by South Africa in Johannesburg May 19-21, 1997, devoted to a ban, mine clearance, and victim assistance issues. The OAU summit meeting in May is also expected to address the matter of a regional mine ban.

International and regional momentum is growing rapidly. The SADC nations should follow the example of the Central American and Caribbean states to become the world's third mine-free zone. This is what their citizens seek. Afonso Lumbala, a thirty-two-year-old farmer from Caxito in Angola has first hand experience with landmines. He stepped on an antipersonnel mine in April 1995. His view is:

> All soldiers lay these mines. They don't care about us, the people. We suffer for them. They never warn us about mines. We find out by losing our limbs. We want them to clear the mine mess and leave us alone. The leaders and their soldiers are responsible for this. So are the people who make these evil weapons.

**Recommendations**

The twelve nations of southern Africa should take steps at the national, sub-regional, regional and international levels aimed at a comprehensive ban on antipersonnel landmines. They should adopt national policies, supported by legislation, to immediately prohibit the use, production, import and export of antipersonnel mines. Plans should be formulated and implemented to destroy existing stockpiles of antipersonnel mines as rapidly as possible, but no later than the year 2000. Each state should commit to the destruction of emplaced mines as rapidly as possible, and to record, mark, fence, and monitor existing minefields until destruction has taken place. All mines removed from the ground must be destroyed, and not retained for future use or re-sale. Each state should make public detailed information about its antipersonnel mine stockpiles and minefields.

The SADC states should use all sub-regional fora to promote a southern Africa mine free zone, and all regional fora to promote an Africa-wide ban on antipersonnel mines, as called for by the OAU. The governments of southern Africa should actively support the Ottawa process, participate in the preparatory meetings in Belgium and Norway, and be prepared to sign an international treaty banning antipersonnel mines in Canada in December 1997.

The international community should devote greater resources to mine clearance and victim assistance programs in southern Africa. Those nations that have manufactured or provided mines used in the region bear a special responsibility. If the region becomes a mine free zone, it should be given high priority for multilateral and bilateral mine clearance and victim assistance funding.

## II. ANGOLA

**Background**

From 1961 until late 1994 Angola was almost continuously at war. In the fighting landmines figured prominently, resulting in tens of thousands of dead and injured. Civilians have in particular suffered from the "plague of landmines." Even with renewed peace the many millions of landmines present a hazard to reconstruction of this war-devastated country. Civilians continue to be victims with terrible frequency. The most common estimates for the number of mines in Angola range from nine to fifteen million.

*The Colonial "First War"*

The nationalist struggle started in February 1961 with an uprising in Luanda. The next month, strikes, uprisings and massacres of white settlers shook the cotton and coffee-growing Bakongo areas of northern Angola. Portuguese reprisals took thousands of lives and generated a huge wave of refugees; about 400,000 fled into nearby Zaire.

By September 1961, the Portuguese military, using napalm and aerial bombardment, and white vigilantes regained control of much of the northern territory. The death toll reached more than 50,000 Africans and 2,000 Europeans. Portuguese forces planted landmines in Cabinda along the Congo border in 1964 during counterinsurgency operations.

In the east the colonial war against the Portuguese began in 1966. With little access to the northern front, the Popular Movement for the Liberation of Angola (MPLA) had been operating in Moxico and Cuando Cubango districts in 1966. The MPLA's actions included ambushing Portuguese convoys and mining roads. By mid-1968 it was estimated that some 500 MPLA guerrillas were operational within the territory.

National Union for the Total Independence of Angola (UNITA) guerrillas also began operating in eastern Angola in 1966 and by the early 1970s were responsible for some attacks along the Benguela railway corridor. In response to expanding nationalist activity the Portuguese retreated into small armed outposts and began resettling the local population into protected villages. By November 1968 Portuguese military officials claimed that over 70 percent of Africans in Lunda and Moxico districts were living in resettlements. The guerrillas also relocated civilians as well.

The guerrilla war in the east, as in the north, was seriously impeded by internecine fighting among guerrilla groups. The MPLA undertook to "liquidate" the National Front for the Liberation of Angola (FNLA) whenever it appeared in the east, and some MPLA units fought UNITA more than the Portuguese. The

16

MPLA drove the ill-equipped UNITA forces out of much of Cuando Cubango district and a number of the UNITA units defected to the Portuguese, who then stopped fighting with UNITA because UNITA was fighting the MPLA.[1]

Landmines were used in Angola in mid-1961 in Uíge province by the Union of the Angola Peoples (UPA) against the Portuguese. Up to the late 1960s the UPA (and its successor, the FNLA) appears to have been very short of weapons, its forces receiving limited supplies of rifles, grenades, explosives and for privileged units a few landmines and machine guns from Congo before trekking with their loads hoisted in woven palm leaves and taken to their respective operational areas in the interior, some as deep as Ucua and current day Uíge city.[2]

Landmine warfare became more widely used by nationalist guerrillas beginning in 1968, a reflection of growing external support for their struggle. The FNLA, UNITA and in particular the MPLA favored their use. The MPLA was responsible for the majority of mine use in the early 1970s. It had reorganized into a more mobile force which emphasized minimal direct contact with the enemy. Mines demoralized Portuguese soldiers and were an important aspect of the MPLA's slow, "unspectacular strategy of attritional warfare."[3] The use of antipersonnel mines by MPLA guerrillas in the Cabindan rain forest has been vividly captured in the classic Angolan novel *Mayombe*, by Pepetela:

> Tugu placed three antipersonnel mines close to the bulldozer.
> When the mines were well camouflaged, Fearless wrote on a
> scrap of paper:
>> Bastard Colonists
>> Go to Hell, Go Home
>> While You Are Here
>> In someone Else's Land,
>> The Boss is Enjoying Your Wife
>> Or Sister, There in The Greens!

---

[1] See, Africa Watch, *Angola: Violations of the Laws of War by Both Sides* (New York: Human Rights Watch, 1989).

[2] John Marcum, *The Angolan Revolution: The Anatomy of an Explosion (1950-1962), vol.1* (Cambridge: MIT Press, 1969), p.229.

[3] John Marcum, *The Angolan Revolution: Exile Politics and Guerrilla Warfare, (1962-1976) vol. 2* (Cambridge: MIT Press, 1978), p.213.

And he left the message well in sight, in the middle of the minefield. The guerrillas smiled. 'Any bastard who wants to read that
will go up in the air,' Ops said.[4]

The Portuguese response in the east of Angola was to increasingly use
helicopters in counterinsurgency operations and by 1972 neither side could gain the
upper hand. In 1970-71 the Portuguese laid some minefields along the Zambian
border in an attempt to stop MPLA infiltration.

The Portuguese suffered their worst landmines casualties in 1970. In that
year landmines reportedly accounted for half the casualties suffered by Portugal's
Angolan forces: 355 dead, 2,655 missing and 1,242 injured.[5] A Portuguese military
intelligence assessment in September 1971 reported over seventy combat actions
that month. The MPLA was responsible for sixty-five, twenty of which involved
the use of mines.[6]

UNITA was ill-equipped and untrained in mine warfare until 1975.
UNITA leader Jonas Savimbi has said that the Namibian nationalist force South
West Africa People's Organization (SWAPO) gave his forces their first four
landmines in 1971 to use on the Benguela railway:

> We got the mines out in the forest—we had only four of them—
> and practiced using the same technique as we had done at the
> ambush. We attached a grenade detonator. Nothing happened. So
> we gave up attempting to use the mines. It took us another four
> years before we got someone who knew you couldn't detonate
> a mine with a grenade detonator. The explosive force of the
> grenade detonator was not enough to make the five kilos of TNT
> in the mine explode. But we didn't know.[7]

---

[4] Pepetela, *Mayombe* (Harare: Zimbabwe Publishing House, 1983), p.16.

[5] John Marcum, *The Angolan Revolution: Exile Politics and Guerrilla Warfare,
(1962-1976) vol. 2* (Cambridge: MIT Press, 1978), p. 214.

[6] Portuguese Military Intelligence report published in, João Paulo Guerra,
*Memória das Guerras Colonias* (Porto: Afrontamento, 1994), p.282.

[7] Fred Bridgland, *Jonas Savimbi: A Key to Africa* (Edinburgh: Mainstream Press,
1986), p.94.

## Landmine Incidents (1962-1972)[8]

| Year | Cabinda prov. | Angola | Total |
|------|---------------|--------|-------|
| 1962 | - | 43 | 43 |
| 1963 | 4 | 55 | 59 |
| 1964 | 6 | 152 | 158 |
| 1965 | 29 | 90 | 119 |
| 1966 | 20 | 72 | 92 |
| 1967 | 13 | 55 | 68 |
| 1968 | 8 | 85 | 93 |
| 1969 | 23 | 259 | 282 |
| 1970 | 29 | 583 | 612 |
| 1971 | 28 | 414 | 442 |
| 1972 | 19 | 584 | 603 |

Casualty reports in 1972 indicated that mines killed forty people and wounded 405 compared with 274 killed and 428 injured by firearms. Landmine explosions were responsible for 39 percent of incidents.[9]

The Portuguese noted during their Angolan operations that their mine detection specialists, whether operating on foot or otherwise, were rarely successful in locating mines. This was often due to their slow movement, which allowed the guerrillas to see them advancing and gave time to dig up the mines in advance to prevent their capture. Because the guerrillas had to transport their military equipment long distances and were often short of replacements, they appear to have wanted to redeploy their mines for re-use elsewhere. To quicken road clearance the Mechanical Engineering Department of the University of Luanda designed a mine exploding vehicle in 1970.[10] This vehicle was never widely used and most mine clearance continued to be by troops walking ahead of convoys probing the roads for mines. Allied to this was a prodigious road building program: 5,000 miles of roads were constructed in Angola by 1974, partly designed to reduce the mine threat.

---

[8] Peter Stiff, *Taming the Landmine* (Alberton: Galago Books, 1986), p.89.

[9] Peter Swift, *Taming the Landmine*, p.90.

[10] Ibid.

## Independence and the "Second War"

Following a military coup in Portugal in April 1974, the colonial government precipitously announced its withdrawal from Angola. In January 1975, the three movements signed the Alvor Accord providing for a joint interim government and an integrated national army. However, as the date for military integration neared, the agreement broke down. By mid-1975, the fronts were at war. The United States, Soviet Union and regional powers rushed to involve themselves. In January 1975 Tanzanian President Nyerere gave UNITA a small amount of military equipment, including landmines.[11] The MPLA was better supplied. The Yugoslav freighter Postonyo in May 1975 docked in Pointe Noire in Congo-Brazzaville, unloading military equipment including TMA antitank mines and some crates of MON and POMZ-2 antipersonnel mines.[12]

The United States had already given covert military aid (including mines) to the FNLA in January 1975. The FNLA had also received military support from China, including shipments of Type 72 and Type 72b antipersonnel mines. The USSR and Cuba supported the MPLA, which was able to seize control of Luanda, but little else. South Africa invaded Angola in support of UNITA and Zaire, with United States assistance, invaded in support of the FNLA. By October, it looked as though Luanda would be captured before the official date of independence, November 11. However, a massive Soviet airlift of military equipment and Cuban troops reversed the military tide. Zaire abandoned its invasion force and the South Africans withdrew. The revelation of South African backing for UNITA and FNLA was disastrous for the reputation of the two movements in Africa, and the MPLA was able to form a one-party socialist government that obtained widespread diplomatic recognition. The U.S., however, refused to recognize the MPLA government until 1993, and waged a covert war against it for many years.

Despite the government's gains in 1976 the war spread. Although UNITA was initially driven out of its Huambo headquarters in central Angola and its forces scattered and driven into the bush, UNITA regrouped and waged a devastating long-running war against the MPLA government, which it portrayed as assimilado (very urban, educated and Portuguese-oriented), mestizo (mixed race), and northern dominated. UNITA described itself as anti-Marxist and pro-Western, but it had its regional roots, primarily among the Ovimbundu of southern and central Angola.

---

[11] Fred Bridgland, *Jonas Savimbi*, p.118.

[12] Human Rights Watch interview with Antònio Baptiste, who claimed to have helped unload this shipment, Luanda, March 1995.

The war spread, with UNITA making steady gains. South African forces intermittently operated in Angola in support of UNITA. The largest South African incursions occurred in 1981-83, in part as retaliation for MPLA support for the South West African People's Organization's (SWAPO) guerrilla war against the South African occupation of Namibia. During this period, South African forces occupied parts of the extreme south of Angola in an attempt to establish an effective UNITA-dominated buffer zone against SWAPO infiltration of Namibia. In late 1983, the U.N. Security Council demanded South Africa withdraw from Angola.

In January 1984 South African forces engaged in another cross-border operation into Angola, Operation Asakari. On January 3, one of the South Africa Ratel-20 vehicles got enmeshed in a minefield near Cuvelai and was knocked out by an Angolan T-54, five of the crew being killed. Operation Askari wound up a few days later, although this went slowly because of the many landmines planted on tracks and roads which the sweep teams had to cover at walking pace.[13] Shortly afterwards, the two countries signed the Lusaka Accords under which South Africa agreed to withdraw if Angola ceased its support for SWAPO. However, in 1985 South Africa launched another invasion to counter a major government offensive against UNITA.

U.S. covert assistance to UNITA, which had been prohibited by the U.S. Congress (the Clark Amendment) in 1976, was resumed after the repeal of the amendment in 1985. U.S. covert aid totaled about $250 million between 1986 and 1991, making it the second largest U.S. covert program, exceeded only by aid to the Afghan mujahidin.

Between September 1987 and March 1988, there were major battles in the Cuito Cuanavale area between some 3-5,000 South African troops and UNITA auxiliaries attempting to stop a larger joint Angolan-Cuban force advance on Mavinga and eventually UNITA's headquarters at Jamba. During these operations the South Africans laid a number of phony and real minefields along their positions. Today, some 27,000 South African-laid mines remain in minefields around Mavinga. South African forces were also deployed and laid antipersonnel mines behind Angolan government lines as these forces advanced in May 1987 and

---

[13] Helmoed-Römer Heitman, *South African War Machine* (Johannesburg: Bison Books, 1985), p.152.

laid antipersonnel mines.[14] Sometimes South African units suffered casualties from antipersonnel mines laid by the MPLA to ambush their operations.[15]

The Angolan and Cuban forces did likewise. Although the fighting over Cuito Cuanavale resulted in military stalemate, the outcome was a psychological defeat for the South African Defense Forces (SADF), which came to believe that it could not militarily succeed in its objectives in Angola. This prompted a significant re-thinking of South African military strategy and a strategic retreat by the SADF, although there were further armed exchanges near the Namibian border at Calueque between Cuban forces and the SADF between April-June 1988 in which real and dummy minefields were laid by the South Africans.

Cuito Cuanavale also marked the beginning of new diplomatic attempts to end the conflict. In 1988, the Soviet Union signaled that it was no longer prepared to arm the MPLA indefinitely. In January 1989, President dos Santos made an offer to Jonas Savimbi which led to a peace process brokered by eighteen African nations. At a meeting in Gbadolite, Zaire, on June 22, 1989 Dos Santos and Savimbi shook hands and agreed on an immediate cease-fire. But it quickly collapsed, as a dispute developed over what was agreed orally and especially over what Savimbi's future role would be.

The following eighteen months saw simultaneously the most sustained efforts to achieve a peaceful settlement and some of the fiercest fighting of the entire war. Between April 1990 and May 1991 six rounds of talks took place between UNITA and the government. The negotiations were hosted by Portugal, with observers from the U.S. and the Soviet Union; these nations were subsequently called the Observing Troika. In May 1991 the talks resulted in an agreement known as the Bicesse Accords, which temporarily ended a conflict that had already taken between 100,000 and 350,000 lives. The agreement was made possible in part by the ending of the Cold War, which facilitated U.S.-Soviet cooperation, and the desire of the Soviet Union and Cuba to reduce their considerable financial commitment to Angola.[16]

---

[14] Fred Bridgland, *The War for Africa: Twelve Months that Transformed a Continent* (Gibralter: Ashanti Publishing, 1990), pp.381-382.

[15] Peter McAleese, *No Mean Soldier: The Story of the Ultimate Professional Soldier in the SAS and Other Forces* (London: Orion, 1994), p.229.

[16] Abiodun Williams, "Negotiations and the End of the Angolan Civil War," in David Smock (ed.), *Making War and Waging Peace: Foreign Intervention in Africa* (Washington DC: U.S. Institute of Peace Press, 1993).

The accords ratified a cease-fire and called for government and UNITA forces to be integrated into a 50,000-strong military force, the Angolan Armed Forces (Forcas Armadas Angolanas, FAA). The accords contained a so-called "Triple Zero" clause which prohibited either side from purchasing new supplies of weaponry. Under the accords, the MPLA remained the legitimate and internationally-recognized government, retaining responsibility for running the state during the interim period and for setting the date of elections. Monitoring this interim period was a small, 576 strong, United Nations Angola Verification Mission (UNAVEM) team.

### Elections and the "Third War"

Held on the last two days of September 1992, the elections provided the first opportunity for Angolans to express their political will in what the U.N. and other foreign observers concluded was a "generally free and fair" process. With a turnout of over 91 percent of registered voters, President dos Santos received 49.6 percent of the vote against 40 percent for Jonas Savimbi. In the legislative election, the MPLA obtained 54 percent of the vote against UNITA's 34 percent. Under Angolan law, failure of the top finisher in the presidential election to receive over 50 percent cast requires an election run-off.

Within a month of the election, Angola returned to civil war as UNITA rejected the results and launched a military offensive. The human cost after the fighting resumed is impossible to determine with precision, but the United Nations estimates that more than 100,000 people died. In addition to the appalling levels of death and destruction, this war was notable for widespread and systematic human rights abuses by both the government and UNITA. As noted by an Africa expert from the U.S. Department of Defense, "This type of warfare bears mainly, cruelly and disproportionately on the populace, which is caught between the warring parties."[17]

Mine warfare also intensified in this third war, with thousands of new mines being laid by both the government and UNITA to obstruct roads and bridges, to encircle besieged towns with mine belts up to three kilometers wide, and to despoil agricultural land. In 1993-94 the government surrounded the cities it held with large defensive minefields. UNITA then laid additional mines at the edges of the government minefields in an attempt to deny those in the besieged towns access

---

[17] James Woods, Deputy Assistant Secretary of Defense for African Affairs, in "The Quest for Peace in Angola," *Hearing before the Subcommittee on Africa of the House Foreign Affairs Committee*, (Washington: U.S. Government Printing Office), November 16, 1993, p.7.

to food, water and firewood. In March 1993 the government also used air-scatterable mines in Huambo to protect its retreating forces from UNITA advances. At UNITA's peak strength in April 1993 the government retained a presence in the towns of Malange and Menongue and in pockets around Kuito and Luena. It also retained control of a sizeable strip from just north of Luanda to the Cunene river border with Namibia. Unlike the previous war, control of urban areas became a primary strategic objective. For UNITA control of urban areas represented legitimacy; for the government loss of urban areas represented humiliation. Not since 1975 had UNITA controlled a significant urban area.

By August 1993 UNITA's fortunes began to change for the worse. The government had mortgaged the next seven years of oil wealth in rearming and rebuilding its army. In 1993-4 the government spent some U.S.$3.5 billion on weapons and foreign military assistance, ironically, in large part from South Africa. UNITA not only faced an improved government army, but was also weakened in 1994 by the drying up of many of its external support networks, particularly from the U.S. and South Africa. The result was reliance on a dwindling pool of its own resources and harsher taxation demands on civilians in UNITA areas, which alienated many. UNITA also found itself unable to administer complex urban centers such as Huambo effectively and the urban areas it held were vulnerable to air strikes. The loss of control of important diamond mines in June 1994 particularly hurt UNITA, as most of its revenue was derived from diamonds sales.[18]

## The Lusaka Protocol and Beyond

Throughout 1993-94 battlefield victories and setbacks determined the pace of international mediation attempts. A series of government offensives in September 1994 finally fragmented UNITA, pushing it from all its remaining significant urban footholds within a month: Soyo (November 1), Huambo (November 5-6), M'banza Congo and Uíge (both in mid-November). In an attempt to stop further territorial losses UNITA signed the Lusaka cease-fire protocol on November 20. But, neither leader signed the agreement, leaving it to subordinates to endorse the accord. It took until February 1995 for most of the fighting to stop.[19] As late as August 1995 the FAA chief of staff questioned whether there was true

---

[18] Human Rights Watch, *Angola: Arms Trade and Violations of the Laws of War Since the 1992 Elections* (New York: Human Rights Watch, 1994).

[19] Alex Vines, "La troisiéme guerre angolaise," in Christine Messiant (ed.), *L'Angola dans la guerre. Politique Africaine*, No.57, March 1995, pp.27-39.

peace, stating, "We do not want peace only for Luanda, we want peace for all Angola. Twenty-five kilometers from the capital there are peasants who die. The roads are mined. There is not freedom of circulation. Ask these peasants whether this is peace."[20]

The Lusaka Protocol envisaged the deployment of over 7,000 U.N. troops (UNAVEM III) for a period of up to fifteen months, dependent on a lasting cessation of hostilities and Savimbi's unequivocal support for the agreement. Only in late March 1995 did the U.N. finally press ahead to prepare the logistics for the expanded deployment of its forces.

Despite the protocol, localized fighting continued in 1994 and 1995. Serious violations continued to decline, although in December 1995 the government's capture of a string of UNITA-held hamlets in the northwest brought deadlock and delayed the peace process. By October 1996 the majority of reported cease-fire violations were isolated attacks on civilians designed either to control the movement of food aid in contested areas or to stop people from moving into areas controlled by the other side.

In late 1996 it became a U.N. priority to reduce UNAVEM's 7,000-strong military component. The withdrawal, which began in earnest in February 1997, was scheduled to be complete by June 30, 1997. There will be a scaled down presence, to be called U.N. Observer Mission in Angola (UNOMA), consisting of military observers, police observers, a political component, human rights monitors and a U.N. special representative to monitor the government of national unity which was formed in April 1997.

With an estimated five to fifteen million mines laid throughout the country and some 70,000 mine amputees nationwide, mine clearance is one of the government's and U.N.'s priorities.

Human Rights Watch in 1997 continues to receive reports of limited planting of new landmines by government and UNITA forces, Cabindan factions, as well as bandits and common criminals. This underscores the urgency of a ban on antipersonnel mines, as well as clearing mines and destroying stockpiles.

### The Continued Laying of Landmines

Landmines still continue to be laid—in violation of the Lusaka Protocol—as part of the continuation of sporadic hostilities, as a barrier to freedom of movement, and in order to mark frontiers in contested areas. Government and UNITA forces, Cabindan factions, and criminals are all responsible for new mine laying.

---

[20] *Publico* (Lisbon), August 4, 1995.

In May 1995 Care International temporarily suspended its humanitarian operations in Bié province because of newly mined roads. On April 19, 1995 nineteen people were killed when a Land Rover detonated an antitank mine on the road between Kuito and Chitepa. This road had been thought to be safe, and another vehicle had traveled down it unscathed just minutes before.[21]

U.N. Security Council Resolution 1008 of August 1995 "Urges the two parties to put an immediate and definitive end to the renewed laying of mines." The U.N. reported in December 1995, "Recently, there had been several accidents caused by mine explosions in the provinces of Benguela, Huambo, Malange and Lunda Norte on roads that had already been in use for several months. The possibility cannot be ruled out that fresh mines are being laid in some areas, though the demining that took place prior to the opening of many access routes was not systematic."[22]

Asked about the laying of new mines in Angola in 1995, U.N. and NGO officials and local people confirmed that it continued. In July 1996 a section of the strategic Malange-Saurimo road had to be temporarily cleared following a mine explosion which resulted in two fatalities and injury to four members of the Zimbabwe contingent of UNAVEM. The provincial government in Lunda Sul also reported that two antitank mines were found on the Saurimo-Cacolo road and promptly deactivated.[23]

The director of the Angolan National Institute for the Removal of Explosive Ordnance ( INAROEE), the official coordinating body for mine clearance, told Human Rights Watch, "There were problems in 1996 with mines laid on roads we believed were cleared, especially in government zones. There have been official investigations, but these have been inconclusive. This tendency is declining in 1997."[24]

The Luena-Lumege road was closed after a mine accident on August 10, 1996 and on September 22, four members of the Brazilian contingent were seriously injured in a mine accident at Chicaunda. While U.N. casualties make

---

[21] Chris Simpson, "Of Mines, Roads and Bridges," *IPS Africa*, May 3, 1995.

[22] United Nations Security Council S/1995/1012, "Report of the Secretary General on the United Nations Angola Verification Mission," December 1995.

[23] *Radio Nacional de Angola*, in Portuguese, 1900 gmt, August 4, 1996.

[24] Human Rights Watch interview with Hélder Da Silva Cruz, director of INAROEE, Maputo, February 27, 1997.

news, many other incidents go unreported. An Angolan truck driver, João Kalulo, survived three explosions from mines set off by his vehicles in 1995 and described the use of mines in economic terms:

> Many of these mines being laid are economic in nature. They keep roads and fields closed and push prices up. They also force us truck drivers along certain routes which make it easier to control and tax. Both sides use this for revenue earning. You'll find the reluctance of some governors to see mines removed less linked to national security and more to their pockets. Tight control is good business. Some places are different. In the Lundas its different, encouraging trade is better business for many officials up there.[25]

Relaying of landmines has been particularly bad in the Lunda provinces where there are UNITA forces, government forces and criminal groups defending their diamond mining interests. On November 7, 1996 about sixty people were killed and others injured when the vehicle they were traveling in detonated an antitank mine on the Lucapa-Dundo road. It was the third such incident on this road in 1996.[26] In January 1996 four expatriate diamond workers, two British, one Russian and one Philippino, were killed on a road between Dundo and Nzaji when their vehicle struck an antitank mine on a road believed to be cleared.[27]

It is not just on roads that new mines are being used. At Cafunfo in Lunda Norte on September 18, 1996 twelve children between six and thirteen years of age were killed by a POMZ fragmentation mine. The incident occurred when they were going to school from their homes in Bairro Muqueneno. This incident was not been reported in the Angolan media because government forces routinely mined the center of town every day between 6:00 p.m. and 6:00 a.m.—to provide an early warning system against UNITA or bandit incursions—and sometimes forgot to remove all the mines.[28]

---

[25] Human Rights Watch interview with João Kalulo, Johannesburg, June 8, 1995.

[26] *Radio Moçambique*, in Portuguese, 0800 gmt, November 7, 1996.

[27] *Jornal de Angola* (Luanda), January 23, 1996.

[28] Letter to Human Rights Watch from eyewitness, posted in Luanda November 11, 1996.

Mines have also been laid to mark frontiers in contested zones. Several local villagers from Uíge province told Human Rights Watch of new mines planted by the government and UNITA during their aggressive patrolling along frontiers. Mine clearance personnel in Bié and Malange provinces also confirmed that routes cleared of mines have been re-mined to slow down their progress or even erode confidence in their operations. While the mine clearance organizations may be using this suggestion to cover up occasional cases where they have failed to clear a field or road properly, the consistency of these incidents suggests that both UNITA and government troops continue to use mines.

Separatist forces in the oil-rich Cabinda enclave in 1996 continued to use landmines in their struggle against the government. Forces of the Front for Liberation of the Cabinda Enclave-Armed Forces of Cabinda, the FLEC-FAC faction, has mined many of the paths in the Mayombe rain forest. A journalist who recently visited the rebels in their rain forest hideaway was told by the head of FLEC-FAC's health department, Dr. Alexandre Batché:

> My children die of malaria, measles and tropical diseases. The drinking water is dangerous and then we have mines.... Outside [the] surgery are twenty people who have stepped on mines. They have no false legs. Some have to walk forty-five kilometers to Zaire for help. One man had lost one leg, one arm and an eye, and he had to be carried for nine days by his comrades to the Zaire border.[29]

Landmines have also been used by poachers to kill elephants. Robert de Bunt of the Kap Anamur NGO told Reuters in June 1994, "The ivory hunters in Huíla province take the antitank mines out and lay them on the elephant paths. I have seen twenty-five carcasses of elephants killed like that."[30] The people of the village of Mulonda took antitank mines from a mine belt surrounding their village and planted them on the traditional elephant migration paths of the Mupa National Park.[31]

---

[29] Peter Strandberg, "Cabinda's Forgotten War," *New African*, January 1997.

[30] Nicholas Shaxson, "Mine Removal Teams in Angola Just Scratch Surface," *Reuters*, June 28, 1994.

[31] "Hunted Elephants," Dumbo internet page of MGM Stiftung Menschen gegen Minen web site (includes photograph), http://www.dsk.de/mgm.

## The Human Dimension

Landmines continue to take their toll in Angola. UNICEF reports that from January to November 1996, ninety-five people stepped on mines in just four of Angola's eighteen provinces (Huambo, Bié, Huíla, and Moxico), resulting in thirty-seven dead, thirty injured and twenty-eight amputations. In one incident, in Kateia, Bié in September 1996, a fragmentation mine killed eleven people.

Angola has one of the highest rates of landmine injuries per capita in the world. Out of a population of about nine million, it has many thousands of amputees, the great majority of them injured by landmines. The most widely used figure is 70,000 people disabled by landmines. That would translate into 1,750,000 injured people in a country the size of the United States. The government claims that there are 100,000 amputees in the country, mostly due to mines. The International Committee of the Red Cross (ICRC) cited a more conservative figure of 15,000 in 1991 based on those it had treated, but that included lower-limb amputees only, excluding those who have been otherwise maimed or disfigured by landmines.[32]

There are no reliable estimates for the total number of people killed by landmines. Because of the lack of medical care for the civilian population, the true figure probably is very high. The government has produced figures only for mine fatalities among its soldiers in the "Second War": between 1975 and 1991, 6,728 were killed by mine explosions.[33]

It appears that the provinces of Bié and Huambo have suffered a disproportionate share of landmines injuries. However, the landmine problem is also very severe in the south and east, particularly in Moxico Province. Before mid-1992 about half of those admitted to the ICRC center for amputees at Bombo Alto, near Huambo, were soldiers and half civilians.

A disproportionate number of those disabled by landmines in Angola are young men, as were the great majority of soldiers, a fact which contributed to the militancy of many amputees in demanding their rights.

Among the civilians, men and women of all ages are affected. Children are an important minority of those affected by landmines. For example, a 1990

---

[32]Africa Watch, *Landmines in Angola*, p.41.

[33]David Sogge, *Sustainable Peace: Angola's Recovery* (Harare: Southern African Research and Documentation Centre, 1992), p.89.

survey of 113 landmine victims by the ICRC found that twenty-nine were children.[34]

Human Rights Watch's 1992 survey of forty-five landmine victims found that all but two had been injured by antipersonnel mines. Interviews in Angola by Human Rights Watch in 1994 and 1995 confirmed that this pattern continued. A 1990 ICRC survey found that ninety-six of 113 victims had been injured by antipersonnel mines.[35] However, incidents involving antitank mines typically caused many more deaths; for example one mine that had been set off by a truck killed five and injured ten passengers.[36]

The ICRC survey distinguished three categories of places where mines were laid: paths, roads, and villages or towns. It found 69 percent of victims were injured on paths, 15 percent on roads and 16 percent in inhabited areas.

. The Human Rights Watch 1990 and 1992 surveys found that out of a sample of fifty-seven cases of civilian injuries, thirty-five occurred on paths, making these the most common sites of civilian mine injury. The victims were walking to fields, schools, markets, or medical centers.

Roads and roadsides are the second most frequent sites of landmine injuries. Both antivehicle mines and antipersonnel mines are common. Eleven out of the Human Rights Watch's sample of fifty-seven civilian victims had been injured on roads, nine of them by antipersonnel mines. The risk of injury from roadside antipersonnel mines is particularly high, affecting people who leave the road to follow a short-cut, to rest, or to urinate.

Many mines have been laid in built-up areas. Five of the fifty-seven civilian victims studied by Human Rights Watch involved people injured inside towns and villages. The ICRC survey of 113 mine victims included eighteen who were injured in this way. On occasion, villages suffered a spate of landmine casualties within a short space of time—usually after a UNITA attack, or after a military presence in the area. Fear of landmines also led to the wholesale desertion of villages. About two-thirds of all mine accidents occurred less than five kilometers from the village or town, giving the lie to the notion that there is a "safe zone" close to habitations.

In addition, many mines have been planted on river banks, especially around bridges. As bridges and their approaches are a well-known location for

---

[34] Africa Watch, *Landmines in Angola*, p.41.

[35] Ibid.

[36] Africa Watch, *Landmines in Angola*, pp. 41-48.

mines, civilians tend to be very careful. Some mines are left on or in the vicinity of railroad tracks. These are intended to disable trains, or to catch people who use the tracks and the embankments as footpaths. Only three out of the fifty-seven civilian victims identified by Human Rights Watch were injured in fields.

### Who Laid the Mines

Victims interviewed by Human Rights Watch believed that the majority of mines were laid by UNITA. In our 1990 survey of forty-seven cases, twenty injuries and five deaths were attributed to UNITA, and some twenty injuries and two deaths to "unknown persons." It may be that in some of those "unknown" cases, people knew the responsible parties but declined to identify them. This would be especially the case if the perpetrator was the government's army (FAPLA), as most interviews were conducted in government-controlled territory. In many cases, however the situation was genuinely too ambiguous to identify who was responsible.

In our 1992 survey of forty-five mine victims, six said that the army was to blame (including one soldier blown up by a mine his colleagues had planted earlier), twenty-seven said UNITA, and twelve said that they did not know. Many of the "don't knows," particularly the six who were interviewed in Luanda, may have been reluctant to mention government forces.

In very few cases were civilians warned that mines had been planted in a certain area. Residents relied solely on observing military activity and on the incidence of mine injuries to discover which areas were safe and which were not.

Jardo Muekalia, UNITA's delegate to the U.S., in June 1995 justified such landmine warfare tactics in a radio interview:

> The purpose of laying a mine in war is definitely to [cause injury], you put it where you expect the enemy to come along, right? Therefore you want the surprise element in it. And so if by fencing them or marking them, then you are basically nullifying the effect you are looking for. The purpose you want it for if for the government, for the enemy, to come and step on it, so you are not going to fence it, because then you identify it.[37]

---

[37] BBC Radio 4, "File on 4," Programme No. 95vY3024NHO, June 13, 1995, 9:20pm.

When asked about legal obligations to protect civilians, Muekalia replied, "Well, I would say that here you are talking about an unconventional, an unconventional world, and it is not always possible to do the right thing."

During interviews with victims in 1994 and 1995 in Huambo, Kuito, Luanda and Caxito, victims blamed both the government and UNITA for planting mines indiscriminately.

### Emergency Care for the Injured

For most civilians injured by landmines who were interviewed, and had survived, first aid was available within a few hours. For soldiers, assistance was usually more rapid, with immediate evacuation often by helicopter or vehicle. The first aid was usually extremely rudimentary, consisting of no more than bandaging the wound and providing comfort and perhaps some pain-killing drugs. For civilians, transport to the nearest first aid post usually involved being carried manually or by cart; onward transport to a hospital was usually by car or sometimes by airplane.

Civilian survivors had to wait on average for about thirty-six hours before arriving at a hospital. One man interviewed by Human Rights Watch believed that it had been six days before he received hospital treatment.

### Medical Care and Rehabilitation

Care and rehabilitation for government forces (first FAPLA, and later FAA) is the responsibility of the Medical-Military Assistance Service (Serviço de Ajuda Medica-Militar, SAMM). It functions well, in part because the government and military attract good people by offering benefits and access to goods.

Civilians receive treatment in civilian hospitals. Adequate treatment is rarely available. Drugs are often in short supply, and the staff are less qualified and motivated than in the governments military  hospitals. The variable quality of medical care means that amputees are not out of danger once they are in  hospitals. Wounds may become infected and secondary or even tertiary amputations often are needed. There has also been a high incidence of osteomyelitides, a bone-wasting disease, which may set in after a bad amputation.

The existing facilities for rehabilitating landmine victims are grossly inadequate. The ICRC ran a center at Bombo Alto, near Huambo, from 1980 to 1992. It included eleven technicians working solely on the manufacture of artificial limbs and seventy-eight workers in all. Injured people came for a five week period to Huambo and were lodged there at the Red Cross shelter. Ironically, those working and receiving limbs and therapy at the shelter could not freely travel between Huambo and Bombo Alto, ten kilometers away, because of the threat of landmines on the road. At the center patients were fitted with prostheses.

Some Angolan students were trained to become technicians at Bombo Alto; others studied at the orthopedic school in Huambo. Artificial feet and limbs were made from wood. Though there were forests nearby, it was not safe to enter them to cut the wood, because of landmines. Hence, the wood had to be brought in from Cabinda. Other raw materials such as resin and nails were hard to find because of the economic situation of the country.

From January to November 1990, 631 new civilian and military patients were fitted with prostheses at the center. In total, 1,127 prostheses were manufactured, and 1,039 major repairs to prostheses were made during the same period. Between 1979 and 1992 ICRC workshops in Angola produced 12,421 prostheses.[38]

In late 1992 the Bombo Alto center closed down because of resumed war and subsequently was looted. In 1993 and 1994 it was used as the ICRC Huambo headquarters. The ICRC also had a center at Kuito which closed operations due to the renewed war.

In 1996, with a fragile peace restored, the ICRC reopened a renovated Bombo Alto orthopedic center in Huambo and also opened a new center in Kuito. An agreement was also signed in June 1995 with the Ministry of Health regarding the provision of orthopedic services. In 1996, the ICRC fitted 1,550 new amputees with prostheses. In addition, it manufactured 2,525 components for other NGO's active in Angola. At the end of 1996 there were seven ICRC prosthetic technicians working in Angola, together with about 120 local employees.[39]

The Swedish Red Cross also runs an orthopedic center at Neves Bendinha. The orthopedic components unit was completely refurbished in 1995 and has started production. The ICRC and the Swedish Red Cross also signed a cooperation agreement for the center. The Dutch Red Cross has one at Viana, Luanda Province. In its Jamba headquarters, UNITA's Special Department for War Wounded was set up in 1989. Up to 1992 it had at least three units caring for war amputees. One of these produced twenty artificial legs per month. The center collapsed in late 1994 due to a lack of resources.

---

[38] ICRC, "Assistance to Mines Victims: ICRC Orthopaedic Programmes," *Landmines in Africa Fact Sheet*, February 1995.

[39] ICRC, "ICRC Physical Rehabilitation Programmes," *ICRC Facts and Figures*, March 1997.

A prosthesis can only be expected to last two to three years, and children require new ones at least every year, as they outgrow the ones they have. Approximately 5,000 new prostheses are required every year, merely to cope with the existing number of amputees. This is more than twice the number currently being manufactured.

Handicap International has a rehabilitation program for disabled persons in Benguela including an orthopedic workshop, physical rehabilitation and an information campaign on the prevention of disabilities.

Angola remains a desperately poor country in which few facilities are available for the physically disabled. Most amputees are reluctant to leave the relative comfort of rehabilitation centers. Their future will consist of being cared for by their families, or attempting to earn a living in one of the few occupations open to them, such as street trading or--for those with education--secretarial or clerical work. The majority, who come from farming backgrounds, are likely to remain a burden on their families for the foreseeable future. Many have been reduced to begging; amputee beggars are already a common sight in Angolan towns. Angola will have to live with the human cost of the landmines war for many years to come.

## The Social and Economic Impact

Landmines have a significant impact on most areas of Angola's society and economy. There are tens of thousands of handicapped people. Thousands of acres of farmland, pasture and forest, and thousands of miles of riverbanks are unusable. For example, the fertile Mavinga valley in Cuando Cubango Province of southeast Angola is largely abandoned because of the vast quantities of mines laid there by UNITA and South Africa. Roads and paths cannot be traveled and rivers cannot be crossed, either by bridge or ford. The return of refugees is particularly hazardous. Commerce and movement is obstructed, and relief supplies can only be delivered with great difficulty. The eradication of landmines is an essential prerequisite for peace and economic development.[40]

The nature of the war in Angola has made the social and economic impact of landmines particularly severe. For the most part, it was not a positional war, with fighting confined to specific heavily militarized areas. At one time or another, almost every part of the country was affected, as the focus of battle shifted rapidly. The disruption of land communication and transport was a major aim of UNITA, and the mining of roads, paths and bridges was consequently an important tactic. UNITA's strategy aimed at destabilizing the government by making any semblance

---

[40] Africa Watch, *Landmines in Angola*, pp. 41-48.

of normal life impossible in as many parts of the country as it could. Outside its base area in the southeast, it consolidated and administrated few areas. Instead, it sought to deny the government free use of whole regions. The wide dissemination of landmines was a central part of this strategy. Meanwhile, government forces laid mines to try and prevent UNITA forces operating throughout the country.

Landmines were generally planted as part of a deliberate military strategy aimed at causing social and economic disruption. They continue to have this effect long after the end of hostilities. Minefields not only hinder freedom of movement and deny land for agricultural production, but around towns like Dondo they act as breeding grounds for malarial mosquitos and tsetse flies which spread sleeping sickness.

**Mine Types and Sources**

As many as fifty-one different types of antipersonnel mines from eighteen countries have been identified in Angola.[41] They include:

- Austria: APM-1; APM-2
- Belgium: M409; PRB M35
- China: Type 72a; Type 72b; Type 69
- Cuba: M57
- Czechoslovakia: PP-MI-SR
- France: MIAPDVM59
- East Germany: PPM-2
- West Germany: DM-11; DM-31
- Hungary: Gyata 64
- Israel: No. 4
- Italy: VS-69; VS MK-2; VS-50
- Romania: MAI 75; MAIGR 1
- South Africa: USK; R2M1; R2M2; Shrapnel No.2 R1M1; Shrapnel No.2; MIM MS-803 (Mini-Claymore); SA Non-Metallic AP.

---

[41] See, Africa Watch, *Landmines in Angola* (New York: Human Rights Watch, 1993), which has a list of twenty types of antipersonnel mines based on physical inspection of the mines themselves or detailed descriptions of them. Other sources include: U.S. Army Foreign Science and Technology Center, Intelligence Report, "Landmine Warfare - Mines and Engineer Munitions in Southern Africa (U)," May 1993, and Central Mine Action Office list of reported landmines, U.N. Humanitarian Assistance Coordination Unit (UCAH), Luanda, November 1996.

- Soviet: PMN; PMN-2;PMD-6; PMD-7; POMZ-2; POMZ-2M; MON-50; MON-100; MON-200; OZM-3; OZM-4; OZM-72; OZM-160
- Spain: PS-1
- Sweden: FFV 013; AP-12
- USA: M16A1; M16A2; M14; M18A1
- Yugoslavia: PMA 1; PMA 1A; PMA 2; PROM-1

Human Rights Watch has documented the following antitank mines in Angola:

M6, M7, M15, M19 (USA); MK7 (UK); TMA2, TMA2, TMA3, TMA4, TMA5, PT-MI-BA3 (Yugoslavia); TM-46, TMN-46, TM-57, TM-62; T72 (China), No.8, Mk3 (South Africa).

### Landmine Records

Existing records on the locations of landmines are extremely scanty. The Angolan army appears to have kept records of the defensive minefields laid around critical economic installations and important military bases, but not those disseminated in the countryside.   Minefield maps remain secret.

The SADF are known to have mapped many of the minefields they laid during their incursions into Angola.   They utilized these records during their clearance operations in the south of the country in 1991. Copies of many of these maps are in the Angolan government's possession. Kap Anamur, the German demining organization, found that in Cunene province the South Africans had effectively cleared many of their  minefields before withdrawal.  Cuban, SWAPO and government-laid mines occupied most of Kap Anamur's time.

Near Calueque in May 1988, South African 102 Battalion reportedly laid a phony mine field around a strong point, going to the extent of using all the customary wire fencing and markers. They also planted tin cans throughout the field.[42]

UNITA appears to have recorded very few of the mines that its forces (known as FALA) laid. British Army Major M.G. Cox, who conducted a 1991 survey of landmines in Angola wrote:

In general, UNITA mines were laid randomly and without record. Their minefields were of the nuisance type designed to

---

[42] Jannie Geldenhuys, *A General's Story: from an era of war and peace* (Johannesburg: Jonathan Ball Publishers, 1995), p.244.

deny key routes and industrial mining facilities to the MPLA. Their most extensive mining operations were along major roads and all of the railways, especially along the Benguela railway. In order to prevent easy clearance of these mines, UNITA extensively used anti-handling/booby trap devices.[43]

More than 1,000 mines were found on the Benguela Railway from 1976 to 1987.[44]

Cuban forces were also responsible for laying landmines, primarily around their military garrisons and the locations where Cuban troops were stationed while on operations. There are varying accounts of the practices used by the Cubans, some claiming that most Cuban minefields were accurately recorded, and others claiming that the Cubans kept no records at all. The Cubans also trained Angolan forces in mine warfare; the standard text for mine warfare for Angolan troops was a Cuban manual.[45]

South Africa's African National Congress (ANC) maintained training bases in Angola for many years, in which weapons for its military operations in South Africa were stockpiled. According to ANC inventories, they held in Angola 19,442 antitank mines and 13,908 antipersonnel mines.[46] Human Rights Watch has not been able to establish what has happened to these.

The United States government was a significant though inconsistent support of UNITA until 1992, providing financial and military support. At least seven types of U.S.-manufactured mines are present in Angolan soil. Major M.G.

---

[43] Africa Watch, *Landmines in Angola*, p.23.

[44] "Benguela Railways and the Development of southern Africa," from Editorial Vanguarda, cited in Phyllis Johnson and David Martin (eds.), *Apartheid Terrorism: the Destabilization Report* (London: The Commonwealth Secretariat in association with James Currey, 1989), p.129.

[45] Human Rights Watch has not seen a copy of the Cuban manual but was told by the CMAO in April 1995 that the manual they had in their possession was typical "Eastern Bloc doctrine."

[46] U.S. Army Foreign Science and Technology Center, Intelligence Report, "Landmine Warfare - Mines and Engineer Munitions in Southern Africa (U)," May 1993, section 2-2.

Cox of the British army noted that "the mines laid by UNITA forces were mainly from the USA."[47]

A U.S. military intelligence report identified the following antipersonnel mines as being used by UNITA forces:[48]

USA: M14; M16; M18A1.
South Africa: No.2.
Belgium: PRB M409.
China: Type 72.
Italy: VS Mk2.

According to statistics from INAROEE, the mine types most commonly found in Angola are from Italy, China, former Soviet Union, Germany, and Romania. INAROEE points to Malange, Bié and Moxico as the provinces most affected by antipersonnel mines and Cunene and Cuando Cubango by antitank mines.[49]

**Mine Clearance Initiatives**
There was a remarkable contrast between the widespread recognition that landmines present an extremely serious threat to Angola, and the actual response to the challenge of eradicating the mines during the period prior to the elections in September 1992, when relative peace prevailed and clearance initiatives were possible. With the exception of Kap Anamur all mine clearance initiatives were suspended. Since the November 1994 Lusaka Protocol there have been renewed attempts to seriously confront the landmine problem.

Approximately 2,500 mines were cleared in 1995 and some 6,000 cleared in the first six months of 1996. INAROEE estimates that some 80,000 mines in

[47] Africa Watch, *Landmines in Angola*, p.25.

[48] U.S. Army Foreign Science and Technology Center, Intelligence Report, "Landmine Warfare - Mines and Engineer Munitions in Southern Africa," section 2-2.

[49] *Jornal de Angola* (Luanda), October 8, 1996.

total have been cleared since 1992.[50] The CMAO estimates that 1.5 million square meters of mined land has been returned to the population.[51]

There is still no comprehensive mine survey of Angola. Before mid-1994 there had been no attempt at a systematic assessment of the extent of the landmine problem, nor any serious attempt to coordinate or plan eradication in an organized fashion. The clearance attempts in 1991-92 by government and UNITA army teams were inadequately supported in technical, financial and logistical terms. An important lesson from 1991-92 is that if future mine clearing efforts are conducted in the same inadequate manner, then not only will there be needless casualties during the clearance operations, but there will be continuing large scale casualties among the civilian population.[52]

The United Nations is expected to make an appeal for $25 million in new funds for mine clearance in Angola, for both Angolan government (INAROEE) and NGO programs.[53]

According to the Angolan government, as of February 1997, mine clearance activities were being conducted in the following provinces by these organizations:

- Huíla: Norwegian People's Aid
- Cunene: CARE
- Cuando Cubango: NPA, UNAVEM, INAROEE
- Moxico: Mines Advisory Group, INAROEE
- Lunda Sol: INAROEE
- Lunda Norte: UNAVEM
- Bié: Halo Trust, INAROEE
- Huambo: NPA, INAROEE, Halo
- Benguela: NPA, Halo
- Cuanza Sul: NPA, Halo
- Bengo: NPA, MGM
- Zaire: Saracem, NPA, CIDEV

---

[50] *Jornal de Angola* (Luanda), October 8, 1996.

[51] Eddy Banks, "Current Mines Situation in Angola," CMAO, Luanda, September 1996.

[52] Ibid., pp.49-57.

[53] U.N. Security Council S/1997/115, February 7, 1997.

- Uíge: NPA, INAROEE
- Cuanza Norte: NPA
- Malange: FAA, NPA, INAROEE

### FAPLA/FALA Teams

Several separate initiatives to clear landmines in Angola were underway prior to the resumption of hostilities in 1992. The intensity of the civil war brought these efforts to a halt.

FAPLA/FALA teams consisted of soldiers from both armies. During the pre-election period, they were working throughout the country with varying success. FAPLA/FALA teams were using manual clearance methods, partly because of the lack of heavy equipment, and partly because they considered it the most effective method. The priorities were to demine the major roads and railways, and the interiors of towns and villages.[54] However, it is questionable how systematically the major roads were cleared.

The Angolan demining effort had a limited impact, largely due to lack of organization, resources, and support. At a meeting on March 4, 1992, the Joint Mine Clearing Commission identified the following problems: serious command, control and communication problems at all levels; none of the mine clearing teams or regional mine clearing commissions had a radio or a vehicle; mine clearance teams lacked basic demining equipment such as helmets, flak vests, mine markers, engineer tape and demolition materials, or adequate, properly functioning detection equipment.

These problems persisted despite the involvement of British military teams in assisting FAPLA/FALA efforts. By mid-1992 most mine clearance had stopped because of this confused situation.

### South African

The South African Defense Forces were active in providing technical assistance and training to FAPLA/FALA clearance teams in the south of the country up to mid-1992. These operations cleared some 300,000 mines. In mid-1992, most sources agreed that the South African contribution was a well-motivated project based on a good knowledge of the general problems and the

---

[54] In the 1980s in Cunene according to ex-FAPLA deminer Albano Costa, "We used to drive cows out in front of us. If one was blown up - food for us. Excellent demining equipment. Heavy enough to blow up an antitank mine, too." Reuters, June 28, 1994.

specific devices (many of which were laid by the SADF itself).[55] All the Angolan parties responded positively to the South African initiative.

The South African firm Mechem has been aggressively seeking mine clearance contracts in Angola. In June 1994 the director of Mechem boasted that, "There are some mines in Angola which no will be able to find without our help."[56] On February 9, 1995 President Nelson Mandela in a meeting with the Angolan ambassador Xito Rodrigues offered South African expertise in mine clearance. In response to a question in the South African parliament in May 1996 about the South African landmine legacy in Angola, the minister of defense responded:

> With the exception of one minefield in the area south of Cuito Cunavale, no mines were left behind by SADF after their withdrawal from Angola. Assistance given by the SADF to facilitate the clearing of mines includes:
> [I] the training of Angolan forces in 1992 in mine/counter-mine warfare.
> [ii] the handing over in 1992 of a complete record to the Angolan government.
> [iii] the handing over earlier this year of two copies of the minefield record to BMATT and the British Military Attache in South Africa for use by the UN in their demining programme in Angola.
> [iv] a further comprehensive De-mining Planning and Management Course to be presented shortly by the National Defence Force for selected personnel in Angola.[57]

In June 1995 Mechem was awarded the $6.5 million U.N. contract to clear priority roads and mine verification.

---

[55] A South African mine specialist told *The Independent* newspaper (London) in June 1994 that the SADF put 27,000 mines, including 9,000 with anti-lift devices, in one minefield alone outside the southeastern Angolan town of Mavinga. *The Independent*, June 6, 1994.

[56] Ibid.

[57] Minister of Defence reply to question, South African parliament, May 15, 1996.

## The United Kingdom

British support for the Angolan mine clearing operations consisted of two-man Royal Engineer teams dispatched to instruct members of the Angolan army (FAA) in mine clearance techniques. The first mission was in December 1991, the second in March 1992. The training appears to have been of very low priority and little practical value.[58]

A second aspect of this British past involvement also deserves mention. The British policy was described by the British Defence Attache Col. Griffiths and his colleagues as solely providing "neutral advice" to the Angolans, but it appears that it was motivated at least in part by the desire to bring commercial advantage to British firms. Griffiths said that "the whole clearance initiative will be under the control of a joint Angolan-UK national coordination body which will be funded by donors such as the EEC." He then went on to explain that the "major work" would be undertaken by a U.K. company and the South Africans. He said that he could not reveal the name of the U.K. company because it was "commercial-in-confidence." Further sub-contracts would be awarded to independent companies.[59]

One of Griffiths' colleagues later confirmed to Human Rights Watch that the UK company involved was Royal Ordnance, and Human Rights Watch was later introduced to a Royal Ordnance representative who said he could be contacted through the British Embassy. Royal Ordnance is the privatized British arms manufacturer that is the major supplier of the British army, as well as an aggressive promoter of arms exports.

The UK continues to fund NGO mine clearance activities.

## United States

In 1991 when Human Rights Watch requested a clarification of planned U.S. involvement in mine eradication, the response indicated that the U.S. did not plan to assist with mine clearance. In 1994 this situation began to change and following the Lusaka Protocol, the U.S. became actively involved in funding mine clearance initiatives in Angola. USAID has funded several projects, including the first mine clearance operations by U.S.-based NGOs: Care International and Save the Children Fund (see below).

---

[58] Africa Watch, *Landmines in Angola*, pp. 52-53.

[59] Ibid.

## The U.N.'s Central Mine Action Office (CMAO)

The U.N. Humanitarian Assistance Coordination Unit (UCAH) began plans to set up a Central Mine Action Office (CMAO) in March 1994 with a $227,000 donation from Canada. Initially a consultant, Guy Lucas, was hired to gather information about landmines and make recommendations on what type of landmine program the U.N. should invest in following the signing of a peace accord. In late 1994 a former Canadian military officer, David McCracken, was hired to replace Lucas and run the office. In February 1995 a Mine Awareness Officer was added. The British Overseas Development Agency (ODA) decided to fund two additional positions within CMAO, a Mine Operation Manager and a Mine Training Officer.

CMAO is a specialized U.N. office operating within UCAH. It is mandated to be involved in capacity-building, act as a coordination point for demining activities of NGOs, UNAVEM, the FAA, UNITA and private contractors. It is also to assist NGOs in seeking funding for mine clearance and awareness activities.[60]

CMAO laid out its four-point mine action plan in mid-January 1995:

- Extensive surveys of mined areas (with priority given to peacekeeper deployment sites and quartering areas);
- Public education and awareness about mines;
- Mine clearance in priority areas; and
- Training Angolans in all aspects of mine action.[61]

The mine action plan argues for an integrated, prioritized approach, with UCAH/CMAO as the focal point. A central committee chaired by the U.N. Special Representative and UNAVEM and UCAH/CMAO was created to harmonize the military and humanitarian aspects of the mine action program in Angola. Two subcommittees were also created to look at, respectively, the specific mine action requirements for U.N. troop deployment and the installation of demobilization quartering areas, in addition to humanitarian assistance requirements.

CMAO and INAROEE work side-by-side in a joint operations center in Luanda. There were problems in 1995 in obtaining funding for this project because UNAVEM wanted to control it. CMAO found itself in a lengthy battle with

---

[60] Creative Associates, "The Status of Mine Action in Angola," report submitted to USAID/OTI, January 1996.

[61] U.N. Humanitarian Assistance Coordination Unit, "Briefing Note: Humanitarian Assistance in Angola," April 1995.

UNAVEM for the release of U.N. Department of Peacekeeping Operations (DPKO)/UNAVEM funds. Although CMAO submitted its first six-month procurement package to UNAVEM in May 1995 it was only in November that equipment was made available, and a senior U.N. Department of Humanitarian Affairs (DHA)New York staff member visited Angola in an effort to eliminate further delays. The visit produced a new document which redefined the roles and responsibilities of the key players.[62] The entire senior staff left the CMAO and a new team took over in early 1996. There has been a lack of continuity and a paucity of Lusophone speakers in the CMAO.

A 1996 report commissioned by the World Bank was highly critical of U.N. mine clearance programs in Angola and of CMAO in particular. The report, which was never made public, reportedly chastised CMAO for its lack of coordination with INAROEE and lack of Portuguese-speaking staff, and concluded that the current management, training and planning structure is unsustainable and unable to be effective. Some who have seen the report have told Human Rights Watch that while many of the criticisms are justified, the report lacked a full appreciation of local dynamics related to mine clearance.

An original objective of the CMAO was to prepare the way for UNAVEM, but it found itself starved for resources because most of the funding for demining in Angola was earmarked for DPKO and UNAVEM.[63] The U.N. Voluntary Trust Fund for Mine Clearance, run by DHA, had little available money. This problem continued throughout 1996 and into 1997.

The long-term U.N. objective was that there should be a national institution capable of managing mine-related issues after the completion of UNAVEM's mandate. A demining school established by the CMAO in Luanda began training its first group of 112 Angolan students in January 1996. Long delays

---

[62] CMAO documents: "Review of Mine action Plan for Angola," cable 3764 dated December 6, 1995; "Implementation Plan for Establishing a National Mine Clearance Capacity in Angola," Cable 3764, December 6, 1995.

[63] Funds for Angolan mine clearance were transferred in and out of accounts four times in 1995. Fault in the initial stages was with the Advisory Committee on Administrative and Budgetary Questions (ACABQ), which had vetoed funds in July, claiming it had heard about a Trust Fund with assets in it for Angolan clearance, although the reality was it had none. The Committee suggested re-submission in September and offered to make a new decision in October 1995. Eventually through lobbying and a strongly worded letter from the U.N. mine specialist, Patrick Blagden, the Fifth Committee of the General Assembly overruled the decision and funds were returned for Angolan clearance.

were experienced in obtaining suitable premises from the government, but in November 1995 a training site without buildings was provided outside of Luanda. By agreement with CMAO the UNAVEM force commander took over responsibility for managing the school and its UNAVEM military instructors in January 1996.

### National Institute for the Removal of Explosive Ordnance (INAROEE)

INAROEE is the national body designed to take over all aspects of the CMAO's work in mine action once the U.N. mandate expires.[64] INAROEE is comprised of an integrated UNITA and FAA team with forty staff members provided by CMAO. INAROEE has been working with the CMAO to design a National Mine Clearance Plan.

INAROEE headquarters is in Luanda. By December 1996, four regional headquarters had been established, with plans to deploy three brigades of sixty-six deminers each to all four regions by the middle of 1997. The total number of brigades might be expanded from twelve to eighteen (one in each province) in 1997 if INAROEE can attract additional funds.

INAROEE has also suffered from the lengthy UNAVEM funding delays. In the revised U.N. plan, the U.N. would provide INAROEE with funds for management support and for the field operations of the twelve brigades. INAROEE's director claimed in October 1996 that in Cazombo in Moxico province an INAROEE brigade was waiting to start clearing the road for repatriating refugees but INAROEE had no funds to fly equipment to them.[65] In October 1996 INAROEE announced that Malange and Bíe provinces were its priority provinces because of the high density population there.

The INAROEE team at Cunje, Bié province spent forty-five days in 1996 clearing a field between two villages that local people said was heavily mined. Only two mines were found, reinforcing the truth that the number of mines is mostly irrelevant—one mine is a problem.

Coordination and cooperation between INAROEE and other agencies has not always been good, in part simply because there are so many organizations involved. Some NGO programs operational prior to INAROEE were not willing to change their priorities as directed by the new agency. There have also been conflicts over competing priorities. One provincial governor wanted a motorcycle

---

[64] INAROEE was formed by government decree of law No.14/95 on May 26, 1995.

[65] *Jornal de Angola* (Luanda), October 8, 1996.

track demined as a high priority, before the scheduled clearance of a water point in a city which had no access to water.[66]

Responsibility for the support of INAROEE is to be transferred from UNAVEM and UCAH to UNDP, subject to the agreement of the government. The original date for transfer, March 1, 1997, was missed.[67] An April 1997 U.N. report stated, "The planned transition of the responsibility for support of the national mine clearance program in Angola from UNAVEM to the UNDP has been seriously delayed primarily because the Government has not yet signed the project document which was submitted for its approval in January 1997.... Unless urgent steps are taken to implement transitional arrangements...the entire program may be undermined and additional effort might be required to sustain it after June."[68]

The U.N. envisions a two-year plan for the development of Angola's national demining capacity, at an estimated cost of $25 million. This will be funded by the remaining funds in the U.N. Voluntary Trust Fund and by a new appeal.[69]

---

[66] Eddy Banks, "Current Mines Situation in Angola," CMAO, Luanda, September 1996.

[67] U.N. Security Council, "Report of the Secretary-General on UNAVEM III," S/1997/115, February 7, 1997.

[68] U.N. Security Council, S/1997/304, Report of the Secretary-General, April 14, 1997.

[69] U.N. Security Council S/1997/115, February 7, 1997. In January 1997 there was sufficient funding for the project until only March 1997. The Voluntary Trust Fund for Assistance in Mine Clearance is the fund established by the U.N. to assist demining initiatives. In addition the U.N. Consolidated Inter-Agency Appeal for Angola had a specific demining component. A request for $13 million for the Mine Action Program for Angola was made in 1995, of which only 24 percent had been met by April 1996. The 1996 appeal called for $5 million for demining, although by July 1996 only $1 million had been received.

## Central Mine Action Training School (CMATS)

CMATS is a joint government and U.N. funded training institute which has trained and equipped Angolan demining teams.[70] In late November 1995 a contract was signed by CMATS to set up operations. The school initially had thirty-five international staff and four Angolan instructors and interpreters. Instructors came from France, Italy, Holland, New Zealand, Pakistan, Sweden, and Uruguay. CMATS has suffered from funding shortages and an unclear chain of command between CMAO, INAROEE, CMATS and UNAVEM III. It planned to train 500 Angolan deminers by the end of 1996, but this was not achieved.

By December 1996, 350 Angolan nationals had been trained. In early 1997, demining brigades had been deployed to the provinces of Cuando Cubango, Uíge, Moxico, Bié, Malange, and Huambo. Another brigade was expected to deploy in Lunda Sul. Delays were attributed to a shortage of international supervisors, lack of equipment and poor cooperation among the parties.[71]

On February 16, 1997 the training school was transferred to INAROEE. UNAVEM III is considering the transfer of its demining equipment to this project when it pulls out.

## UNAVEM III

UNAVEM III has also engaged in mine clearance. On May 19, 1996 an engineering company of 206 Indian troops arrived in Angola as part of UNAVEM III. The Indian engineers engaged in mine clearing and the repair of bridges and roads, among other tasks. An advance party of British engineers which arrived in April 1996 also engaged in mine clearance of priority roads and cantonment areas for demobilizing troops. Namibia and Brazil have also provided 200 troops with

---

[70] In the January 1995 Chipapa meeting between UNITA and government military both sides agreed for the first time to form Joint Mine Clearing Teams and provide the U.N. with all necessary assistance in terms of mine information, reconnaissance, survey and clearance. Both sides also appointed Mine Liaison officers to the Joint Commission. By April UNAVEM had received limited information from FAA and UNITA concerning minefields, as well as confirmation that the parties will make available the necessary mine clearance personnel. Both sides believed, however, that the U.N. should equip and train the personnel. The government had allocated U.S.$3 million for the procurement of mine clearing equipment. The U.N. reported in December 1995 that, "the government/UNITA mine sweeping operation is still limited, owing mainly to mistrust between the two parties."

[71] "Progress Report of the Secretary-General of the United Nations Angola Verification Mission (UNAVEM III)," S/1996/827, October 4, 1996. See also, *Noticias* (Maputo), February 17, 1997.

mine clearing experience. As of February 1, 1997, United Nations troops had demined 4,505 kilometers of road.[72]

### Commercial Firms

Because of the lack of its own capacity to clear mines quickly, the U.N. awarded the South African firm, Mechem, a $6.5 million contract in June 1995 to clear mines along more than 7,000 kilometers of priority roads and to offer quality assessment of other road clearance operations.[73] Although scheduled to start in September 1995, a mixture of bureaucratic delays, Mechem's refusal to pay bribes and suspicion of Mechem by military officials resulted in a delay in off-loading its equipment in Luanda harbor.[74] Although the government gave Mechem permission in early December to become operational, the project only got underway on January 11, 1996. The German government also provided quality assessment officials to assist CMAO to supervise the Mechem contract.

Mechem's operations are based upon twenty-five air-sensing, armor-plated Caspir vehicles working in tandem with dog demining teams and other manual methods. Mechem deployed two teams, one in the northern and the other in the southern region of Angola. The teams of seventy-five deminers include sub-contracted personnel of other demining companies, such as Ronco, Gurkha Security Guards and Mine-Tech. Eleven Angolan deminers also worked with the Ronco team.

Mechem completed its clearance contract in the southern sector in August 1996. Mechem had to repeat its minesweeping operations on the Saurimo-Luena road when old mines were discovered there.[75]

From June 1995 to December 1996 over 4,000 kilometers of road had been cleared and twenty-four bridges re-opened. Mechem encountered a series of delays, including one that lasted several months. These were caused by UNITA

---

[72] U.N. Security Council, "Report of the Secretary-General on UNAVEM III," S/1997/115, February 7, 1997.

[73] The roads in the north, center and south of the country slated for clearance were in the following priority: Luanda to N'dalatando, Malange and Saurimo; Luanda to Lobito, Huambo and Luena; Lobito to Lubango and Menongue; Namibe to Lubango and Huambo; Huambo to Kuito; Huambo to Bailundo.

[74] The Star (Johannesburg), October 21, 1995.

[75] Telephone interview with CMAO, October 11, 1997.

because of alleged "security concerns." In fact, UNITA was reluctant to see roads opening up through the zones it controlled. For example, on May 19 the Mechem demining team was forced at gunpoint by UNITA forces to return to its point of origin east of the bridge over Rio Luí, even though the team had received authorization from UNITA's General "Bok" and Arlindo Pena "Ben Ben." The team was forced to return in darkness, resulting in one of the vehicles rolling off the side of the road. Fortunately there were no injuries but the vehicle had to be left at the site of the accident. Mechem completed its contract in Angola in early 1997 failing to have cleared certain roads, such as the Malange-Andulo-Kuito road. [76]

Other commercial firms are clearing mines around the Soyo oil installations, employed by FINA and SONANGOL. Saracen, linked to the South African firm Executive Outcomes, is working in Soyo, replacing the French firm Cofras and its successor CIDEV. The South African firm Shibata Security and the British firm, Defence Systems Limited, have also engaged in small-scale demining exercises in the Soyo area. CIDEV has distributed a proposal for a mechanized demining operation of Huíla province but has failed to attract funding to date.

### NGO Initiatives

#### Kap Anamur

The Kap Anamur Committee is a German humanitarian NGO founded in 1979. After one of its nurses became a landmine victim in Somalia, the organization decided to branch into humanitarian mine clearance. Kap Anamur set up a mine clearance project in Angola in May 1992 and operations began in August. Through agreement with the Angolan government the town of Xangongo (Cunene province) was chosen as a starting point. The German government provided former East German military equipment, including a number of T-55 tanks with KMT-5 rollers and off-road trucks. [77]

Former employees of Kap Anamur admitted that the importing of the T-55s was a bad idea because these tanks were readily available in Angola. The T-55s, moreover, functioned poorly in trial mine clearance operations. After a

---

[76] Interview with Vernon Joynt, Managing Director of Mechem, Harare, April 22, 1997. Joynt argued that it was not only UNITA politics that had hampered the completion of the contract but that the U.N. had also run out of funds to pay for his clearance costs.

[77] Committee Kap Anamur, German Emergency Doctors "Field Activity Report," April 1994.

mechanic died when a TM-62 mine exploded under the belly of T-55 tank equipped with KMT-5 rollers, the continued use of the tanks was scrapped.

The army and UNITA each sent a group of well-trained sappers (mine experts) to work jointly on the project, but the FALA members left the project after the October 1992 elections. In 1993 the operation had five Germans, twenty-five local sappers from FAA and twenty mechanics, at a cost of $20,000 a month. In addition to the T-55 casualty there were two other casualties by mid-1994. One sapper died when lifting a TM-62 mine with a shovel and another died in a probable UNITA ambush while clearing a road.

Between mid-1992 and 1994 Kap Anamur cleared minefields and mine clusters around Kahama, Humbe, Mulondo, Matala, Xangongo, Mongua, Cuamato, Ondjiva, Namakunde and Chitado. Kap Anamur claims to have cleared 50,626 antitank mines and 25,338 antipersonnel mines by mid-1994, in addition to large amounts of other types of unexploded ordnance. The most common mines cleared were TM-46, TM-57, and TM-62B antitank mines and PPM-2 and PPM-6 antipersonnel mines.

According to Kap Anamur the majority of minefields in Cunene were laid by Cubans, the army and SWAPO. The South Africans had cleared most of their minefields although not up to humanitarian clearance standards. Kap Anamur kept few records of what was cleared, and cleared areas were not marked.

Kap Anamur employed a sapper who said he had planted 1,835 antitank mines in a minefield around Xangongo in 1987. In 1993, working for Kap Anamur, he found only 300 mines. Many of the mines had apparently been lifted by local people in the late 1980s; many were reportedly then planted in roads in northern Namibia so as to claim lucrative South African reward offers for reports of mines because of acute poverty in the area. People would lift and carry the primed mines in rucksacks across the border. Although mines have exploded in transportation, the trade continues today. In the late 1980s Angolan and Cuban forces tried to protect their antitank mines from theft by protecting them with a cluster of antipersonnel mines. But this was not a regular pattern nor a successful deterrent.[78]

In early 1995 Kap Anamur attempted to move its operations from Cunene to Benguela province with fatal consequences. Kap Anamur had cleared the Benguela, Catengue, Caimbambo, Cubal and Calondende stretch of road, but had encountered problems at Calondende. On March 1, 1995 five people, including one

---

[78] Hans Georg Kruessen, "Landminen in Angola: Raeumen, Zestoeren...und danach?," in "Landminen in Angola und Mosambik," seminar report (Bielefeld: KoordinierungsKreis Mosambiek, July 1995), pp. 29-31.

German attached to the Kap Anamur project, were killed by unidentified gunmen at Solo, one hundred kilometers from Benguela, between Catengue and Caimbambo, while traveling along the Catengue-Caimbambo road. The gunmen also took all the victims' personal belongings and the organization's technical equipment. The attack appears to have been aimed at keeping the road closed because the clearance team had received several indirect warnings not to work in the area prior to the incident.

Kap Anamur was also involved in controversy when one of its expatriate staff was arrested in 1995 for involvement in the illegal export of munitions to Namibia. Kap Anamur ceased operating in Angola in 1996.

### Mines Advisory Group

The Mines Advisory Group's (MAG) presence in Angola dates to mid-1992 with the start of a Community Mine Awareness poster campaign in cooperation with UNHCR. Following a specialist mission by MAG to Angola in November 1993, MAG began operations in April 1994, setting up a base in Luena, Moxico Province. Luena was chosen because of its critical location for returning refugees from Zambia and Zaire following a cease-fire. The UNHCR estimated that up to 200,000 refugees would use four mined routes to travel to or through Luena. Additionally there is a shortage of land for the communities and for agricultural projects of relief agencies because of mines.[79]

By October 1994 the construction of a demining school was finished and by October 1996 134 deminers were operational and thirty more had just been trained. Nine minefields are prioritized for initial clearance operations. MAG has concentrated on one minefield in particular. One hundred and forty families, including a camp of internally displaced, live within one hundred meters of this minefield; two hundred and forty families, as well as a school and three churches are within 500 meters. The local community has already farmed every inch up to the minefield boundary and some people have entered the area searching for firewood. Several U.N. officials have criticized MAG's focus of resources on this one minefield as being extravagant and have advised that MAG should be working on clearing priority routes in the short term.

Mine clearance operations in Moxico province were suspended in mid-January 1995 until late March 1995 because of a dispute with the governor of Luena although all the minefields prioritized for clearance serve no military role. This problem was eventually resolved with the intervention of the Minister of Social Assistance, Albino Malungo.

---

[79] Mines Advisory Group Annual Report 1994/95.

MAG is now part of a larger comprehensive rehabilitation project in Moxico in coordination with the Vietnam Veterans of America Foundation and Medico International (Germany). It involves an integrated approach to the full range of needs of individuals and communities affected by landmines. The overall project includes mine clearance and mine awareness, as well as physical, psycho-social and socio-economic rehabilitation components.

In October 1996 MAG also expanded its clearance operations to Lumeje, UNITA's "capital" in Moxico province. In coordination with INAROEE and the CMAO teams operating in Cazombo, MAG also plans to further expand its activities in Luau, which has a severe mine problem and will be a focal point for repatriation from Zaire.[80] MAG has also formed Mine Action Teams (MATs), which are mine awareness and minefield survey personnel who work together in gathering information and marking mined sites in order to assess the local priorities for clearance.[81]

Initial funding for these MAG clearance operations was contributed by CAFOD, OXFAM and Christian Aid. The British ODA funded a mine survey and marking project in the second half of 1994. In 1996 MAG funding came from USAID, DanChurchAID and the U.N. DHA Mine Clearance Trust Fund.

**Halo Trust**

The British NGO Halo Trust began operating in Kuito in late 1994. One of its deminers was killed on November 11, 1994. In January 1995 the government, through the Ministry of Defense and the Ministry of Cooperation, issued a permit to Halo Trust for demining operations in Kuito, Benguela and Huambo provinces. Britain's ODA has provided funds for mine clearance in Benguela. Halo Trust's initial work was in the city of Kuito itself with a team of twenty-six Angolans and twelve expatriates. Between November 1994 and February 1995 Halo destroyed 1,200 mines in central Kuito. In May 1995 Halo Trust faced a crisis over its operations, following a dispute with the governor of Kuito, who indicated that he wanted the team removed from Bié province. The Halo Trust manager in Luanda told Human Rights Watch that government confidence in them has improved, but

---

[80] The 180,000 Angolan refugees in Zaire are fearful of returning home because of landmines. See, Berthuel Kasamwa-Tuseko, "Les Réfugiés angolais ne veulent pas rentrer sur des champs de mines," *Propeace* (Kigali), no.1, January 1996, pp.47-48.

[81] Human Rights Watch telephone interview with MAG Angola desk officer, Cockermouth, November 11, 1996.

that UNITA is still distrustful, and refuses to share information about where UNITA mines are located.[82]

Halo has also conducted limited local surveys in Benguela and Huambo and began clearing mines in Huambo on January 26, 1996. It maintains nine clearance teams and three survey teams in Angola. Halo claims to have cleared 3,000 mines in 1995. In October 1996 Halo cleared mines around pylons in Kunje, at an average of seventy mines a day. In Bié province, Halo has a team of 127 deminers.[83]

### Norwegian People's Aid

Norwegian People's Aid (NPA), a nonprofit mine clearance organization, in January 1995 obtained a permit to clear mines in Malange province from the Ministry of Defense and the Ministry of Cooperation. NPA encountered difficulties in starting up, including instances when government forces planted mines to block NPA's attempt to become fully operational. [84]

In February 1995 NPA began to deploy its first team of deminer platoons in two locations along the Malange-Luanda corridor as part of an agreement with the World Food Program and SwedRelief. By March 1995 NPA had cleared two bridgeheads over Rio Macuso and Rio Lombe. By August NPA had still not been able to start work on its principal mine clearing tasks because the military situation was too tense. In 1996 NPA gradually starting clearing land around Malange. Mark Buswell of NPA stated, "We want to prioritize fertile areas, and if they are not of great military significance, the parties gradually accept that we will clear the areas. The military also gain advantages when areas around water stations and health stations are cleared, so in such cases it is easier to get permission."[85]

Five specially trained dogs were brought in from Mozambique in 1996 but fell ill with sleeping sickness because they had not been vacinated and needed to be replaced. NPA expects the number of dogs deployed to grow to up to fifteen in 1997. On October 3, 1996 NPA announced the start of its clearance operations in

---

[82] Human Rights Watch telephone interview with Halo Trust in Luanda, November 6, 1995.

[83] *Jornal de Angola*, November 11, 1996.

[84] Human Rights Watch telephone interview with NPA in Luanda, August 1995.

[85] Norwegian People's Aid, *Mines: The Silent Killers* (Oslo: NPA, 1996), p.16.

Cuanza Norte province around Dondo and Ndalatando.[86] In February 1997 NPA planned to train 300 sappers to clear mines in Malange, Kwanza Norte and Benguela provinces. Mine clearing teams were working in Benguela, Bengo, Malange and Kwanza Norte provinces in 1997 and were considering extending their activity to Cabinda, Zaire, Uíge and Huíla provinces.

NPA was also contracted by the U.N. to conduct a nationwide survey of the landmine problem in the northern eleven provinces, to map the presence of mines, consequences for local trade and the extent of damage. After a series of delays NPA began work on the survey in June 1995, but progress was slow. Both sides were reluctant to give real information about landmines and access to the area was difficult. Serious work got underway in the spring of 1996. By February 1997, field work was completed in four provinces (Bengo, Cuanza Norte, Benguela, and Malange). Field work was underway in Uíge and Zaire provinces with three survey teams, one supervisor and one data base analyst. NPA hoped to survey eleven of the eighteen provinces. The INAROEE emphasis had since moved away from a nationwide survey to survey work by the respective mine clearance organizations in the areas in which they operate.

### Save the Children Fund (USA)

Save the Children Fund (USA) won a mine clearance contract from USAID in 1995. SCF initially funded expanded NPA teams to clear mines in Cuanza Sul and Bengo and Moxico provinces with the goal of making agricultural land accessible to the internally displaced, refugees, demobilized soldiers and residents. Save the Children established a demining school near Sumbe and commenced in January 1996 to train 170 deminers through NPA. A total of 250 deminers were trained and Save the Children took over management of the operations from NPA.[87]

However, their clearance operation ran into problems following a serious accident on November 28, 1996 in Bengo province in which three deminers were severely injured. Save the Children suspended its mine clearance operations pending a review. Reportedly, a group of deminers all approached a recently uncovered mine, when it exploded. The medical evacuation was described by a U.N. official as a "comedy of errors," with the vehicle carrying the injured crashing

---

[86] *Noticias* (Maputo), October 3, 1996.

[87] Human Rights Watch telephone interview with CMAO, October 11, 1996.

and no senior supervisory staff on location at the time of accident.[88] Save the Children has subsequently pulled out of Angola, but it is unclear what will happen to its teams.

### Care International (USA)
Care International (USA) was in 1997 funding Greenfield Consultants, a new commercial firm based in the U.K. and run by the former Halo Trust manager in Mozambique. Greenfield first signed in 1995 a twelve month contract with Care which called for two clearance teams operating in Cuando Cubango province, plus mine awareness programs in Bié, Cunene, Huíla and Cuando Cubango provinces. The clearance teams were deployed in December 1995.[89] They cleared mines in Huambo in late 1996.

### Other NGOs
MGM, a German-based NGO, received charitable status on July 5, 1996. It is run by former members of Kap Anamur who left that organization because of increasing controversy over its safety and ethical record. MGM, funded mainly by the German government, was awarded a contract from the World Food Program in August 1996 to clear roads for the internally displaced in Caxito, Bengo province. The first clearance operations commenced in November around Dange bridge, resulting in four mines cleared.[90]

Sankt Barbara is also a German-based mine clearance organization, run by Gerhart Bornman. Like MGM, Sankt Barbara is funded by the German government and has been awarded a contract by the WFP to clear route ways that will be used for the return of internally displaced persons in Benguela province. Sankt Barbara was not yet operational as of April 1997.[91]

---

[88] Human Rights Watch telephone interview with U.N. DHA official, New York, December 11, 1996.

[89] Human Rights Watch telephone interview with David Hewitson of Greenfield Consultants, London, January 30, 1996.

[90] MGM web page, http://www.dsk.de/mgm.

[91] Human Rights Watch interview with Hélder Da Silva Cruz, director of INAROEE, Harare, April 21, 1997.

Humanitarian Aid Medical Development (HMD International) is a London-based NGO that plans to carry out mine clearance training and mine awareness activities, starting in Saurimo region in 1997.[92]

**Mine Awareness Initiatives**

Coordinated by the CMAO, a national mine awareness program was started in 1994, using media and messages printed on bags and clothing. The campaign was led by Norwegian People's Aid in coordination with UNICEF, Catholic Relief Services, the International Federation of Red Cross and Red Crescent Societies and the Norwegian Refugee Council.[93] It was originally planned to train 390 local mine awareness instructors spread over eleven cities in nine provinces between May 1, 1995 and May 1, 1996. This was extended to September 1996 and another 240 local mine awareness instructors were trained. According to the CMAO, by September 1996 an estimated 920,000 people received mine awareness training and eighty-two supervisors and more than 620 instructors had been trained in thirteen provinces.

The Mines Advisory Group has also conducted a mine awareness program in the refugee camps in Zambia and has attempted to run a program in Zaire. For a brief period in 1996 MAG clashed with the Lutheran World Federation in Meheba camp in Zambia, which was concerned that Mines Advisory Group mine awareness campaign was frightening Angolans out of repatriating. Organized repatriation programs were eventually postponed, and rescheduled from 1996 to mid-1997.

In 1996 there were also increased efforts by CMAO to strengthen the links between mine awareness and survey programs. Information (Level I) gained in these sessions was collated in the national data base at CMAO/INAROEE and was to be the foundation for more detailed survey work (Level II and Level III). The aim was to locate accurately danger points and reduce them to the smallest possible size so that the limited resources available were not wasted. The data base was also used to provide information to any new organization planning to move to a new location. In preparation for the resettlement of internally displaced persons (IDPs)

---

[92] UCAH News, November 28, 1996.

[93] World Vision and Care International were also to be involved but Care International pulled out in April 1995.

and refugees in the eastern sector of Moxico province a Level I survey in mid-1996 identified seventy-eight minefields.[94]

As with mine clearance, there have been problems of coordination in mine awareness operations. MAG criticized NPA efforts in Luena. NPA, in turn, has complained about Care International efforts in Menongue, which it said duplicated already existing services. NPA also claimed that CARE paid three times NPA wages, destroying local salary structures and undermining confidence and momentum in the NPA program.

**Antipersonnel Mine Ban Position**

While Angola had been receiving much international attention for several years because of the extent of its landmine problem, the Angolan government had little to say about the growing global effort to ban antipersonnel mines. The Angolan government came under increasing international and domestic pressure in 1996 to make a serious effort toward banning antipersonnel landmines.[95] At the end of the Convention on Conventional Weapons review conference on May 3, 1996 in Geneva, Angolan Ambassador Parreira, signaled an official shift. In the final plenary session he announced that "as recommended in article 4 of the resolutions 1593 and 1628 of the Organization of African Unity, I am honoured to avail of this singular opportunity to declare that the Government of Angola supports a total prohibition of all types of antipersonnel mines."[96]

This commitment was reiterated by Angola's foreign minister on September 23, 1996 when he told the U.N. General Assembly in New York that Angola supported all efforts aimed at the complete elimination of the production, use and trade of antipersonnel mines in both international and domestic conflicts.

Angola attended the first ever meeting of fifty pro-ban governments in Ottawa, Canada in October 1996 and agreed to the final declaration calling for an urgent and comprehensive ban on antipersonnel mines. Angola also attended the conference in Vienna, Austria in February 1997 to discuss the elements of a total ban treaty. A representative of the Angolan government was present throughout the

---

[94] Eddy Banks, "Current Mines Situation in Angola," CMAO, Luanda, September 1996.

[95] *Folha 8* (Luanda), No.106, May 10, 1996 in a feature article called on the government to sign the CCW and ban landmines for example.

[96] Permanent Mission of Angola to the U.N. in Geneva, "Statement, by H.E. Prof. Dr. Adriano Parreira Permanent Representative of Angola," Geneva, May 3, 1996.

4th International NGO Conference on Landmines, held in Mozambique February 25-28, 1997, and told the conference that Angola supports a regional mine-free-zone in southern Africa.

The verbal commitment to a ban has not been followed up with concrete actions, however. No unilateral steps have been taken with respect to a moratorium or ban on use, import or export of antipersonnel mines, or with respect to destruction of stockpiles of mines.

Brian Atwood, the head of USAID, visited Angola in February 1996 and asked President dos Santos and UNITA leader Savimbi to blow up their stocks of landmines. U.S. Senator Patrick Leahy subsequently made the same request. It is a request that the Security Council has also made to both parties in Angola. U.N. Security Council Resolution 1087 (December 11, 1996) "Calls upon both parties to intensify their demining efforts, and reiterates the need for continued commitment to peace by destruction of stockpiles of landmines monitored and verified by UNAVEM III...."

On November 28, 1996 a group of Angolan NGOs coordinated by the Forum Das ONG's Angolanas (FONGA) began the Angolan Campaign to Ban Landmines. The campaign is supported by some twenty NGOs. A petition circulated by the campaign had already gathered about 30,000 signatures by March 1997, including that of Henrik Vaal Neto, the Minister of Information. The need for an antipersonnel mine ban was also underlined by Britain's Diana, Princess of Wales, when she visited Angola in January 1997 on behalf of the British Red Cross.

## III. BOTSWANA

Botswana (formerly Bechuanaland) obtained independence on September 30, 1966. Botswana provided sanctuary to nationalist guerrillas fighting for independence in what was then Rhodesia (now Zimbabwe), Namibia and South Africa. This resulted in occasional raids by Rhodesian troops into northern Botswana in the late 1970s and covert raids by the South African security forces against ANC and SWAPO guerrillas in the 1980s.

Only the Rhodesians used landmines during their cross-border incursions. They planted a limited number of Rhodesian-made RAP 1, RAP 2, and Shrapnel No. 2 mines in northern Botswana in 1978-79. All of these are believed to have been cleared and there has not been a reported landmine incident in over a decade.

The Botswana Defence Force maintains a small stockpile of landmines.[97] The government of Botswana has been largely silent on the issue of an international ban on antipersonnel mines, but encouragingly attended the February 1997 conference in Austria aimed at developing a ban treaty, and voted in favor of the December 1997 U.N. General Assembly resolution recognizing the need for the conclusion of such a treaty "as soon as possible."

---

[97] Botswana Defence Force official, Harare, March 3, 1995.

59

# IV. MALAWI

Malawi became independent on July 6, 1964. Two years later Malawi officially became a one party state with President Hastings Banda as president. For the next twenty-five years Banda ruled ruthlessly, no political opposition was tolerated, and the government was responsible for using detention without trial, torture and assassination to suppress political opposition.[98] Only in 1994 did opposition become more vocal. In mid-June 1993 a referendum on multi-party democracy resulted in 63 percent of voters demanding an end to one party rule. Multi-party elections were finally held in May 1994, with Bakili Muluzi, leader of the United Democratic Front, winning the presidential contest with 47 percent of the vote to Banda's 34 percent.

Malawi's foreign policy during the Banda era was complex and Machiavellian, especially regarding Mozambique and South Africa. For example, Malawi permitted Renamo rebels from Mozambique to maintain rear bases in Malawi until late 1986. Yet, on December 4, 1986 the Mozambique and Malawi governments set up a security commission, then signed a Joint Security Pact later that month.

From April 1987 until mid-1993, Malawian troops deployed along the Nacala railway corridor to protect it from Renamo attack, using landmines in their operations. Many of the mines were supplied by the United States as part of a broader military assistance package to the Malawian Defence Force.[99]   U.S. supplied mines found in Malawi include M14s, M16A1s, and M18A1 Claymore mines.

Malawi does not have minefields. Most of the mines on Malawian soil have spilled across the Mozambique border where they were laid by Frelimo or Renamo. There have also been a few reported incidents where landmines have been brought across from Mozambique and used in criminal activities. Edmund Chimaliro of the Malawi Red Cross works as a project coordinator in Dzaleka refugee camp. He told Amnesty International in November 1996 that:

---

[98] See, Africa Watch, *Where Silence Rules: The Suppression of Dissent in Malawi* (New York: Human Rights Watch, 1990).

[99] U.S. Army Foreign Science and Technology Center  Intelligence Report, "Landmine Warfare - Mines and Engineer Munitions in Southern Africa (U)."

Landmines are not really a problem in Malawi, but there have been been several incidents on Malawi soil. In Chikwakwa at Changambika refugee camps, Mozambicans planted landmines for killing each other. During my time in these camps we had three incidents. In one incident, they had hung up a poster up on a tree to attract people to read what it said. The landmine was placed under the poster and a person was blown up for his curiosity to read what was on the poster. In Nsanje, another person was blown up by a landmine planted outside the bathroom.[100]

There were mine awareness campaigns in 1993 and 1994 in the refugee camps for returning Mozambicans. The Malawi Red Cross Society in 1996 carried out a poster campaign with the slogan, "This is What Landmines Tear Off Every Twelve Hours."[101]

The government of Malawi had not actively participated in international efforts to ban antipersonnel landmines before 1997, although it co-sponsored the December 10, 1996 U.N. General Assembly Resolution. However, at the 4th International NGO Conference on Landmines in Maputo in February 1997, General O.B. Binauli, High Commissioner of Malawi to Mozambique, stated that Malawi "condemn(s) the manufacture, export, import, use and stockpiling of any type of mines." He indicated Malawi's support for the Ottawa process aimed at the signing of a total ban treaty in December 1997, and said, "Malawi is now working on draft legislation to join the world community to ban landmines subject to approval by Parliament; and Civil Society is committed to campaign for the ban and eradication of landmines in the world."[102]

---

[100] Interview transcript provided by Amnesty International researcher Casey Kelso, London, December 19, 1996.

[101] *The Nation* (Lilongwe), September 11, 1996.

[102] "Malawi Government's Position on Landmines," presented by H.E. General O.B. Binauli, High Commissioner of Malawi to Mozambique, to the 4th International NGO Conference on Landmines, Maputo, Mozambique, February 27, 1997.

# V. MOZAMBIQUE

## Background

Mozambique was at war almost continuously from the mid-1960s when the independence struggle erupted against the Portuguese until October 1992, when the Mozambican government and Renamo rebels signed a cease-fire accord. In October 1994 the first multi-party elections ever were held, won by the ruling party, Frelimo, and the country has remained at peace. Prior to the 1992 cease-fire combatants on both sides used landmines, often directly against civilians. Mines have claimed thousands of victims and continue to do so even though the war has ended. Since the October 1992 General Peace Accord over 1,000 people have been injured by landmines.

Mines have taken a terrible human toll in Mozambique. There are an estimated 10,000 amputees who have received some form of medical treatment. Medical facilities are quite primitive, and rehabilitation services inadequate. Landmines also constitute one of the most immediate obstacles to postwar redevelopment. They affect delivery of relief aid, resettlement and agricultural and commercial reconstruction.

## The Colonial War

The guerrilla struggle against the Portuguese began in earnest in September 1964, led by the Front for the Liberation of Mozambique (Frelimo). The Portuguese colonial authorities had already deployed some 30,000 troops in Mozambique by then. On June 14, 1965 in Cóbuè (Niassa province) and on November 25, 1965 in Muidumbe (Cabo Delgado) antipersonnel mines were used for the first time by Frelimo.[103] The use of antivehicle mines began in October 1965 in both provinces. In December 1966 the Portuguese military claimed to have captured 157 foreign manufactured mines from Frelimo. By 1967 the Portuguese began to admit that mines in particular were responsible for a number of casualties and that there had been a loss of some territory in the far north to the rebels.[104]

In 1967 the Portuguese created a "no man's land" inside the northern frontier, abandoning to the rebels the thinly populated areas along the Tanzanian

---

[103] Military Intelligence, "Supintrep No.18 - Potência de Combate das Forças da Frelimo," March 1968.

[104] Alex Vines and João Paulo Borges Coelho, "Trinta Anos de Guerras e Minas em Moçambique," in Arquivo Histórico de Moçambique (ed), *Moçambique: Desminagem e Desenvolvimento* (Maputo: Arquivo Histórico de Moçambique, 1995), pp.11-49.

border. Below this zone the local population was concentrated in *aldeamentos* (fortified villages). As early as 1965 a small nationalist group, the Mozambique Revolutionary Committee (COREMO), had laid a limited number of landmines in Tete province. [105]

Frelimo increasingly mined roads north of the Lúrio river in the late 1960s. Portuguese soldiers nicknamed the area "Minas Gerais," (General Mines) playing on the name of the Brazilian state. Frelimo's landmine campaign contributed to the Portuguese decision to launch the biggest offensive of the war thus far, "Operation Gordian Knot," against Frelimo strongholds in Cabo Delgado. [106]

The conflict escalated seriously in early 1969 when Frelimo opened a new front in Tete province in an effort to bypass attempted Portuguese containment in the north and to threaten Portugal's plans to complete the Cahora-Bassa hydroelectric project. The Portuguese reported the use of many landmines in 1971 and 1972. [107]

The Beira-Moatize railway line was a frequent target for Frelimo attack as the main supply line to Cabora-Bassa until 1974. From 1970 Frelimo's forces carried out an increasing number of hit-and-run raids without confronting the enemy directly. Simultaneously, Frelimo increasingly used landmines to attempt to cut road communications.

A Frelimo fighter described use of landmines in ambushes:

> There was not a day without an ambush. When we were in the
> dry season we used another strategy. In that dry season when a
> person could not be without thirst, we would sabotage with one
> big mine here, for a vehicle, and then at a shady point, put small
> mines. When they came there with the injured they would come

---

[105] João Paulo Borges Coelho, lecturer, Department of History, University Eduardo Mondlane, interview, Maputo, February 26, 1997.

[106] Rodrigo de Silveira, "Ataque a Minas Gerais," in José Freira Antunes, *A Guerra de África 1961-1974, Vol. II* (Lisbon: Circulo de Leitores, 1995), p. 804.

[107] According to Portuguese military intelligence document AHM,FGT, Cx S/n GG/SCCIM, 1972 the following landmine incidents were reported for 1971 and 1972: Niassa, 126/111; Cabo Delgado, 283 / 213 ; Tete, 167/390. Landmines deactivated in the same period were Niassa, 159/143; Cabo Delgado 852/650; Tete, 395/1040.

to dance amongst themselves, eh eh eh. The situation for them worsened greatly.[108]

Security of the Cahora-Bassa project was one of the main preoccupations of the Portuguese colonial authorities, who boasted that the complex was surrounded by the "largest" minefield in Africa, with some 80,000 landmines in it.[109]

However the situation was always more complicated than it appeared. In his 1988 memoirs Portuguese General Kaúlza Oliveira de Arriaga, the Portuguese commander for Mozambique, described the daunting task he faced to protect Cahora-Bassa in 1971-72 with limited resources:

The security plan for Cahora-Bassa around the dam and the hydro-electric installation required the mounting of an obstacle of three circular fences of barbed wire, inside which would be continuous antipersonnel minefields. This obstacle was constantly watched and regarded by the terrorists as impenetrable. But despite there being two or three establishments in the metropol [Portugal] producing at reasonable prices these mines, they were never sent to Mozambique in minimally sufficient quantities. This drew protests from the Commander-in-Chief, inclusive within the High Command for National Defense. As a result the President of the Council of Ministers and the Minister for National Defence ordered without ambiguity the immediate despatch of mines. However, these mines never reached Mozambique. We had therefore to lay at one point or another the small number of mines we had from existing stocks in the province and operate a psychological operation to convince all those interested of the existence of effective minefields. The result of this psychological operation was excellent, convincing the residents and enemy that

---

[108] João Paulo Borges Coelho, "Entrevista com a Associação dos Antigos Combatantes de Tete," *Arquivo*, no.13, April 1993.

[109] *The Daily Telegraph* (London), July 2, 1973.

impenetrable minefields had been established around Cahora-Bassa.[110]

Although antipersonnel mines in the numbers sought from Portugal were not forthcoming, Arriaga purchased additional stocks from South Africa. Journalists traveling in Cabo Delgado and Tete in 1973 were warned by Frelimo to keep to set paths because Portuguese forces had laid mines along suspected Frelimo infiltration routes.

In March 1970 Frelimo began "Operation Estrada" in Cabo Delgado, which involved mining and booby trapping roads south to Rio Messalo. The Portuguese response was to increase the tarring of roads and, in 1970, they launched the largest military operation of the war. "Operation Gordian Knot" penetrated deep into the northern areas of Cabo Delgado and Niassa districts, resulting in the destruction of many Frelimo rear bases. Although the campaign demonstrated the Portuguese ability to still inflict tactical defeats on Frelimo, it also illustrated the overall Portuguese inability to maintain control of a combat zone of over 400,000 square kilometers. By 1972 the Portuguese army in Mozambique peaked in size at 60,000 men, including 40,000 Africans. However, Frelimo was still able to improve its military position in 1972 and 1973, and began in 1974 to carry out regular attacks in the Vila Pery District (present-day Manica province). This brought the war for the first time within striking distance of the main white population centers.

To cope with Frelimio mines the Portuguese took measures ranging from tarring roads to placing sandbags underneath the driver and passengers to lessen the force of a mine blast. Frelimo guerrilla units in Tete began using charcoal to disguise the mines put in tarred roads, making visual detection more difficult. Portuguese attempts to clear roads and tracks were infrequent until near the end of the conflict. A Rhodesian liaison visit to Nampula in 1971 found the Portuguese had only one mine detector in their possession, and it was non-functional.[111] Portuguese patrols relied almost entirely on men walking ahead of military convoys, prodding with long sharp implements ("Picas"). Frelimo guerrillas began

---

[110] Kaúlza Oliveira de Arriaga, *Guerra e Política: Em Nome da Verdade. Os Anos Decisivos* (Lisbon: Edição Referendo, 1987), p.231. Arriaga's estimate of landmines planted arround Cahora-Bassa could be incorrect as Norwegian People's Aid has uncovered large numbers. It could also be that the post-independence government planted additional mines.

[111] Peter Swift, *Taming the Landmine*, p.41.

to plant mines with anti-prodding devices, often simple tin contacts kept apart by paper that detonated a mine once prodded.[112]

Frelimo targeted more than just railways, convoys and soldiers with landmines. In Tete province Frelimo began a "dirty" war, aimed at preventing productive life in the aldeamentos. Antipersonnel landmines were planted on the paths used by the population to collect water, on the *Machambas* (plots of land) themselves or on access roads. Portuguese military reports of landmines casualties in Tete province show that the vast majority of mines planted by Frelimo were targeted against civilians on access paths out of the *aldeamentos*.[113]

### Independence and Beyond

The war came to a close following a military coup in Lisbon in April 1974, brought about in part by growing disillusionment with Portugal's colonial wars. Portugal quickly decided to grant independence to its five African colonies, including Mozambique. The Frelimo leadership formed a transitional government in September 1974 and led the country to independence in June 1975. Frelimo has ruled Mozambique ever since. For a number of years Frelimo ruled ruthlessly as a Marxist-Leninist party which tolerated little opposition domestically, and which developed close links with communist and socialist countries.[114]

In 1977, a long-running war began with the Mozambique National Resistance (Renamo or MNR), which was created that year by the Rhodesian Central Intelligence Office (CIO) in response to Mozambique's support for Zimbabwe nationalist guerrillas. Just before Zimbabwe gained independence in 1980, the management of Renamo was transferred to South Africa and run by South Africa's Military Intelligence Directorate (MID).[115]

The transfer marked a turning point in the war, which soon began to escalate. The South African government used Renamo as a tool for destabilizing

---

[112] Ibid.

[113] Portuguese Military Intelligence, 4° Secção/CMD/ZOT, situation report from May 1972 to July 1974.

[114] Africa Watch, *Conspicuous Destruction: War, Famine and the Reform Process in Mozambique* (New York: Human Rights Watch, 1992).

[115] Alex Vines, *Renamo: From Terrorism to Democracy in Mozambique?* (Oxford: James Currey in association with the Centre for Southern African Studies, University of York and the Eduardo Mondlane Foundation, Amsterdam, 1996).

Mozambique and as a counter to Mozambique's support for the African National Congress (ANC). South Africa's aims were to disable Mozambique's infrastructure and economy, thereby bringing Frelimo to the negotiating table, and making it more compliant to South African objectives. Pumped up with ample military supplies from South Africa, Renamo's strength increased between 1980 and 1982 from less than 1,000 to 8,000 fighters. The first combat areas were Manica and Sofala provinces, but Renamo quickly expanded its military operations throughout most of the country. By 1982 fighting had spread to Gaza and Inhambane provinces and to the country's richest province, Zambézia.[116]

In the early 1980s, Renamo acquired its reputation for savagery. It became particularly well-known for its practice of mutilating civilian victims, including children, by cutting off ears, noses, lips and sexual organs. Renamo also engaged in numerous attacks on civilian targets such as transportation links, health clinics and schools.

The government made a bid to end the war in 1984, when it signed the Nkomati non-aggression pact with South Africa. South Africa said it would halt its support of Renamo if Maputo stopped its support for ANC military operations. A series of South African-mediated negotiations followed between the government and Renamo, with some positive results, but the talks quickly collapsed.

The Mozambican government largely abided by the Nkomati Accord, while, by their own admission, the South Africans did not. Foreign Minister "Pik" Botha conceded that "technical violations" of Nkomati had occurred after Mozambique publicized the contents of rebel diaries found by Zimbabwean and Mozambican troops when they overran Renamo's Casa Banana headquarters (near Gorongosa, Sofala province) in 1985.

In 1983, Frelimo began to change its policies, moving toward free market capitalism, pursuing nonalignment internationally, and developing increasingly good relations with many Western nations. At the same time, Renamo began operating with greater autonomy from South Africa, expanding its operations, and becoming increasingly brutal, killing thousands of civilians as it carved territory for itself.

By 1986, Renamo units had pushed deep into Zambézia province and routed poorly supplied government positions in Tete, especially in Mutarara district. At one point it appeared as if Renamo would capture the city of Quelimane (Zambézia), cutting the country into two and giving Renamo the opportunity to set

---

[116] Ibid.

up an alternative government. These Renamo gains and the fears of even more severe famine caused tens of thousands of refugees to flee to Malawi.[117]

As the Mozambique Armed Forces weakened, the government took steps to reverse the situation. Diplomatic pressure was put on Malawi to halt Renamo operations on its soil. Tanzanian and Zimbabwean troops were brought in to help government forces to regain lost territory.

During this period, President Samora Machel was killed in a mysterious plane crash. Joaquim Chissano, Mozambique's foreign minister since independence, became president. Chissano undertook a major review of Frelimo's economic, foreign and human rights policies. This ultimately led to reforms and peace negotiations which began in 1990.[118]

The armed forces launched a major counter-offensive along the Zambezi river in 1987. Soviet-trained Red Beret commandos, with air support, toppled one rebel-held town after another on the north bank of the Zambezi river. An estimated 3,000 Tanzanian soldiers took up defensive positions along the river valley, guarding the recaptured settlements. Elite Zimbabwean paratroopers launched an offensive in Manica and Sofala, and pounded rebel strongholds in the mountainous Gorongosa region. The tide had clearly turned and Renamo was increasingly on the defensive.

This counter-offensive and the continuing actions of Renamo sent hundreds of thousands of refugees into the neighboring countries of Malawi, Zambia and Zimbabwe. Renamo committed the biggest massacres of the war in late 1987 in Inhambane and Gaza provinces apparently in a desperate attempt to stop military reverses in the area.

In April 1988, the U.S. State Department released a report on Renamo's treatment of civilians, as told by refugees. In this report, Robert Gersony, a specialist in refugee affairs, accused the rebels of killing at least 100,000 people and running what were effectively slave labor camps in zones they controlled. He reported that only a fraction of the armed attacks against civilians in Mozambique could be attributed to the government army.[119] While the report accurately detailed

---

[117] Africa Watch, *Conspicuous Destruction*, p.33.

[118] Ibid.

[119] Robert Gersony, "Summary of Mozambican Refugee Accounts of Principally Conflict Related Experiences in Mozambique" (Washington D.C.: Department of State, 1988).

the horror of much of Renamo's military methods and human rights abuses, it minimized abuses by government armed forces.

South Africa continued to support Renamo with arms and intelligence until former President de Klerk took over the government in late 1989. By late 1988 it had become clear that there could be no military solution to the war. After several failed diplomatic initiatives and false starts, direct peace talks began in July 1990 and culminated in the General Peace Accord signed on October 4, 1992. Under the terms of the accord, demobilized Renamo forces and government troops were to form a 30,000 strong joint army. A 6,400 United Nations Operation in Mozambique (ONUMOZ) force oversaw what became a two year transition period.[120]

The U.N. withdrew in December 1994 following the peaceful October multiparty elections. Although President Chissano and Frelimo retained power, the Renamo opposition party did well in the legislative elections.

One of the U.N.'s main tasks was to coordinate the clearance of landmines, but the initial program was unsuccessful. In an attempt to correct matters, the U.N. has pledged extra resources for additional landmine clearance and training in Mozambique.

### Landmine Use—Tactics and Strategies
Landmines were deployed by the parties in a variety of ways. Frelimo and Renamo in the 1980s and 1990s frequently disseminated landmines in a random fashion. In many other cases it appears that civilians were the main target and that mines were used deliberately to terrorize civilian communities and to deny them access to fields, water sources and fishing points. In the southern provinces, Human Rights Watch found that Renamo was largely responsible for laying mines specifically to discourage or make impossible the return of displaced persons to their homes.

Renamo's war against the government was aimed at the devastation of the economy and the isolation of government forces to garrisons and towns. As part of this campaign Renamo used landmines extensively. Rhodesian military officials began training Renamo combatants in landmine use in 1977. Route denial was a frequent objective through mining of major roads, supply routes, and rural tracks. Airstrips were also an important target of Renamo mining. Ambush mining, particularly on roads and tracks, was extensively employed by Renamo.

Government forces began using mines to protect border installations against Rhodesian incursions in 1977. Many of the technicians had received

---

[120] Alex Vines, *Renamo*, pp. 148-163.

training in mine laying years before when they trained as nationalist guerrillas in Tanzania, China, and Algeria. Government forces primarily used defensive mining, for the protection of key economic installations and strategic locations.

In the town of Namaacha, on the border with Swaziland, a minefield was laid around the Canada Dry bottling factory in 1984 after an attack by Renamo rebels. The soldiers did not formally warn the local population and in 1992 when the General Peace Accord was signed the soldiers protecting the factory were withdrawn, leaving behind a large minefield that was not marked or mapped. In 1995 deminers at the site found seventy-five antipersonnel mines in one area of fifty square meters.[121] Sir David Steel, the former president of the Liberal International and a British parliamentarian, visited the site in late 1995 and wrote:

> It has been protected by surrounding the grounds with no fewer than six varieties of mine, almost all of Russian or Chinese origin. These varied from tiny, cheap, round plastic mines which could be thrown out of vehicles and helicopters to disappear into undergrowth and sand, to crude cigar-box variations, left lying with lids ajar, waiting to be stood upon. The most vicious variety was one of the type they had found on the morning of my visit.... This heavy metal object the size of a pint milk-bottle lay buried in the ground with only its dark green top protruding. It was linked by an almost invisible thin copper trip wire to a tree and possibly some ten yards further on to another mine. On disturbing the wire this nasty little number jumps three feet into the air attached by cable on the ground. It then explodes sending deadly shrapnel in all directions. One of these mines had killed a soldier in the forty-five-man unit [clearing the mines] only a fortnight before.[122]

The Komatipoort electricity power lines were another example of defensive mining of economic installations. When these power lines came under attack by Renamo in 1980, the Mozambican power company (Electricidade de Moçambique, EDM) in cooperation with the Ministry of Defense decided to protect the lines with mines. Landmines were planted in three phases, first very close to the

---

[121] Fernando Gonçalves, "Landmines: Seeds of Death," *Southern Africa Political and Economic Monthly,* vol.9, no.5, February 1996.

[122] *The Scotsman* (Edinburgh), April 24, 1996.

pylons, but sabotage continued. Then the mined area was increased around the pylons to four meters, but the attacks still continued. Finally ring minefields of a radius of forty meters were laid around each of the 202 pylons, each with 200 to 300 antipersonnel mines (mostly Soviet made PMN, PMN-2, PMN-6, and OZM-4). These large minefields reduced the sabotage attempts but did not stop them.

The power company has said that they can not afford to close the line to allow total mine clearance because lost business would bankrupt the company. They also say that "the majority of mines are now outside the zone they were assigned because the rains displace the mines, and this poses a threat to EDM personnel and local people, especially because the zones these lines pass through are populated. There have already been people and livestock killed."[123]

Frelimo also laid large defensive minefields along the border with South Africa in the early 1980s. In addition, government patrols laid mines around their positions when they stopped at night. Many of these mines were left behind when patrols moved on, posing a lethal danger to civilians.[124]

Government forces and allied militias also planted mines indiscriminately, aimed at denying Renamo access to food or water sources. In 1988 or 1989 in Pebane district, Zambézia province, government forces spread Italian AUPS mines from the air during counterinsurgency operations against Renamo under the overall command of the now current joint head of the new army, Lagos Lidimo.[125]

Portuguese forces in the independence war also used landmines in Mozambique to protect economic and strategic installations and during counterinsurgency operations. Rhodesian and South African forces planted mines in cross-border raids in the late 1970s and early 1980s. Tanzanian troops laid defensive minefields around their bases in Zambézia province. Malawian troops planted mines along the Nacala railway and Zimbabwean regular forces mined the Beira and Limpopo transport corridors.

---

[123] Faude Sultuane, "A Electricidade de Moçambique e O Problema das Minas na Região Sul do Pais," in Arquivo Histórico de Moçambique (ed), *Moçambique: Desminagem e Desenvolvimento* (Maputo: Arquivo Histórico de Moçambique, 1995), pp.127-129.

[124] Human Rights Watch interview with FAM commander, Maputo, April 11, 1995.

[125] Ibid.

## The Continued Use of Landmines

A limited number of landmines have been planted since the General Peace Accord. Both government and Renamo local commanders appear to have used mines to slow down mine clearance through their areas, or to wage local vendettas. Freelance bandit groups in Manica and Tete also used landmines in a number of ambushes reported between 1994 and 1997.

The mine clearance firm Mine-Tech has reported several incidents of new mine laying. In early 1996, on the Dakata-Espungabera road, Mine-Tech lifted a newly-laid French-manufactured MAPDV-59. They also reported new mine laying on the Mavonde road in Manica province.

Efforts to reconstruct the country have been threatened by the continued use of landmines by criminal groups. A bulldozer belonging to the Italian consortium Italia 2000, which is responsible for refurbishing the Cahora Bassa power lines, hit a landmine on a dirt road in Manica province in the Macuiana area of Mossurize district on July 7, 1996. The road had been declared cleared by Mine-Tech. This was the second incident in a fortnight. In the first case the mine was removed before any damage was done. On April 9, one Mozambican employee of the consortium was killed and a second lost both legs when an Italia 2000 truck struck a mine in the Vanduzi area. A couple of days before, a caterpillar truck hit a mine. It absorbed the blast and there were no casualties. A third mine was found in April but deactivated. These incidents also took place on roads which had been demined. A commission of inquiry was set up, and it concluded that there was a 70 percent chance that the mine was new.[126] In another incident, an antipersonnel mine boosted by ammunition exploded on July 10, 1995 at Ressano Garcia railroad station killing two people. Police believe the mine exploded prematurely, killing the person who planted it.[127]

Many caches of weapons, including landmines, remain scattered around the country. Joint South African and Mozambican Police arms seizure operations in the south of the country have also found landmines. Mine-Tech has reported that in Manica province landmines have been removed by unknown individuals from weapons caches slated for destruction. At Save, Chidoko on November 10, 1995, some of the 119 POMZ-2 mines they recorded in a cache were removed. On November 13 at Machaze/Chitobe one of the ten Type 72A and two of the MON-50 mines they registered were removed before they could destroy them.

---

[126] *Mozambiquefile* (Maputo), May 1996.

[127] *Noticias* (Maputo), July 12, 1995.

Landmines have also been used by poachers. In Manica province, Mine-Tech has seen POMZ-2 antipersonnel mines laid across game parks and found an Italian VS-50 that had probably been removed from the Zimbabwean border minefield and laid by a poacher several kilometers inside Mozambique.

These incidents demonstrate the urgency of destroying all stockpiles of antipersonnel mines. Not only do they maim and kill innocent civilians but the use of landmines threatens political stability and the economic reconstruction of the country.

## The Mines

While systematic mine laying occurred from 1965 until 1992, most mines were laid by Mozambican government armed forces and Renamo between 1978 and 1990. No one knows the true extent of the landmines problem but most surveys so far suggest that it is a patchy, but nevertheless, serious problem. The most widely cited estimate of the number of mines is the December 1992 U.N. estimate of two million mines. However, this figure has no independent basis; it was reached by simply taking the average of estimates being circulated at the time. Human Rights Watch was unable to conduct a comprehensive assessment of landmine numbers, but its 1994 study found that the U.N. estimate was considerably high, and the figure was better thought of in the tens or hundreds of thousands. Then-U.N. mines expert Patrick Blagden had told Human Rights Watch, "It is likely that our initial figures were over-pessimistic. However, Mozambique has a serious mines problem and we are concerned to improve this situation."[128]

Sergio Vieira, the rapporteur of Frelimo's parliamentary group, stated in July 1996 that during the independence war (1964-1974) Frelimo received at most 5,000 mines a year from its allies, and that subsequently between 1974 and 1992, Frelimo never imported more than 20,000 mines a year—which would translate into acquisition of less than 400,000 mines in twenty-eight years, although Vieira fails to mention the use of improvised mines by both sides during the war.[129] Regardless, Human Rights Watch believes that the number of mines is not the most significant factor—it is their impact. Mozambique has a serious landmine problem which threatens to kill innocent civilians daily and is curtailing the economic

---

[128] Human Rights Watch, *Landmines in Mozambique* (New York: Human Rights Watch, 1994).

[129] *domingo* (Maputo), July 16, 1996; Vieira was secretary to Frelimo's first president, Eduardo Mondlane, and has held several posts in government, including security minister and deputy defense minister.

construction of the country. In some cases the number of mines proves to be irrelevant. The very threat of mines, especially antipersonnel mines, can depopulate an area or close a road network. During an Norwegian People's Aid mine clearance operation in Maputo province a team was sent in 1994 to clear the village of Mapulenge, which had been the center of a community of about 10,000 people. It had been deserted for some four years because it was locally believed to be heavily mined. After three months of work, the clearance team reported finding four mines; these, and the rumor of many more, were sufficient to depopulate the area.[130]

### Types and Sources

Former Soviet mines remain the most commonly found in Mozambique. Some mines came through circuitous routes. The French MAPDV-59 appears to have originally been used in Algeria: after independence the Algerians reportedly lifted many and resold them to Mozambique.[131] This demonstrates the necessity of immediately destroying mines during clearance operations. The South Africans also 'recycled' mines captured in Angola and gave them to Renamo for its operations.

The following is a list of landmines reported in Mozambique:

- Soviet: PMN, PMN-2, POMZ-2, POMZ-2M, PMD-6M, OZM-3, OZM-4, OZM-72, MON-50, MON-100;
- Czechoslovak: PP-MI-SR II;
- East German: PPM-2;
- Yugoslav: PROM-1;
- Chinese: Type 69, Type 72, Type 72B;
- Italian: VAR-40, VAR-100, Valmara V-69;
- Belgian: PRB-M409;
- French: MAPDV-59;
- British: No.6;
- Portuguese: M-969;
- United States: M18A1, M14;
- South African: M2A2, No.69 Mk1, Shrapnel Mine No.2, MIM MS-803 (mini- Claymore);
- Rhodesian: RAP-1, RAP-2, RAPS (PloughShear);

---

[130] NPA report to U.N., March 1994.

[131] Handicap International, Paris, January 1995.

•      Zimbabwean: ZAP-No. 1, ZAPS (PloughShear).

Antitank mines found in Mozambique include: TM-46, TM-57, TMN-46, TM-62D, TM-62M, TM-62P, TMK-2 (Soviet); Mk5, Mk7 (UK); M19, M24 (USA); Type 72 (China); Pt Mi Ba III (Czechoslovak); T-AB 1 (Brazilian); DNW ATM 2000E (Austrian); PRB M3 (Belgium); No.8 Mk1 (South Africa); 'Chocolate Box' (Rhodesia).

Human Rights Watch was told by Mechem that Renamo received thirty TMA-3 antitank mines in the 1980s from the South Africans and that not all these mines have been accounted for.

**Mined Area by Province[132]**

| Province Area (Sq Km) | Est'd Population (WFP-1994) | Population Density (Inhab./sq km) | Extent Mined |
|---|---|---|---|
| Cabo Delgado 77,867 | 1,416,000 | 16 | Moderate |
| Gaza 77,450 | 1,313,000 | 16 | Moderate |
| Inhambane 68,615 | 1,493,000 | 19 | Severe |
| Manica 61,661 | 858,000 | 11 | Severe |
| Maputo City 300 | 1,069,000 | 3,236 | Outskirts |
| Maputo 23,276 | 1,073,000 | 40 | Severe |
| Nampula 78,197 | 3,199,000 | 38 | Moderate |
| Niassa 122,176 | 820,000 | 6 | Moderate |
| Sofala 67,218 | 1,529,000 | 20 | Severe |
| Tete 100,724 | 938,000 | 7 | Severe |
| Zambézia 103,127 | 3,322,000 | 29 | Heavy |
| TOTALS 778,611 | 17,030,000 | - | |

Over 70 percent of all 1,652 mine fields officially reported so far consist of areas mined to prevent access to local community infrastructure and tracks and trails used by villagers. Such areas are not heavily mined, but mines are a

---

[132] Shawn Roberts and Jody Williams, *After the Guns Fall Silent: The Enduring Legacy of Landmines* (Washington: Vietnam Veterans of America Foundation, 1995), p.218.

significant obstacle to the normalization of life in rural areas. A peasant farmer from Inharrime in Inhambane province, when asked about what he thought of landmines replied curtly, "The most important thing for us is not the identification of them [mined localities], but their clearance.[133]

### Analysis of Reported Mined Areas In Mozambique[134]

| PROVINCE | | | | CATEGORY | | |
|---|---|---|---|---|---|---|
| | 1 | 2 | 3 | 4 | 5 | 6 |
| Niassa | 8 | 10 | 4 | 12 | 39 | 26 |
| Cabo Delgado | 1 | 8 | 3 | 12 | 74 | 21 |
| Nampula | 3 | 19 | 5 | 25 | 63 | 9 |
| Zambézia | 6 | 72 | 2 | 141 | 202 | 55 |
| Tete | 3 | 37 | 4 | 31 | 106 | 38 |
| Manica | 14 | 14 | 0 | 7 | 6 | 1 |
| Sofala | 7 | 32 | 2 | 5 | 10 | 2 |
| Inhambane | 46 | 25 | 6 | 30 | 118 | 25 |
| Gaza | 6 | 15 | 1 | 10 | 18 | 0 |
| Maputo | 35 | 36 | 25 | 32 | 84 | 1 |
| **Total** | **129** | **268** | **52** | **305** | **720** | **178** |

Mined Area Categories: 1. Minefield Rings; 2. Roads/Tracks;
3. Key National Infrastructures (dams, bridges, power lines etc);
4. Local Infrastructure; 5. Local High Use Areas (schools, health posts, wells etc);
6. Local General Areas.

### The Human, Social and Economic Impact

The human cost of the landmine problem in Mozambique has been high. There are an estimated 8,000 amputees who have received some type of medical treatment, but neither the government nor Renamo has kept detailed records of the numbers of people killed or injured.

In 1993 Human Rights Watch reviewed records of victims receiving treatment at the ICRC's Beira clinic between January 1990 and mid-1993. These figures indicated that 54 percent of the landmine victims were civilians, and 80

---

[133] *domingo* (Maputo), August 7, 1995.

[134] Produced by the Maputo-based Plans Office UNDP/DHA/Accelerated Demining Program, 1996.

percent were male. Children constituted six percent of the victims. Bush paths were a far more prevalent location for mine accidents than roads, tracks or fields. A random survey of 160 ICRC files in Maputo from its national data base revealed a similar ratio of civilian to military victims, and male to female victims. The bush paths were once again the scene of the greatest number of accidents.[135]

A Physicians for Human Rights survey in early 1994 in Metuchira subdistrict, Sofala province, an area with a high incidence of landmine incidents, estimated that there were a 20.2 landmine deaths and injuries per 1,000 inhabitants in the subdistrict.[136] This ratio is comparable with that of mine casualties in Afghanistan and Cambodia. The survey also showed the average number of victims per landmine detonation was greater among soldiers (5.7) than civilians (4.1), probably because fragmentation antipersonnel mines were more frequently used in "bush" areas where soldiers tended to patrol in groups. However, civilians were more likely to die from landmine injuries as they did not have rapid access to medical attention.

Despite the high incidence of landmine casualties mine awareness was low. For example, only 37 percent of households sampled were aware that mines had been laid in Metuchira. A nationwide survey for the Vietnam Veterans of America Foundation (VVAF) of the social and economic costs of landmines in Mozambique, conducted from December 1994 to July 1995, has shown a similar low awareness of landmines.[137] Fear of landmines and their effect on economic activity was far less than expected, averaging only a few percent.[138]

Halo Trust also published a survey of "Landmine Casualties in Mozambique" in October 1993 based on 3,400 recorded cases of deaths and injuries. The vast majority came from files in the Ministry of Health in Maputo,

---

[135] The ICRC kindly permitted access to medical files for landmines research purposes.

[136] Alberto Ascherio etal, "Deaths and injuries caused by landmines in Mozambique," The Lancet, Vol. 346, September 1995, pp.721-724.

[137] Shawn Roberts and Jody Williams, After the Guns Fall Silent, Appendix Nine, pp.497-522.

[138] A critique of the study is in: César Palha de Sousa, "Notas Sobre o Impacto Sócio-Económico das Minas em Moçambique," in Arquivo Histórico de Moçambique (ed), Moçambique: Desminagem e Desenvolvimento (Maputo:   Arquivo Histórico de Moçambique, 1995), pp.61-70.

although the authors said it drew upon an extensive nationwide search.[139] The survey differs from Human Rights Watch's in that records that stated cause of injury as "Arma de Fogo" were taken by Halo's researchers to mean a mine, due to the related injury. This interpretation can be inaccurate as many health workers used this term to describe other war-related injuries—serious gunshot or grenade wounds for example. According to the survey of casualty records from 1980-1993, 78 percent of all mine accidents occurred in just four provinces: Maputo, Inhambane, Sofala and Zambézia, although this may well have reflected the greater level of reporting in the better communicated provinces. Twelve percent of the casualties were military personnel and 88 percent civilians. Eighty-four percent were male and 16 percent female.

Handicap International's Inhambane clinic's statistics up to 1993, in contrast to the sample cited in the Halo Trust report, show 97 percent of mine casualties who received treatment were civilians, and only 40 percent were male. The tradition of migrant labor in Inhambane and the past preference of soldiers to go to ICRC clinics rather than Handicap's could explain this difference.

Many of the landmines laid by Renamo in southern Mozambique in particular were deliberately intended to cause maximum social and economic disruption, including random dissemination of mines in fields and along their access paths to stop peasants from producing food. In some areas, farmland, pastures, forests and riverbanks remain dangerous because of mine infestations.

Mines still restricted the free movement of people in certain districts such as Maringue, in Manica province in 1996.[140] In Niassa province local authorities continued to call for help because mines limit agricultural production.[141] Mines put at the bases of bridges by government forces to stop sabotage posed a serious problem. These mines significantly slowed down efforts to repair road bridges, many of which were in urgent need of attention.[142]

Mines were also a particular hazard to returning refugees. Alice Simbane's story was not unique. In December 1992, in a Maputo hospital she told Human

---

[139] Elizabeth Sheehan and Mike Croll, "Landmine Casualties in Mozambique," Halo Trust, October 1993.

[140] *Noticias* (Maputo), May 26, 1996.

[141] *Noticias* (Maputo), July 1, 1996.

[142] "Estradas e Pontas clamam pela desminagem e reabilitação," *Tempo* (Maputo), October 13, 1996.

Rights Watch of her family's return in 1992 after three years in a refugee camp in Zimbabwe:

> I was excited by the peace. I and my family hoped to return to peace. We wanted no memories of war. However, my brother on the long walk home stepped on a landmine and has lost his foot. What have I done to deserve this? They had told me we had peace.

Facilities for the evacuation, emergency treatment, hospital treatment and physical and social rehabilitation of landmine victims are poor. This situation was up to 1994 exacerbated by Renamo's failure to allow some mine victims to travel freely to obtain medical care in some of their zones.

The Mozambican government has relied heavily on nongovernmental organizations and foreign aid to meet the rehabilitation needs of mine victims. For example, the U.S. Agency for International Development gave $5.5 million to the Mozambican Ministry of Health between 1989-1993 for the provision of artificial limbs.

Two organizations, Power and Handicap International, have offered prosthesis treatment. The ICRC also ran an orthopedic program in Mozambique from 1981 to 1995 and had four workshops, in Maputo, Beira, Quelimane and Nampula. These workshops fitted over 4,000 people with orthopedic devices and produced over 23,000 elbow crutches before the program ended. In 1994, 790 prostheses were manufactured and 311 new patients came for treatment. The ICRC withdrew in 1995 and the British-based NGO Power took over the management of the workshops and has opened some new ones.[143]

Handicap International also runs an orthopedic operation in Mozambique. It has expanded its operations in recent years in northern Mozambique and is expected to expand into mine clearance operations in 1997 (see below). Another British-based NGO, The Jaipur Limb Campaign will become operational in Mozambique in 1998.

**Mine Awareness Campaigns**

In order to warn returning internally displaced and refugees of the dangers of landmines, a large-scale mine awareness campaign was run between mid-1993 and 1994. Mine awareness training had been conducted by Handicap International

---

[143] ICRC, "Assistance to Mines Victims: ICRC Orthopaedic Programmes," *Landmines in Africa Fact Sheet*, February 1995.

in Tete, Inhambane and Zambézia provinces; Medicenes Sans Frontiers Switzerland in Maputo province; the Norwegian Refugee Council and Cemirde in Gaza and Maputo provinces; Norwegian People's Aid, UNHCR, and Food for the Hungry International in Sofala province; and Mine-Tech in Manica. Niassa, Nampula and Cabo Delgado provinces have so far been neglected. The International Rescue Committee is considering operating in Niassa in conjunction with UNHCR and NPA.

Mine awareness campaigns by the UNHCR, often in cooperation with other local or international NGOs, were also conducted in neighboring countries, including in Swaziland beginning in July 1993 and Zimbabwe in August 1993. The International Rescue Committee ran a lengthy campaign in Malawi between September 1993 and June 1994. Other campaigns took place in South Africa in March 1994 and in Tanzania in May 1994.

The Mozambican Red Cross intends to create committees at the local level all across the country to educate and warn people about landmines.[144] In order to alert the rural population about the presence and dangers of landmines, and thereby minimize the number of victims, Radio Mozambique has also conducted an awareness campaign, calling on the people to be suspicious of any strange objects. "It could be a landmine," says an advertisement broadcast ten times a day in the various national languages and in Portuguese, the official language. Radio Mozambique emphasizes that it is best to be suspicious about objects that may seem to be buried in the soil. "Immediately alert the authorities, because it could kill you."

Handicap International also worked closely with the Associação dos Deficientes Moçambicanos (ADEMO) and Associação dos Deficientes Militares de Moçambique (ADEMIMO) in mid-1994 to conduct an effective advertisement and signature campaign calling for destruction of stockpiles of landmines in Mozambique and guarantees that cleared mines will be destroyed. The petition also called for an international ban on landmine production, transfers and sales. Over 100,000 signatures were gathered through this campaign nationwide.

Handicap International also received support in April and May 1995 for an awareness campaign from the U.S. Army's Humanitarian Demining Program, with assistance from members of the U.S. Army's 4th Psychological Operations Group. This effort produced 300,000 posters, 300,000 booklets and 500,000 pamphlets in Portuguese which were used by Handicap International in its awareness campaign.

---

[144] *Noticias* (Maputo), May 13, 1996.

## Mine Clearing Initiatives

In addressing the 4th International NGO Conference on Landmines in Maputo on February 25, 1997, President Chissano provided these statistics: since 1992, about 30,000 mines have been removed from Mozambican soil; currently, about 11,000 mines per year are being removed; between January 1993 and January 1997, 7,400 kilometers of road, 1,700 kilometers of railway, 1,800 kilometers of electricity transmission line, and 2,300 square kilometers of farmland were demined.[145] Still, many minefields remain across the country. Some 2,000 areas have been recorded as mined. In Zambézia province alone in 1995 over 300 mined zones were reported.

Even though it has been more than four years since demining began, Mozambique's director of mine clearance, Osório Mateus Severino, when recently asked what problems exist, stated, "First, we must have a clear idea of what the landmine situation in Mozambique is. We are in the dark about that, and without a sound knowledge of the situation, it is impossible to define a strategy, let alone determine the cost and resources needed for clearance operations."[146]

### Gurkha Security Guards

In their first joint attempt to deal with the landmine problem, the Mozambican government and Renamo agreed at the December 31, 1992 meeting of the U.N.'s Supervisory and Control Commission (CSC) to hire a British company, Gurkha Security Guards Ltd. (GSG) to remove mines in central Mozambique. The agreement ended a dispute over who should be contracted; Renamo wanted to hire the South African security company Minerva (Mechem), and the government favored having the Zimbabwe army clear mines.

At the end of January 1993, GSG began a formal mine clearance operation in Mozambique in cooperation with Lomaco (Operations Electric and Lincoln). The program was initially funded by the European Community. The aim was to clear roads of mines and unexploded ordnance, in order to allow relief vehicles carrying food and other forms of aid to reach more remote regions. GSG's clearance efforts first concentrated on roads north of Beira. Its contract was

---

[145] Cited in Mozambique News Agency, "Mozambique calls for total landmine ban," Report no. 104, February 27, 1997, p. 4. Mozambique's director of mine clearance, Osório Mateus Severino, gave these figures a day later: 6,300 kilometers of road and 3,000 hectares of land were cleared; 25,000 antipersonnel and 270 antitank mines were disabled. *Radio Moçambique*, Maputo, February 26, 1997.

[146] *Radio Moçambique*, Maputo, February 26, 1997.

extended in July 1993 for five months so that additional roads could be cleared for the World Food Program.[147] When the project finished in February 1994, GSG had cleared 160 kilometers of road. Only six mines were found, mainly at the bases of bridges, at a cost to the E.U. of $1,683,000.

### The United Nations Program

In January 1993, U.N. mine expert Patrick Blagden unveiled ONUMOZ's mine clearance plan for Mozambique. The plan's long-term objective was for Mozambique to carry out its demining operations and then serve as a source of expertise for other mine clearance operations in Africa. The first stage called for identifying some 2,000 kilometers of road as a priority for clearance. These roads were to be those necessary for the humanitarian transport of food to feeding centers in the areas most seriously affected by drought; the establishment and administration of transit centers for refugees; and access to assembly areas for demobilized soldiers. Subsequently, the ICRC and the World Food Program identified twenty-eight roads as priorities for demining, and the joint government/RENAMO Supervisory and Control Commission (CSC) agreed. Eighty percent of these roads were in the central provinces of Manica and Sofala.

The second stage of the U.N. plan called for identifying and clearing routes necessary for the return of refugees to Mozambique from neighboring states and routes necessary for the economic development of Mozambique. The third stage called for establishing a school in Mozambique to train mine clearers who would then complete the clearance of the remaining mines.

According to the original time frame, contractors were to be on the ground in Mozambique at the end of May 1993 to begin road clearance. During June and July 1993 the mine clearing school was to be established, and the first group of students were expected to complete their eight-week course in August. Under the plan, 140 Mozambicans were to be trained in 1993, with a total of 570 students certified as mine clearers by 1994.

However, with the exception of the GSG pilot project, no professional demining took place in Mozambique until mid-1994 because of delays by both Renamo, the government and the U.N. on matters largely unrelated to demining.

### Mine Clearance Delays

U.N. plans for demining had to be approved by both sides in the Supervisory and Control Commission but little of substance was agreed to after December 1992. Subsequent U.N. initiatives were blocked or delayed by either the

---

[147] Human Rights Watch, *Landmines in Mozambique*, pp.80-83.

government or Renamo. After the original U.N. "Mine Clearance Plan for Mozambique" failed to get government approval, U.N. demining expert Patrick Blagden and U.N. Demining Project Manager Andre Millorit redrafted the proposal. Government officials told Human Rights Watch that they did not like the plan because it suggested that the government had been as responsible as Renamo for laying mines. In the formal discussions of the control commission, however, the government claimed it disapproved of the plan because it did not offer sufficient mine clearance training.

Following U.N. lobbying, both sides agreed that individual mine clearance initiatives could go ahead before the overall Mine Clearance Plan was approved by the control commission although all individual initiatives still required its clearance.

From March 1993, the government became increasingly cooperative towards the U.N. with respect to mine clearance, perhaps recognizing that open roads were to its advantage, and also seeing the political advantages if only Renamo could be blamed for hampering clearance efforts. In contrast, Renamo became less enthusiastic and was increasingly responsible for serious delays and the postponement of decisions in the control commission.

Some progress was achieved in late August 1993 following a visit to Mozambique by Patrick Blagden. Blagden issued both sides an ultimatum and threatened to withdraw U.N. support for mine clearance if some headway was not made. In response both sides agreed to a nationwide survey of the mines problem by Halo Trust and on November 24, 1993, the control commission finally approved the U.N. clearance plan in a revised form.

However, the problems with the control commission forced the U.N. to adhere rigidly to clearance of the twenty-eight roads already approved by the commission. U.N. officials acknowledged that with the end of the drought and further information about needs, the priority of roads had changed, but they feared that any change would cause further delays. They believed it better to get a core of projects underway before a new agenda was pushed. Only in late 1994 did this situation improve.

### Independent Government and Renamo Mine Clearance

During 1993 and the first half of 1994, while the U.N., government and Renamo were responsible for delaying mine clearance initiatives in the CSC, uncoordinated mine clearance by both sides occurred across the country. The government had been clearing roads through areas under its control since November 1992. The government's mines expert for Manica and Sofala provinces, Captain Boaventura Chupica Gavalho, told Human Rights Watch that the government had made Manica and Sofala a priority area for its own clearance. Government soldiers had also been active in mine clearing in many other areas. The government had also been pressing for certain strategically important roads to be cleared by GSG.[148]

Renamo was also reluctant to see some roads opened through its areas as it feared that the government could then move armored units through the areas. Particularly sensitive was the Macossa-Maringue-Canxixe stretch of road; Maringue was Renamo's main headquarters. But as Renamo's confidence grew in the post-election period it facilitated access to more and more roads to be cleared through its areas.

In 1994 the French military trained a company of soldiers from the new joint Defense Armed Forces of Mozambique (FADM) in mine clearance techniques at the Boquisso Centre for Sapper Training. In early 1995 the first company of trained sappers started to locate mined areas in Maputo province. In September 1996 the FADM announced another unit of its soldiers had been trained in mine clearance techniques but refused to reveal its total mine clearing capacity.[149]

The Direcção Nacional de Estradas e Pontes (DNEP) was also active in mine clearance through its emergency "Project After War (Projecto depois guerra)." Under pressure from commercial entrepreneurs to re-open lucrative trade routes quickly, the DNEP had been using demobilized soldiers on short contracts.

Although Renamo also has cleared mines along roads in its zones, the international agencies have found evidence that the standard was particularly poor. Renamo denied this, claiming that the government had continued to lay mines in an attempt to denigrate Renamo's reputation.

### Funding for Mine Clearing

Between 1993 and 1995 some $31.3 million was spent on landmine clearance, and pledges for 1996-1998 stand at around $20.6 million. Seventeen donors have given funds for mine clearance in Mozambique, the top three being Norway, the U.S. and the Netherlands.

Funds have been slow to come in, and even slower to be spent. By the end of 1992, $7 million from the ONUMOZ budget and another $7 million from the U.N. Department of Humanitarian Affairs (DHA) Trust Fund were earmarked for mine clearance in Mozambique. The U.N.'s Humanitarian Assistance Coordination Office in Maputo announced on February 19, 1993 that Norway ($1.1 million), the

---

[148] Human Rights Watch, *Landmines in Mozambique*, p.37.

[149] *Noticias* (Maputo), September 17, 1996.

Netherlands ($2.7 million) and Sweden ($4.2 million) had contributed to the DHA Trust Fund. Italy also announced it would provide $800,000. Yet by April 1994, only $1.5 million had been spent on mine clearance. The little demining which had been done had been accomplished only by bypassing the U.N. system.

## Project Caminho

According to U.N. minutes, UNOHAC had short-listed five companies for mine clearance contracts in early 1993.[150] But for over a year there was indecision. Finally, after countless delays, the U.N. reached a decision in early May 1994. A consortium of Royal Ordnance of the UK, Lonrho de Moçambique and Mechem of South Africa was awarded a $4.8 million contract to clear 2,000 kilometers of priority roads. GSG provided some personnel and Mine-Tech did some contract work for this clearance operation, called "Project Caminho."

The award of this contract prompted widespread international criticism of the U.N., including from Human Rights Watch, for employing firms that had manufactured and designed mines. Subsequently U.N. officials said that the contract award was a mistake. David Gowdey, then an official in the U.N. Department of Humanitarian Affairs, stated, "It is now our view that no arms producer can ever again receive a U.N. mine clearance contract."[151] Regrettably, this was not to be the case.

The Dutch government expressed its concern at the award since the Netherlands had contributed funds to the U.N. Trust Fund. In July 1994 the Dutch government requested a return of what was left of their $2.7 million in the Trust Fund. However, the funds were not repaid and the Dutch government has taken the U.N. to court over the matter. According to a Dutch diplomatic source, Dutch funds in the future will be given directly to mine clearance operations and will not be paid to the U.N. Trust Fund.[152]

It seems that the award of this contract was the result of infighting within the U.N. system, especially between U.N. agencies in New York and their Maputo offices. A key problem was the creation of two new U.N. coordinating structures in Maputo, ONUMOZ and UNOHAC, which eroded the influence of existing U.N. structures in Maputo. In particular a battle between UNDP and the Department of Humanitarian Affairs contributed to the crisis. UNDP had won control of mine

---

[150] Human Rights Watch saw a copy of these minutes in Maputo in May 1993.

[151] *World Press Review*, September 1994, p.48.

[152] Dutch diplomatic source, August 10, 1995.

clearance funds in 1993 and refused to approve projects and programs proposed by UNOHAC for demining, creating a paralysis. UNDP also blocked Patrick Blagden from re-visiting Mozambique until late August 1993. There was also deliberate backpeddling on mine-related requests for projects that were not operating through the U.N. Trust Fund. Only in March 1994, when the DHA sent Felix Downes-Thomas, a DHA deputy director, to head up UNOHAC did the situation improve. Finally in May 1994 a decision was made. On May 20, the secretary-general agreed that the remaining $7.5 million for mine clearance would be taken away from UNDP's Office for Project Services (OPS) in New York and put under the control of UNOHAC. [153]Six months later, however, UNDP replaced UNOHAC.

The selection of Mechem was particularly controversial. Mechem's director, Vernon Joynt, previously designed mines for the SADF, including, in all likelihood, some of those now found in Mozambique. Mechem was attached to the South African Council for Scientific and Industrial Research until the U.S. boycott of South Africa, when it became part of Armscor. Mechem remains a subsidiary of Denel Ltd. In Mozambique, Mechem used a technique first tried in northern Namibia during the South African occupation: Casspir mine-protected trucks drove over the road to be demined and sucked up air samples onto filters which were then given to sniffer dogs in a safe environment. Mechem claimed this is twenty times quicker than other methods. Between July 27 and December 15, 1994, the "Project Caminho" consortium cleared in Manica, Sofala and Maputo province some 2,051 kilometers of road, destroying twenty-one antipersonnel and two antitank mines.[154]

In the run up to full UNOMOZ withdrawal after the October 1994 elections, U.N. management of mine clearance changed once again. An "Understanding" was signed between UNDP and DHA on November 2, 1994 on improving coordination. The UK, U.S. and Norway committed themselves to support continued NGO mine clearance operations.

*The Accelerated Demining Program (U.N./ADP)*
        Part of the original 1992 U.N. demining plan was to establish a Mine Clearance Training Center. The U.N. aimed to replace the foreign companies with Mozambicans. Aldo Ajello, the U.N. special representative in Mozambique, estimated that the demining plan could provide employment for up to 2,000 people

---

[153] Diplomatic sources, Maputo and New York, August 1995.

[154] Comissão Nacional de Desminagem, "Sumário de Registos Concernentes a Operação de Desminagem em Moçambique," March 1, 1997.

with these jobs designated for demobilized soldiers. The MCTC was to become operational in August 1993, but because of U.N. delays was only formally opened in Beira in January 1994. Its first thirty students graduated on May 9. Beira proved to be unsatisfactory as the facilities were shared with RONCO, which was training its own mine clearers there. In July 1993 the school was moved to larger premises in Tete, previously used by Norwegian People's Aid for its demining program. In August the MCTC relocated to Maputo to take responsibility for mine clearance in the south.

Because of the delays in U.N. mine clearance efforts, DHA decided in August 1994 to create an Accelerated Demining Program as part of the MCTC. At the end of the ONUMOZ mandate, in January 1995, an agreement was signed between the UNDP and DHA for joint responsibility of the ongoing mine clearance operation.[155] The U.N.'s Accelerated Demining Program awarded two technical assistance contracts in August, to Special Gurkha Services (SGS) for ten field-level supervisors (at an annual cost of $600,000) and to Defence Services Ltd (DSL) to provide middle-management trainers. In October 1995 the Accelerated Demining Program commenced. The German government provided technical assistance and support staff to the project at a cost of $800,000 per year. The majority of the staff were initially former East Germans. This technical assistance project was also supported through the German NGO Solidaritatsdienst-International.[156] In 1996 the German government ran this program directly through its German Project Coordination program.

By August 1996 the U.N. Accelerated Demining Program had trained 450 mine clearers with the support of nine expatriate advisers (seven of which had been provided under in-kind arrangements by Australia, Germany and New Zealand) as well as a team of ten Ghurka field supervisors. More recently, five platoons have been working in Maputo province and another five in Inhambane Province.

Plans to make the Accelerated Demining Program a national NGO in 1997 have been postponed until proposed Mozambican legislation on NGOs is introduced. Accelerated Demining Program staff hope that it will remain an autonomous organization, engaging in field operations across the country.

---

[155] At a meeting in Copenhagen in March 1995 at the World Summit for Social Development, U.N. Secretary-General Boutros Boutros-Ghali assured President Chissano that the U.N. remained strongly committed to providing continued assistance for its mine clearance efforts. U.N., *The United Nations and Mozambique, 1992-1995* (New York: U.N. Department of Public Information, 1995), p.53.

[156] Interview with Lt. Col Steve Ransley, ADP Manager, Maputo, March 1995.

By February 4, 1997 1,541,088 square meters had been cleared of landmines under the U.N.'s Accelerated Demining Program. A total of 9,102 antipersonnel mines and sixty-one antitank mines had been cleared.[157] The majority of mines were cleared from ring minefields in north and south Moamba and Sabie town. The choice of these guaranteed mine-rich locations such as Moamba was made less from an urgent humanitarian needs analysis and more from the need to show a high landmine clearance tally as a demonstration of productivity for current and future donors.[158]  These locations also did not overstretch the Program logistically.

*National Mine Clearance Commission*
Following the October 1994 elections, the government, with U.N. encouragement, indicated that it would form a National Mine Clearance Commission (CND) which would take over responsibility for mine clearance. In May 1995 the CND was established by government decree, comprising seven ministers and the director of the executive body of the commission.[159] The commission was to be chaired by the minister of foreign affairs and cooperation and was mandated to:

•    collect, process and analyse information and data relevant to demining, elaborate a strategy and action plans for mine clearance, and establish procedures for setting priorities at local and national levels;

•    monitor and coordinate all ongoing demining activities;

•    act as the approval and licensing authority for new operators wishing to start mine clearance activities in the country, as well as ensure quality control and uniform standards;

•    adjudicate public tenders for service contracts in the field of mine clearance;

---

[157] Comissão Nacional de Desminagem, "Sumário de Registos Concernentes a Operação de Desminagem em Moçambique," March 1, 1997.

[158] Diplomatic and mine clearance sources, Maputo, August 1995.

[159] Council of Ministers Decree No. 18/95 of May 3, 1995. The ministries of economy, interior and defense are represented on the commission.

• promote and oversee the implementation of a national program to improve public mine awareness.[160]

The commission was also mandated to "promote national demining capacity, through national companies and nongovernmental organizations, as well as through a subsidiary national demining operative unit." This provision was for the transfer of the Accelerated Demining Program to the government in 1997.

The commission has not been very successful. A year and a half after its launch it had failed to hold a formal meeting and the executive arm of the Commission has been slow to organize. A July 1996 U.S diplomatic cable stated that "the CND has failed to develop as expected, is poorly led, and has yet to produce a long-awaited national demining policy. Nonetheless, efforts to strengthen the National Demining Commission and develop a national mine clearance policy continue."[161] A report on landmine clearance in Mozambique for the Swedish development agency, SIDA, by the Stockholm Group for Development Studies reached a similar conclusion stating that "the directorate still lacks capacity to direct any mine clearance work in the country."[162]

A draft proposal circulated to proposed donors in early 1996 by the commission envisaged its rapid expansion in size and scope after the Accelarated Demining Program wound down in 1997. It proposed an increase in demining platoons from ten to thirty-five over a five-year period and converting the Accelerated Demining Program into a government agency reporting to the commission at a cost of $12.3 million for the first two years. Unfavorable donor response resulted in these plans being scaled down to a modest increase in size and additional mine clearance responsibilities only in the south, particularly in Gaza province.

In June 1996 the Commission's executive director Osório Mateus complained that the government had released only $445,000, which were

---

[160] Bernt Bernander and Christer Westerberg, "The Mine Clearance Programme in Mozambique," unpublished report by the Stockholm Group for Development Studies, June 1996.

[161] U.S. Embassy, Maputo cable, Message ID4505486, July 1996.

[162] Bernt Bernander and Christer Westerberg, "The Mine Clearance Programme in Mozambique."

inadequate for the CND's full-scale operations. He blamed the commission's failure to set up regional delegations on the lack of funds.

Also in June, the U.N. put out an international tender for consultants to assist the CND as part of an agreement signed (after a lengthy delay) between the U.N. and the Mozambican government. Four experts are to set up a data bank, administer the CND's manpower resources, and assist in management and civic education. The Netherlands and Sweden have pledged $1 million towards this.[163]

With the Accelerated Demining Program ending, the government is determining whether to transform it into a private commercial company or an NGO. Donors remain suspicious. The U.S. embassy reported, "We are in a good position to influence the drafting of a national policy on how the CND operates and to protect foreign NGOs from efforts (some within CND) to turn the Mozambican program into a milk-cow for local companies or NGOs with little or no experience."[164]

Much of the decision-making on mine clearance remains at local and provincial level without CND participation. The Accelerated Demining Program holds weekly demining meetings in Inhambane and Maputo with the governors who have set up provincial liaison demining committees. In these committees the provincial priorities are discussed and agreed upon. A decentralized approach, which devolves decision-making to the local level, is likely the best guarantee that humanitarian priorities are addressed first.

Mine clearance was given prominence by the government during the Paris Club donors meeting in early 1995 and during 1996. The government's apparent increased interest in mine clearance is probably attributable in part to the hope that it will attract large sums of money.

*Commercial Firms*

### RONCO

From March 21 to 30, 1993 the U.S. Department of Defense sent a mission to Mozambique to assess whether U.S. Army engineering teams could contribute to the rebuilding of roads and infrastructure. The team's conclusion was

---

[163] "Lack of funds threatens success of demining operations," AIM Reports, no.87, June 21, 1996.

[164] U.S. Embassy, Maputo cable, Message ID4505486, July 1996.

that direct U.S. Army involvement would be too costly and that funds channeled to the private sector would be more cost effective.[165]

The USAID in mid-1993 invited U.S. companies to bid for a contract to clear the outstanding 2,170 kilometers of ICRC/WFP priority designated roads in Sofala and Zambézia provinces. It had earmarked $3,962,970 for this demining. Some of the roads were also chosen to complement AID's Rural Access Road Project. At least a dozen U.S.-based demining companies bid for the contract, with RONCO Consulting Corporation winning in late September 1993.

RONCO Consulting Corporation was founded in 1974. It boasts that in partnership with the Global Training Academy of San Antonio, Texas it introduced and perfected a system for use of Mine Detecting Dogs (MDDs) to locate mines in Afghanistan in 1989. The dogs are trained to detect explosives and such things as trip wires for booby traps using their acute sense of smell and hearing. Once the dogs have detected mines and other ordnance, the deminer pinpoints its location using detectors or prods and disposes of it using standard techniques. RONCO claims that dogs are much faster than other techniques of locating mines and proving that a suspected area is free of mines.

In late December 1993 RONCO began hiring ex-combatants from the army and Renamo and started the renovation and construction of a Demining Training and Operations Facility outside Beira. In January 1994 the first mine detecting dogs arrived. On April 15 RONCO graduated the first group of Mozambican deminers and dog handlers, which was formed into six demining teams. Demining operations began on May 3, 1994. On August 8, the full contingent of twelve demining teams were deployed, each with seven deminers and thirty-two dogs. In mid-November 1994 RONCO was clearing seventy kilometers of road per week at a cost per kilometer of approximately $3,150. When it completed its contract in June 1995, RONCO had cleared 2,176 kilometers, destroying thirty-one antipersonnel and five antitank mines.[166] Dogs, equipment and trained deminers—a contribution valued at $1,150,000—were transferred to Norwegian People's Aid at the end of the contract.

### Mechem

The South Africa firm, Mechem, first cleared mines in Mozambique in July 1991 through a front company named Minerva. Minerva was awarded a

---

[165] Human Rights Watch, *Landmines in Mozambique*, p.37.

[166] Commissão Nacional de Desminagem, "Sumário de Registos Concernentes a Operação de Desminagem em Moçambique," March 1, 1997.

contract by Electricidade de Moçambique to clear fifty-one minefields around damaged Maputo to South African pylons. A total of more than 12,000 mines were cleared in six weeks, using Caspirs with steel wheels which were driven in a methodical criss-cross pattern. The project cost R500,000.[167]

In February 1994 Mechem engaged in road mine clearance for a Murray and Roberts road-building project, clearing 133 kilometers in three weeks for R220,000. In April 1994 Mechem cleared 107 kilometers in two weeks for Basil Read Mining for R727,586. Mechem was also funded in May and June 1995 by the Italian NGO MOLISV/MOVIMONDO to conduct a small clearance operation in central Mozambique. This NGO had raised US$13,000 from the sale of T-shirts in Italy for mine clearance of ten tracks to water sources in Manica province. Mechem cleared twenty-three kilometers in which it removed twenty-one antipersonnel mines and two antitank mines. [168]

Following high-level government exchanges between South Africa and Mozambique in 1996, the CND formally invited Mechem to participate in mine clearance in Mozambique. Mechem has drawn up plans for two projects: a $34 million initiative to clear 90 percent of all remaining main minefields over two years in partnership with the Portuguese firm, Carlos Gassman-Technologias de Vanguardia Aplicadas, LD; and a $3 million project to clear Maputo province in five months. [169]

### Mine-Tech
Mine-Tech is a Zimbabwe-based mine clearance firm founded in 1993. Mine-Tech uses demobilized Zimbabwean soldiers and is run by Col. Lionel Dyck, a former Rhodesian army officer who stayed in Zimbabwe after independence and commanded an elite Zimbabwean paratroop unit which operated in Mozambique against Renamo. In December 1993, Mine-Tech conducted a survey of the Gorongosa region of Sofala province for GTZ, a German development agency. Throughout 1994 and early 1995 Mine-Tech conducted nine surveys and cleared 375 kilometers of road in Manica province for GTZ in support of UNHCR at a cost of some $175,000. Seventy-one mines were cleared, including fifty-seven

---

[167] Mechem, "Memorandum: Mine Clearing in Angola," dated February 16, 1995 and sent to the Director General, Department of Foreign Affairs, Pretoria.

[168] Ibid.

[169] Information provided by National Demining Commission, Maputo, February 27, 1997.

antipersonnel.[170] Mechem also sub-contracted to Mine-Tech some work during Project Caminho in areas that were inappropriate for mechanized clearance.[171]

On July 29, 1995 Mine-Tech was awarded the prime contract for a $7.8 million project for clearance of the 932 kilometer Cahora-Bassa power line from Songo substation in Mozambique to the Apollo substation in South Africa. It was funded primarily by a loan to Hídroelectrica de Cahora-Bassa from the European Investment Bank. Controversy abounded over this contract. The competition had been fierce with firms spreading rumors and false stories about each other orally and in the press. The consortium Italia 2000 initially commissioned Mine-Tech for the whole contract but its decision was challenged by the losing consortium Lincaba, which included the French company Cofras and South Africa's Mechem. The South African government then intervened at ministerial level pushing for Mechem involvement and threatened to withdraw its funds for the project. A compromise deal was finally worked out in mid-July after the E.U. threatened to declare the whole project null and void because of tender irregularity. Mine-Tech became the main contractor, with Mechem sub-contracted under the Portuguese company Carlos Gassman-Technologias de Vanguarda Aplicadas, LD. Mechem was to be responsible for surveys, mechanical clearance and quality control. The contract was completed in May 1996. [172]

By January 20, 1996 Mine-Tech had reportedly cleared a total of 1,518 kilometers of road and a surface area of 15,079,071 hectares in which 298 antipersonnel mines and twenty-five antitank mines were discovered.[173]

In 1996 Mine-Tech was awarded a $100,000 contract by UNICEF to clear two village neighborhood locations. Mine-Tech also in 1996 cleared some mines on the Dondo to Muaza stretch of the Sena railway line. In 1997 it continued to do village clearance work in Manica province and was hoping to expand into Sofala.

---

[170] U. Weyl and C. Pearce, "GTZ(MARP) & Mine-Tech: Integrated Humanitarian Demining, Explosive Ordnance Disposal and Security Management in the Context of the Peace & Reintegration Process," briefing paper, 1996.

[171] Interview with Chris Pearce, director of Mine-Tech, Harare, November 12, 1996.

[172] Diplomatic and mineclearance sources, Maputo and Harare, September 1995.

[173] Commissão Nacional de Desminagem, "Sumário de Registos Concernentes A Operação de Desminagem em Moçambique," March 1, 1997.

**Special Clearance Services (SCS)**
Like Mine-Tech, SCS is a Zimbabwe-based company that uses Zimbabwean personnel. In 1996 SCS won a UNICEF contract to survey and clear a village neighborhood for $60,000. In mid-1996 SCS proposed to the Swedisn development agency, SIDA a $2,360,000 project to clear three different areas of Manica province and to establish a local demining capability. In 1997 SCS was engaged in some commercial road clearance work in Zambézia, Tete and Sofala provinces. SCS has carried out limited survey work in Zambézia, Tete, Sofala, Gaza and Maputo provinces.[174] As of August 28, 1996, SCS is recorded by the CND as having cleared 7,730 square meters and destroying eighteen antipersonnel mines.[175]

**Krohn Demining Enterprise**
Krohn is a private firm from Germany engaged in a mechanical mine clearance test program in Maputo province. It is German funded and liaised with the U.N./Accelarated Demining Program. It uses two caterpillar machines equipped with spiked, heavy rollers, operating in succession and detonating mines as they move forward, followed by a tractor plow. The results are verified through conventional mine detection, and remaining mines are removed manually. As with other mechanical methods, clearance is limited to areas judged topographically suitable. In early May 1996 a test area was artificially planted with 264 mines of different types to assess performance. One hundred and seventy mines were audibly detonated and a number of others deactivated by the passage of the machines.[176]

By March 29, 1996 Krohn had reportedly cleared 340,940 square meters of land, and 3,870 antipersonnel mines.[177] In early 1997 the Accelerated Demining

---

[174] Human Rights Watch interview with Bernie Auditorie, director of SCS, Maputo, February 27, 1997. See also, SCS, "Company Profile," no date given.

[175] Commisão Nacional de Desminagem, "Sumário de Registos Concernentes a Operação de Desminagem em Moçambique," March 1, 1997.

[176] Information provided by the Accelerated Demining Program, Maputo, February 1997.

[177] Commissão Nacional de Desminagem, "Sumário de Registos Concernentes a Operação de Desminagem em Moçambique," March 1, 1997.

Program drafted an agreement with the German government under which management of this project was to be taken over by the Accelerated Demining Program and the Krohn machines to be used as part of an integrated demining program.[178]

### NGO Mine Clearance Programs

#### Halo Trust

The Halo Trust, a London-based non-profit mine clearance consultancy, obtained in 1993 a $470,000 U.N. contract, after a year delay in approval, to conduct a nationwide assessment of the landmines situation in Mozambique. Six teams were sent with questionnaires to every district and municipality in an attempt to make a scientific assessment of the worst areas for landmines. Halo's nationwide survey results, published in mid-1994, recorded 963 reports of landmines. The survey was criticized for being too superficial, and for being published a year too late and only in English, when Portuguese is the official language in Mozambique. The survey did not, despite its intention, form the basis of a long-term landmine program for Mozambique.[179]

Months after publication, USAID provided the Mine Clearance Training Center funds for a consultant for two months (January-March 1995) to analyze Halo's original survey data. The consultant's report concluded that although the Halo data did project some general trends, more detailed surveys of affected areas were needed to work out a priority list for humanitarian clearance. This remains an important task for the National Commission for Mine Clearance two years later with the data base now recording some 2,000 mined sites.[180]

The British Overseas Development Administration allocated UK £700,000 in 1993 in support of the plans of Oxfam UKI, Save the Children Fund UK and Action Aid to contract three Halo demining teams in Zambézia. By mid-1996 Halo had received $450,000 from the DHA Trust Fund (for National Survey), $2,500,000 from the U.K., $450,000 from Ireland (via Concern), and $65,000 from International Organisation for Migration (for employment of ex-soldiers).[181]

---

[178] Ibid.

[179] Human Rights Watch interview with U.N. official, New York, March 12, 1995.

[180] Diplomatic sources, Maputo, February 27, 1997.

[181] Information provided by Overseas Development Agency, December 1996.

Halo has focused its attention on the northern region, training some 150 demining personnel and deploying four platoons of thirty men each, three in Zambézia province and one in Niassa. It has only two expatriate staff in a managerial capacity.[182] Halo had by January 31, 1997 cleared 144 kilometers of road and 1,641,477 square meters of mines. A total of 3,833 antipersonnel mines and 180 antitank mines were reportedly cleared.

Halo is considering whether to expand its operations into Cabo Delgado and Nampula provinces. USAID had reprogrammed the $1 million remaining after the completion of the RONCO contract to make a grant to World Vision, which had a strong presence in central and northern Mozambique. World Vision was likely to subcontract for a Halo team to operate in Nampula for two years and possibly Cabo Delgado. Halo expected to pull out of Mozambique before the year 2000.

Halo claims to have developed a new technique for clearing roads, Labor-Intensive Road Verification (LIRV). Unskilled local labor is used to excavate sideways the surface of dirt roads from a one meter wide central furrow cleared by trained deminers. According to Halo this method is applicable on soils made soft after rains and brings down costs and significantly speeds up the pace of clearance. Halo had declined various requests for independent verification of this claim and on October 9, 1996 a heavily-laden truck detonated an antitank mine at Caronga in Niassa province on a road cleared by Halo using the LIRV technique.[183] Halo in its report of the accident failed to mention that one person was killed and two others injured.[184]

### Handicap International
Handicap International (HI) has been active in Mozambique since 1986. After opening a prothesis workshop in Inhambane in 1986, it has since expanded, opening additional workshops in Nampula, Tete, Vilanculos (Inhambane) and, in 1993 and 1994, in Pemba (Cabo Delgado) and Lichinga (Niassa).

---

[182] In March 1995, Chris Moon, a Halo Trust project manager, lost his right arm and lower leg in the explosion of a Portuguese M966 antipersonnel mine during mine clearance activities in Zambézia province.

[183] Bernt Bernander and Christer Westerberg, "The Mine Clearance Programme in Mozambique," Stockholm Group for Development Studies, June 1996, p.16.

[184] Nick Bateman, "Anti-tank mine accident Cuamba/Mecanhelas road," The Halo Trust, Quelimane, fax dated October 11, 1996.

HI was considering entering into mine clearance operations in 1997. It has been talking to SGS and other firms about setting up a low cost two or three year project aimed at four districts in Inhambane province at a cost of $1,640,000. The objective was to train local teams, making them self-sufficient in "proximity clearing" of scattered landmine clusters. The HI program also envisioned setting up a Mine Clearance Bureau within the provincial government, to provide management, communications and logistical support. Operating at district level, the demining teams would act on requests prioritized by district authorities, making "fire brigade" sorties to identified mine locations. [185]

### Norwegian People's Aid

NPA began training Mozambican mine clearers in July 1993. By mid-1994 NPA had trained over 250 Mozambican deminers in Tete province to work on roads, tracks and areas for the safe return of refugees from neighboring countries. In late 1994 NPA set up a training center for mine dogs in Tete province. NPA progressively strengthened its operational capacity to six platoons, with two platoons deployed in each of the provinces of Tete, Sofala and Maputo. In 1996 the platoons assigned to Maputo province were redeployed to Manica province. Another two platoons were trained in 1996 to work in Sofala province.. By February 7, 1997, NPA was recorded as having cleared 104 kilometers of road, some 4,164,411 square meters of land and destroyed 8,214 antipersonel mines and fifteen antitank mines in Maputo, Manica, Sofala and Tete provinces.[186] In January 1997 alone, according to national radio NPA disabled 214 mines while clearing a two kilometer stretch of road. [187]

In late 1996 NPA employed 450 Mozambican sappers and a Mozambican director along with fifteen expatriate staff (mostly administrative). NPA planned to reduce its expatriate staff in 1997 to ten, and in 1998 to five. The aim was to establish a fully Mozambican NGO as NPA's successor organization.

NPA's operations have been funded mainly by the Norwegian Agency for International Development and ONUMOZ, which provided the maintenance budget for deminers. However, in its first seven months of mine clearance, NPA did not receive any U.N. payment because of bureaucratic delays. The U.S.,

---

[185] Information provided by Handicap International, Maputo, November 20, 1996.

[186] Commissão Nacional de Desminagem, "Sumário de Registos Concernentes A Operação de Desminagem em Moçambique," March 1, 1997.

[187] *Radio Moçambique*, Maputo, February 10, 1997.

Netherlands, Austria and Italy have also provided funds. NPA also inherited mine-detecting dogs, dog handlers and deminers trained by RONCO when it completed its contract.

*Other Mine Clearance Initiatives*

The Mines Advisory Group (MAG), a British-based mine clearance nongovernmental organization, sent an assessment mission to Mozambique in March and April 1993, which visited Maputo, Tete and Inhambane provinces. MAG sought but failed to raise funds to establish a mine awareness and survey project in Inhambane province in conjunction with Handicap International. MAG was considering re-applying for funding to work in Inhambane province.[188]

The Canadian International Demining Center (CIDC) is a Canadian NGO devoted to mine clearance. At the request of the National Mineclearing Commission it has drawn up a project proposal for creating indigenous mine clearance capacity in Nampula, Niassa and Cabo Delgado provinces over a period of two years at a cost of $2,820,000. A request for funding has been submitted to the Canadian government.[189]

HGM, a German mine clearance NGO proposed a clearance project in 1995 but failed to attract funding. British-based Mine Clearance International was also seeking contracts in Mozambique, as was the French firm CIDEV which signed on September 5, 1996 a memorandum of intent with the Caixa Francesa de Desenvolvimento to offer its services for mine clearance. The Caixa Francesa allocated around $2.5 million for clearance of the Komatippoort/Maputo and Songo-Matambo power lines. Another private firm, OGS, has signed a similar memorandum of intent.[190] In September 1996 the Iranian Minister of Defence Abdol Ali Tavakoli also offered Iranian teams to clear mines in Mozambique.[191]

On March 26, 1997, the South African and Mozambican foreign affairs ministers signed a demining agreement, which proposes a R12 million project for clearance in Maputo province. The demining was to pave the way for a number of

---

[188] Information provided by MAG, November 1996.

[189] Information provided by the National Mineclearance Commission (CND), Maputo, September 12, 1996.

[190] *domingo* (Maputo), December 1, 1996.

[191] *Noticias* (Maputo), September 11, 1996.

large joint projects, such as an aluminum smelter and the Maputo development corridor project.

**Antipersonnel Mine Ban Position**
On October 24, 1995 President Chissano announced in New York after meeting with then U.N. Secretary-General Boutros Boutros-Ghali that Mozambique was prepared to head an international campaign against landmines. Chissano stressed that "many people are demanding that Mozambique should head a world campaign against the production, sale and use of landmines." He pledged that Mozambique was prepared to play such a role.[192]

However, the government took little concrete action in the next year, as it appeared that there was a split on the landmine issue, with the Ministry of Foreign Affairs and Development increasingly supportive of a ban, but the Ministry of Defence opposed. Some in the Mozambican military clearly wanted to retain the option of using landmines, believing that they have a useful role in Mozambique's defense strategy.

It has also appeared that in some cases the government was reluctant to see some minefields cleared. The Songo minefield around the Cahora Bassa dam illustrates this contradiction. A cursory survey of the field in 1994 concluded that it held "several hundred thousand" antipersonnel mines although the authorities have never provided a map of the minefield to the mine clearers. In September 1995, NPA began mine clearance operations at Songo and found that the minefield consisted of a circular perimeter around Songo and the dam wall, estimated to be thirty kilometers long and forty meters wide. In eight months seventy Norwegian People's Aid sappers cleared 46,000 square meters, destroying some 3,000 mines. However on July 24, 1996 the CND faxed Norwegian People's Aid saying mine removal operations at Songo must stop immediately "until an agreement has been reached between the Mozambican government and the Cahora Bassa hydroelectric dam board of directors."[193] The CND Director Osório Mateus justified this suspension by saying that the Cabora Bassa dam was a major economic and strategic project. He said that "the removal of this security system necessarily implies the introduction of another that is at least as good and preferably better."[194]

---

[192] "Chissano/Boutros Ghali Meeting," New York, *AIM*, October 24, 1995.

[193] *Imparcialfax* (Maputo), August 19, 1996.

[194] Ibid..

Mine clearance was only resumed again several weeks later.[195]  Mine-Tech was stopped from clearing the last fifteen mined pylons near Cahora Bassa for the same reason.

In November 1995 the Campanha Moçambicana Contra as Minas (CMCM)—Mozambican Campaign to Ban Landmines—was launched. In May 1996 the CMCM started a newsletter and three editions were published that year. The campaign also took on a full-time coordinator. The CMCM has grown to over seventy organizations and has been increasingly active in lobbying for a ban of landmines. In 1996 the CMCM lobbied the Commission for Defence and Public Order for a law to ban landmines in Mozambique. It also held meetings with the foreign minister and the speaker of the assembly. It encouraged letter writing to the press, in particular in response to an article by parliamentarian Sergio Vieira justifying landmines in the June 16 edition of *domingo*.[196]  The CMCM also gathered over 100,000 signatures on a petition calling for a total ban.

Mozambican Foreign Minister Leonardo Simão in October 1996 spoke at the U.N., saying, "We look forward to continue working together with a view toward eliminating these horrible weapons, not only in Mozambique but also in all countries affected by this evil." He said his government supported a worldwide ban on the production, stockpiling and distribution of landmines.[197] Mozambique also played a constructive role in supporting the U.S.-sponsored U.N. General Assembly resolution calling on nations "to pursue vigorously" an antipersonnel mine ban, and to conclude an international ban treaty "as soon as possible." The resolution passed on December 10, 1996 by a vote of 156-0, with just ten abstentions.

As the 4th International NGO Conference on Landmines (held in Maputo February 25-28, 1997) approached, the government's position on landmines received greatly increased attention domestically, regionally and internationally. President Chissano, after repeated delays, agreed to meet with the Mozambican ban campaign the week before the conference. He accepted their petition with more

---

[195] Human RightsWatch interview with NPA official, Maputo, February 27, 1997.

[196] See, *domingo*, July 16, 23 and 30, 1996;. Also a page of letters in the November 17, 1996 edition from academics, journalists, the Rector of the University, Brazão Mazula and Graça Machel, the widow of late President Samora Machel, complaining about the Vieira article.

[197] "Mozambique Says More Resources Needed to Cope With Landmines," *South Africa Press Agency*, October 4, 1996.

than 100,000 signatures, and told them to expect a significant announcement on a mine ban soon. He also agreed to open the conference on February 25. His speech strongly endorsed an international ban, but did not commit Mozambique to any new steps. However, the following day, February 26, Mozambique's foreign minister addressed the NGO Conference and announced an immediate ban on the use, production, import and export of antipersonnel mines. (Apparently, Chissano could not make the announcement the day before because the Council of Ministers had not yet approved the decision). Foreign Minister Simão's statement said:

> Accordingly, under the provisions contained in paragraph 1 of article 153 of the Constitution of the Republic, the Council of Ministers determines:
> 1. With immediate effect, the production, commercialization, utilization and non-authorized transportation of antipersonnel landmines is hereby prohibited in the national territory.
> 2. The Government shall continue to promote all efforts aimed at ensuring mine clearance activities, with a view to guaranteeing greater security to the citizens.[198]

Regrettably, destruction of Mozambique's stockpile was not addressed. Foreign Minister Simão later told the press, "A thing we in government haven't yet reached a decision on is where shall we put the mines that are today stockpiled. We may decide that at some point we will need to destroy them."[199]

Foreign Minister Simão has also said, "The government took its decision because of the mobilization work undertaken by the Mozambican Campaign Against Landmines. The campaign collected 100,000 signatures from citizens who think that antipersonnel mines should be banned throughout the world. They spoke with me. The head of state received them. They were received by other members of government. They told us what the aims of the campaign were, and we thought we should support them."[200]

---

[198] Statement by H.E. Dr. Leonardo Santos Simão, Minister of Foreign Affairs and Cooperation of the Republic of Mozambique, before the 4th NGO International Conference on Landmines, Maputo, February 26, 1997.

[199] domingo (Maputo), March 2, 1997.

[200] Mozambique News Agency, "Foreign Minister praises local campaign," Report no. 105, March 7, 1997.

The announcement puts Mozambique at the forefront of the ban movement in the region. President Chissano told parliament on March 17, 1997, "In addition to this internal action, measures are being taken, under our proposal, to convince the summits of the SADC and the OAU to include in the agendas of their next sessions the problem of landmines, aiming to a ban in the continent and region." In announcing their new demining agreement on March 26, 1997, the foreign ministers of Mozambique and South Africa said, "In taking this step South Africa and Mozambique affirm their partnership in the campaign for a mine-free southern Africa and in the International Campaign to Ban Landmines."[201]

President Chissano has also shown that he intends to play an active role internationally. In his speech at the Islamic Conference in Pakistan on March 23, 1997, Chissano called on all member states to support a ban and proposed such language in the final declaration of the gathering, but his proposal was opposed by Pakistan and Indonesia.[202]

---

[201] South African Ministry of Foreign Affairs Press Release, March 26, 1997, carried by SAPA news agency, Johannesburg, March 26, 1997.

[202] *Radio Moçambique*, March 25, 1997.

# VI. NAMIBIA

Namibia became independent in 1990 from South Africa, which had administered Namibia under a League of Nations mandate from 1920 to 1966, and illegally since 1966 on a de facto basis. A low level guerrilla war, in which landmines were frequently used, was fought from 1966 until independence. Landmines continue to pose a threat to civilians.

## Background

The war typically involved hit and run attacks by the South West Africa People's Organization's (SWAPO) military wing, the People's Liberation Army of Namibia (PLAN), and counterinsurgency sweeps against the guerrillas by South African forces. The northern war zone, the "Operational Area," was divided into three zones by the South African command: Sector 20 (Kavango), Sector 70 (Eastern Caprivi) and Section 10. Sector 10, covering Ovamboland and Kaokoland, was the scene of most military activity and had at least eighty permanent army and police bases. Sector 10's headquarters were in Oshakati. South of the "Operational Area," the "Red Line" as it was also known, were the white farming areas, where the military structure was different. Towns such as Grootfontein acted as rear military supply and logistics bases. The farms also had small military units based on them and the farmers mustered into Area Force Units, largely white part-time militia units.

South African military activity consisted mainly of intensive patrolling by relatively small groups scouring the bush for signs of PLAN combatants and searching in the Kraals and Cuca shops (general stores which also doubled as pubs). On making contact with PLAN combatants, the patrols would pursue them and, when necessary, radio for reinforcements. In case of contact with a large PLAN unit, mobile reaction forces would be dispatched in armored personnel carriers. PLAN actions included attacks on military bases, sabotage, planting of landmines, bombings and assassination of "homeland" leaders, those who had decided to collaborate with the occupation. PLAN's offensives were usually timed for the wet season, when bush cover provided guerrillas greater camouflage protection.[203]

---

[203] Africa Watch, *Accountability in Namibia: Human Rights and the Transition to Democracy* (New York: Human Rights Watch, 1992).

### Armed Insurgency Begins

The armed insurgency began on August 26, 1966, when SWAPO fighters engaged in a shootout with South African forces near a guerrilla training camp that had been established at Omgulumbashe. The war escalated after May 22, 1971, when a mine planted by SWAPO forces exploded under a police vehicle near Katima in the Caprivi strip, killing two white South African policemen and injuring nine others, including two African trackers. The landmine blew a crater in the road measuring about two meters in diameter and half a meter in depth, hurling the vehicle a good fifteen meters; the body of one policeman was thrown some twenty-five meters. This incident was the first landmine incident in Namibia, and also marked the first time white South African officials were killed by a landmine on soil controlled by South Africa.[204]

Another police vehicle detonated an anti-vehicle mine several miles from Katima on October 4, 1971, seriously injuring four constables. The following day a policeman inspecting the scene stepped on an antipersonnel mine and was killed. Police tracking the SWAPO unit came across three more antipersonnel mines in their path. In 1972 and 1973 anti-vehicle mines in Eastern Caprivi killed two policemen and injured three others. SWAPO reported in July 1972 that during the preceding four months its mines had destroyed thirteen South African military vehicles, killing twenty-five to thirty South African personnel.[205]

By mid-1973 SWAPO was engaging South African forces directly in combat rather than just planting mines. The result was that in June 1974 South Africa pulled its police units out of Caprivi and replaced them with army units.

By the early 1970s, SWAPO had established several guerrilla bases in Zambia along the border of the Caprivi Strip. All the 1971-74 Caprivi attacks appear to have been launched from rear bases in Zambia by small units of up to five guerrillas. After the collapse of Portuguese colonial rule in Angola in 1975, SWAPO was able to move PLAN armed units into southern Angola, where they mingled with the Ovambo people living north of the border. SWAPO was soon able to infiltrate large numbers of combatants into Namibia. In a skirmish in 1975, sixty-one PLAN guerrillas were killed along with three South Africans. By the spring of 1976, the military threat was sufficient for the South African colonial authorities to declare emergency rule in the country's northern tier-Ovamboland, Kavangoland and the Caprivi Strip.

---

[204] *The Guardian* (London), May 25, 1971.

[205] Michael Morris, *Armed Conflict in Southern Africa* (Cape Town: Jeremy Spence, 1974), pp.10-11.

By late 1977, PLAN guerrillas were engaging in frequent clashes in Ovamboland; the South Africans claimed there were one hundred clashes every month. In 1977, South African forces cleared a "free-fire zone" (where any living creature was liable to be shot on sight), a one kilometer wide strip in front of a 450 kilometer ten-foot-high security fence designed to halt infiltration from Angola. The creation of the strip involved the forcible removal of dozens of villages and homes and the closure of an Anglican mission station. Nevertheless, SWAPO continued its hit and run tactics, including the laying of landmines.

The sabotage of strategic installations, particularly communications, power and water supplies, became a common PLAN tactic; according to the South African Defence Force (SADF) it increased tenfold during 1978. A particular target was the Ruacana hydroelectric facility on the Angolan border. Constant sabotage of the power lines from Ruacana forced the administration to link the north of Namibia with the Cape grid. To deter the use of landmines, the major roads in the north were tarred, and armored military escorts were used.

By the late 1970s landmine warfare was becoming a serious concern for the South African forces. In December 1977 Major-General Wally Blad, the South West Africa Defence Force (SAWDF) Director General reported that South African casualties had increased during the past year following a "significant" rise in the use of landmines. He noted that sixteen soldiers had been killed by landmines. By February 1979 there had been 324 confirmed landmine incidents.

### The War in the 1980s

While South Africa built up its forces and conducted an aggressive counterinsurgency campaign in the years immediately after 1978, SWAPO's numbers and capabilities continued to grow. SWAPO's growth was assisted by Cuban, Angolan and East European instruction. Some SWAPO members were also sent to Chinese and Russian military academies. SWAPO equipment was mainly Soviet, Czech, Yugoslav, and East German origin, notably AK-47 rifles, RPG-7 grenade launchers, POMZ antipersonnel mines and TMA-3 anti-vehicle mines (nicknamed cheese mines by South West African forces).[206] Interviewed in 1986, PLAN's deputy chief of engineering and demolition justified SWAPO's dependence on landmine warfare by saying that mines are "designed to cope with the situation

---

[206] Denis Herbstein and John Evenson, *The Devils are Among Us: The War for Namibia* (London: Zed Press, 1989), p.41.

in which the enemy is infinitely superior in relation to every conventional factor of warfare."[207]

South African officials reported in June 1980 that SWAPO guerrillas had changed their mine warfare tactics. In the 1970s SWAPO had concentrated on laying its mines within fifteen kilometers of the Angolan/Namibian border. But in 1980 landmines were used for the first time in Kaokoland, causing several deaths. In late 1979 SWAPO also had begun to lay mines along the Oshivello-Oshakati tarred road.

By mid-1979, PLAN fighters were operating in the area of Grootfontein, a white farming district in the northeast. By 1981, a number of the farms in the Outjo, another white farming area, had been abandoned. The effect of landmines on the isolated administrative post of Opuwo was described by journalist Helen Gibson in 1981:

> Opuwo and its 8,000 inhabitants live behind high fences and none of the thirty white civil service families ever leave the perimeter unless they travel in Dakota aircraft or Buffel mine-protected vehicles.... The reason for this isolation is that SWAPO guerrillas regularly mine the dirt road that leads south to the town of Outojo, 270 miles away.... The mines find targets sometimes more than six times a month.[208]

Despite the difficulties of carrying mines long distances, PLAN specialized in mine warfare, including techniques of tunneling under or lifting sections of tarred roads. Antipersonnel mines were often laid alongside antitank mines to hamper mine clearance. The SADF with its sophisticated mine-proofed vehicles, usually escaped heavy casualties. Civilians were the most frequent victims. In 1980, 220 Ovambos were killed and another 256 injured in mine related incidents.[209]

In the summer of 1980, the South African military launched attacks across the border against SWAPO targets deep in Angola. The attacks resulted in numerous casualties and logistical difficulties for SWAPO, which was forced to

---

[207] *The Combatant,* July 1986.

[208] *The Financial Times* (London), March 1, 1981.

[209] Paul Moorcraft, *African Nemesis: War and Revolution in Southern Africa 1945-2010* (London: Brassey's, 1990), p.227.

launch its attacks from ever greater distances. As a result, fighting dropped off and South African officials predicted a speedy demise of PLAN as a military force. Nevertheless, in April 1982, a detachment of some 1,000 guerrillas penetrated 130 miles south of the Angolan border to Tseumb, the site of a large copper mine, where they killed nine South African soldiers and a smaller number of civilians.

In April 1982 South Africa's Brigadier Jan Klopper announced that SWAPO forces had planted a trail of landmines in the farming regions bounded by the Tseumeb, Tsintsabis and Oshivello, south of Kavongo. A Tseumb farmer had been killed in April when his vehicle detonated a mine. Several soldiers who were with him checking his fences were injured. Earlier another farmer had been injured by a mine and flown to Pretoria. The South Africans reported that during 1982, 1,268 SWAPO guerrillas had been killed compared to seventy-seven members of the South African and South-West African forces. They also claimed that 139 civilians had died, mainly in landmine accidents, that year.[210]

But the insurgency did not escalate qualitatively. SWAPO was unable to mount the kind of armed struggle that had taken place in Zimbabwe. The strength of the South African forces, as well as Namibia's terrain, made that impossible. Though the SWAPO insurgency could not defeat the South Africans militarily in Namibia, neither could the South Africans eliminate PLAN without enormous cost to themselves.

PLAN activity during 1983 continued to feature the use of mines. Between January and March SWAPO landmines in Owambo, northern Namibia, killed eight black policemen, two South African soldiers and some twenty-six civilians. In July 1983 a powerful mine exploded in the center of Windhoek, causing extensive property damage but no injuries. That same month two landmines killed six and seriously injured ten passengers in a civilian vehicle near Ruacana.

In 1984 and 1985, the war continued at a rate of nearly one incident a day, with a marked increase in sabotage by PLAN forces, often using mines. The progress of the war became increasingly hard to track with accurate information of troop strength and casualties difficult to obtain. The two sides supplied widely varying estimates of both. By 1984, South West Africa Territorial Forces (SWATF) reported PLAN casualties at a ratio of twenty-one to one (PLAN to SWATF). SWAPO countered by publishing statistics of South African forces killed in action that the SADF denied. Both sides continued to dispute the other's claims of casualties.

---

[210] *The Times* (London), April 30, 1982; *The Guardian* (London), December 30, 1982.

Landmine warfare continued. The main road to Oshikango got nicknamed "Landmine highway" in the press because of SWAPO's frequent planting of mines in it. The South African authorities also stepped up their attempts through a reward system to gain intelligence about the location of landmines. In 1985 leaflets dropped in the north amongst Ovambo villages offered rewards of R20,000 for information leading to the capture of SWAPO commanders, and R200 for information about landmines. South African units were also offered a similar, but financially higher incentive package. Jim Hooper traveled with Koevoet, a special counterinsurgency unit known for its violence, in hot pursuit of a PLAN unit in the mid-1980s:

> Not long after the contact, the trackers found a POMZ-2 AP mine the insurgents had set alongside a bush trail. The green, pineapple-sectioned bombs had been hidden behind a tree, the thin, almost invisible trip wire stretched across the path. The pin to detonate had been drawn most of the way. The slightest pressure would have allowed it to drop out, followed by an almost instantaneous explosion of deadly shrapnel.[211]

PLAN's use of mines to stop hot pursuit sometimes resulted in the desired lethal effect. The *Namibian* newspaper reported in November 1986 that a Koevoet unit lost two men in a landmine explosion when following a guerrilla trail.[212]

When units like Koevoet caught prisoners alive they would often immediately force them to show them where mines had been placed or where hidden arms caches were located. The hidden caches, too, were sometimes protected by landmines.

Civilians, as well as soldiers from both sides, suffered from the mines. A Lutheran pastor and four members of his family were killed in a landmine explosion on a narrow track north of Oshakati in June 1982. The indiscriminate nature of landmine warfare in Namibia was clearly recognized by those writing about the war. Herbstein and Evenson wrote in 1989, "Though the guerrillas always attempted to lay mines where they thought military vehicles or so-called

---

[211] Jim Hooper, *Koevoet!* (Johannesburg: Southern Book Publishers, 1988), p.97.

[212] *The Namibian* (Windhoek), November 14, 1986.

'puppets' would pass, there was an inevitable element of indiscrimination in their targeting."[213]

Another writer on the conflict in Namibia, less sympathetic to SWAPO than those above, Helmoed-Römer Heitman, described landmines as "the ideal weapon of random terror. Rendering the normal use of Owambo's dirt roads an extremely hazardous undertaking, the landmine serves both to spread fear and uncertainty among the population and to undermine confidence in the authorities' ability to offer meaningful protection. Additionally, it hinders economic development that might have gone some way toward negating SWAPO propaganda."[214]

PLAN favored the use of mines because it minimized contact with the security forces. It was also a popular assassination tool. A landmine laid in the driveway or under the wheel of a parked car leaves very little room for counteraction. At least one member of the Owambo Government, Thomas Shikongo, was killed in this way together with his daughter and some friends.

In April 1987, PLAN succeeded in infiltrating the farming areas around Etosha National Park for the first time since 1983. Throughout 1987, military communiques maintained that SWAPO was being forced to concentrate on sabotage operations and mortar and rocket attacks against military outposts because it was otherwise militarily ineffective. Yet, the 1987 wet season infiltration by PLAN became one of the bloodiest campaigns of the conflict for both sides. By the late 1980s, the war had reached a stalemate. The South Africans succeeded in preventing serious cross-border attacks, while guerrilla activities were sufficient to tie down large numbers of South African troops.

While most of the PLAN mines were laid on the many gravel roads, and on their verges to catch those trying to avoid the mines, there were also attempts to lay under the tar of the main north-south road. This included tunneling under the road from the verge and also heating a 200-liter drum and using it to lift out a section of the surface like a cookie cutter. Antipersonnel mines were also sometimes laid with the anti-vehicle mines in an effort to hamper clearing work.

Between 1974 to 1989 the South African Engineer Corps reported having lifted and disarmed a total of 1,743 landmines in northern Namibia. Between 1979-89 some 1.13 million kilometers in Sector 10 (mainly Ovambo) was reportedly swept by a mine detecting vehicle or by a sapper on a motor bike looking for road

---

[213] Denis Herbstein and John Evenson, pp.43-44.

[214] Helmoed-Römmer Heitman, *South African War Machine* (Johannesburg: Bison Books, 1985), p.158.

disturbances, while over the same period, according to the same sources, foot teams swept 430,000 kilometers by foot with mine detectors. The projected repair costs by the SADF would have been R97 million.[215] In some cases, according to the local population planted mines from Angola just in order to later claim the attractive rewards for "finding" them.

The South African Defence Forces in the 1980s also laid a series of minefields in northern Namibia around military encampments and installations. These minefields quickly proved to be difficult to maintain and dangerous. Maintenance was necessary for a variety of reasons, such as the removal of the carcasses of animals that had wandered into the minefields. SADF soldiers involved in these maintenance operations suffered accidents not only because of lapses in procedure but because the mines had been displaced from their original location. Some mines moved as much as thirty centimeters in the ground over time; others rose to the surface after heavy rains and were seen floating.

In part because of this experience, the SADF abandoned plans in 1988 to construct a thirty kilometer barrier minefield along a stretch of the Namibian border with Angola. The original plan had been to construct a barrier minefield combining antipersonnel and antitank mines and antitank ditches, in order to delay a possible attack by joint Angolan and Cuban forces on two Namibian towns. The SADF's engineering staff convinced the command to abandon the plan for a number of reasons. They argued it would require too many combat engineering regiments, would take many months to complete, would cost millions of Rand in terms of man-hours, machines and material, and that maintenance would also be costly and dangerous. From a tactical view, covering the whole obstacle belt with constant observation and fire would be practically impossible. The barrier minefield was likely to be ineffective because the terrain involved was flat and without any natural obstacle. An enemy force could outflank the obstacle in an estimated thirty minutes. The alternative of good intelligence, early warning and a higher state of armed force readiness was seen to be a cheaper and better solution.[216]

### Negotiations, the U.N. and Independence

In 1976, the U.N. Security Council unanimously adopted Resolution 385 which called on South Africa to withdraw from Namibia and allow free elections. The following year, South Africa and SWAPO agreed that the five Western nations

---

[215] Jannie Geldenhuys, *A General's Story*, p.184-5.

[216] International Committee of the Red Cross, *Anti-personnel Landmines: Friend or Foe?*, pp.31-32.

then on the Security Council—the United States, France, United Kingdom, West Germany and Canada—would serve as mediators to negotiate an internally acceptable solution. In 1978, the U.N. Security Council adopted Resolution 435, providing for internationally supervised elections. Resolution 435 also restated the need to end "South Africa's illegal administration of Namibia and transfer power to the people of Namibia with the assistance of the United Nations in accordance with resolution 385."

Resolution 435 also envisaged a United Nations Transition Assistance Group (UNTAG) to be deployed for twelve months to assist the secretary-general's special representative in ensuring the early independence of Namibia through "free and fair elections under the supervision and control of the United Nations."

In the early 1980s the process leading toward the implementation of Resolution 435 stalled. In 1981, the U.S. had introduced "linkage" between the withdrawal of Cuban troops from Angola and the departure of South African forces from Namibia. In 1982, eight additional points were added to Resolution 435 by Security Council members. These included constitutional guarantees for a Bill of Rights, multi-party democracy and an independent judiciary.

In December 1988, the Brazzaville Protocol was signed. It set April 1, 1989, as the date for implementation of Resolution 435. To prepare, UNTAG personnel began to arrive in Namibia in January 1989. As the date for implementation drew close, SWAPO announced a policy of "national reconciliation" to heal the divisive wounds caused by the independence struggle, but on April 1, 1989, a large scale movement of PLAN fighters into northern Namibia provoked widespread fighting in which many PLAN combatants were killed. Implementation of Resolution 435 was suspended until May 1989.

Following the election of a Constituent Assembly in November 1989 (in which SWAPO received a majority of the votes) and the drafting of a constitution, Namibia achieved independence on March 20, 1990.

**Post-Independence**

In late 1989 before the South Africans withdrew from Namibia they made limited efforts to clear the main minefields around their bases by hurriedly driving Olifant tanks, and other heavy vehicles, back and forth repeatedly over the minefields. Although this detonated many mines, it was clearly not up to humanitarian standards, under which civilians could safely return.

Landmine clearance was not part of UNTAG's mandate, although mined roads initially posed a threat to effective U.N. deployment. UNTAG privately conceded that Caspir anti-mine vehicles were needed. A U.N. official said, "We are urgently seeking further mine-resistant vehicles so that the operational effectiveness of the U.N. police monitors can be increased."[217]

The U.N. decided to rent Caspirs and a Buffel vehicle from South Africa for UNTAG. Landmines were the responsibility of an Australian engineer unit which cleared some of the minefields in Ondangwa. In March 1990 the Australian contingent announced that it was winding up its operation by fencing and repairing fences around ten minefields near former SADF and police bases in the north. A publicity campaign followed asking local residents to leave the fences, parts of which had been stolen, intact.[218] A year later most of these fences were gone.

U.N. police monitors also uncovered a series of arms caches during their stay. In early January 1990 the U.N. announced the discovery in December of a cache of weapons, including antipersonnel fragmentation mines at Ondangwa, probably taken from a nearby abandoned Koevoet camp.

## Landmine Types and Sources

The U.S. Department of Defense data base "MineFacts" (available on CD-Rom) claims that the Namibians have produced PMD-6 antipersonnel mines.[219] When asked about this by Human Rights Watch, Namibian officials and Namibian Police (Nampol) have denied it.[220] Told of the denial, a U.S. expert involved in compilation of the landmines data base insisted on the veracity of the information, which he stated was based on visual identification of the weapon.[221]

Aside from the disputed Namibian PMD-6, twenty-five types of antipersonnel mines have been reported in Namibia originating from nine countries:

---

[217] The Natal Mercury (Durban), May 3, 1989.

[218] The Namibian (Windhoek), March 9, 1990.

[219] U.S. Department of Defense, Minefacts CD-Rom, 1996.

[220] Vernon Joynt, director of Mechem, claimed that South Africa had produced PMD-6 mines in the past and assembled them in South West Africa. The MUV fuzes were produced in South Africa. According to Joynt, assembly stopped prior to Namibian independence in 1990. Human Rights Watch interview with Vernon Joynt, Harare, April 22, 1997.

[221] Human Rights Watch interview, Geneva, May 1996.

- Portugal: M-969; PRB M409.
- Soviet Union: OZM-4; PMD-6; PMN; POMZ-2; POMZ-2M.
- Yugoslavia: PMA-1; PMA-2;PMA-3; PMR-1;PMR-2A; PROM-1.
- Czechoslovakia: PP-MI-BA; PP-MI-SR.
- East Germany: PPM-2.
- Belgium: PRB M409; PRB M966; PRB 966 B/Type 1.
- Rhodesia: RAP No.1; RAP No.2.
- South Africa: R2A2; SA Non-Mettalic AP.
- Zimbabwe: ZAP No.1; ZAPS.

The following antitank mines have been reported: Mk-7(UK);No.8 (South Africa); PT-MI-BA II, PT-MI-BA III, PT-MI-K (Czechoslovakia); TMA-2, TMA-3, TMA-4, TMA-5 (Yugoslavia); TM-46, TM-57, TM-62B, TM-62M, TMD-44, TMD-B, TMK-2 (Soviet Union); UKA-63 (Hungary).

Human Rights Watch has obtained copies of two confidential documents indicating that the arsenal at the Namibian Defense Forces Grootfontein Military Base is poorly maintained, and contains explosives, including several mine types, that are unstable and very hazardous. The stores include antitank mines, Claymore mines, POMZ-2 mines, and "obviously suspect wooden PMD-6 mines that had previously been soaked by constant exposure and wet." According to both of these reports, the condition of the arsenal is so unstable that even moving the weapons could cause an accident. Despite domestic press exposure of Grootfontein Military Base's condition the government has not openly confronted the problem.[222]

**The Minefields**

The SADF left no detailed records of where the mines were laid in the minefields, although there are records of the number planted. PLAN did not keep accurate records of where it laid mines and its ex-combatants have generally been reluctant to assist the police in trying to relocate them. Generally, fences and warning signboards were erected around minefield perimeters. These minefields were all in the far north, around former army and police bases, water towers and electricity pylons.

The 200 kilometer Omburu-Ruacana (SWAWEK) power line has 401 pylons, all of which were mined in late 1980 by the SADF to protect them from

---

[222] PROC GEN/EOD/93/4. Confidential Report on Inspection of Ammunition and General Visit, Groofontein Military Base, by Col. D.W.J Radmore, March 17-18, 1993.

PLAN sabotage attempts. Each pylon had a minefield covering an area of approximately thirty meters by thirty meters around it, containing between 200 and 400 antipersonnel mines.

There is some controversy about these minefields around the pylons and who is responsible for them. In a reply to a question in the South African parliament on May 15, 1996, the defense minister claimed that in 1989 it was decided by the interim Namibian government and SWAWEK (South West Africa Water and Electricity Commission) that the minefields protecting the power lines should not be lifted. However, in a 1991 memorandum by Nampol on rendering safe these minefields, Nampol stated that the SADF had been asked on several occasions to clear the minefields prior to their withdrawal:

> SAWECK maintains that the corporation can not be held responsible for the safety of these minefields, nor can it be held liable for any loss of lives or property as a result of people or livestock being killed by any mine or explosive device inside, or around any of these minefields, whether a fence has been removed or not.... [T]he South African Defence Force has never been requested by the corporation to lay mines around any pylon at any place whatsoever and...the South African Defense Force has been requested on several occasions after the implementation of Resolution 435 to remove these mines and have the area rendered safe.[223]

In March 1991 a controversial twelve month R3.4 million contract was awarded to Namibian Blasting Agents, a Windhoek based firm, run by the former head of the infamous Koevoet counterinsurgency unit, Ben Vermaak.[224] Only three companies bid for the job to remove several thousand SADF-planted landmines around the pylons. The mines turned out to be much more numerous than expected: 8,122 R2M2 and 1,082 No.69 South African-manufactured antipersonnel mines were reportedly found and destroyed.[225] The Namibian Blasting Agents used

---

[223] Nampol, "Memorandum. Rendering Safe of Minefields: Omburu-Ruacana (SWAWEK) Powerline," June 18, 1991.

[224] See, *The Namibian* (Windhoek), March 15,16, 25 and 28, 1991 for details about the Ruacana power line contract controversy.

[225] Information provided by Nampol, April 1996.

a bulldozer and roller method to clear many of the mines. Two deminers were killed during these operations and several mines were found afterwards.

### Northern Namibia's Eleven Minefields[226]

| Place | Size SQ.M. | Cleared SADF | Fence and Signs | UNTAG | Rate % |
|---|---|---|---|---|---|
| 1. ALPHA TOWER | 20750 | X | X | Fence Repair | 89 |
| 2. BRAVO TOWER | ? | ? | ? | ? | ? |
| 3. CHARLIE TOWER | 4560 | X | X | Neg | 97 |
| 4. EENHANA BASE | 36900 | X | X | Part Prodded | 95 |
| 5. HURRICANE BASE | 55000 | X | X | Neg | 95 |
| 6. ETALE | 39200 | X | X | Part Swept | 96 |
| 7. MAHENE NKONGO OGONGO | 56000 | X | X | Fence Repair | 86 |
| 8. OHANGWENA | 11600 | X | X | Fence Repair | 76 |
| 9. OKALONGO OKANKOLO | 45500 | X | X | Fence Repair | 95 |
| 10. OMBALANTU OSHIGAMBO | 27000 | X | X | Neg | 82 |

[226] Figures provided by Nambian Explosive Police, 1995.

11. RUACANA   56000 X          X        Part Swept              92
TOWN

| Area | 353510 sqm |
| Mines Laid | 44594 |
| Mines Neutral | 40779 |
| **MINES Remain** | **3719** |
| **Clearing Rate** | **88%** |

### Records of Mines Laid and Lifted by September 1995

|  | Mines Laid | Mines Cleared | Mines Not Accounted For |
|---|---|---|---|
| 1. ALPHA TOWER | 1687 | 1502 | 182 |
| 2. CHARLIE TOWER | 2291 | 2223 | 65 |
| 3. EENHANA | 5094 | 4789 | 281 |
| 4. HURRICANE | 7564 | 7156 | 401 |
| 5. ETALE | 5426 | 5209 | 206 |
| 6 OHANGWENA | 1991 | 1513 | 478 |
| 7. OKALONGO | 4160 | 3934 | 212 |
| 8. OMBALANTU | 2326 | 1908 | 414 |
| 9. RUACANA | 8796 | 8022 | 750 |

### Continued Human Cost

Landmines continue to be a lethal legacy of the armed struggle. Although the ICRC estimated in 1995 that there are some 2,000 uncleared mines in Namibia, the U.N. now estimates that some 50,000 landmines remain to be cleared. A Namibian official told Human Rights Watch in July 1995 that he believed that this was an over-estimate, claiming that 4,000 uncleared mines in the eleven known minefields of some 352,400 square meters is a better assessment.

All the minefields were originally fenced. However, once these sites were abandoned the local population removed fencing for its own use. At independence Nampol officials advocated constant monitoring and maintenance of the perimeter fences, but this has not occurred. As a result the minefields now pose a greater threat to people and livestock as they can easily stray into unmarked, partially-cleared minefields. Today, Nampol officials advocate complete clearance of these fields.

Landmines continue to take a toll in Namibia. Residents of Ohaiha, 120 kilometers east of Opuwo in Omaheke district are the most severely affected. Seven cattle were recently killed by mines. The villages of Onaiso, Otjororo, Otjomukandi, Okomahuara, Omakange and Okambombena have also reported recent landmine incidents. These communities have called on the government to clear the landmines or fence of the contaminated areas, because they fear that their grazing cattle will detonate more mines.[227] Even while Namibians were at the ballot boxes voting in their first ever multiparty election, landmines posed a lethal threat. Johanne (age nine), Johanna (age two), and Filleman (age nine) Nangolo were killed by a antipersonnel mine they found while playing when their parents had gone to vote at the nearby polling station.

Ben Tjimu was killed on April 24, 1991 and three others injured while trying to remove an injured cow from a minefield around one of the pylons, eighty kilometers southeast of Opuwo. Nine cattle were killed on the same day.

Antipersonnel mines left behind by the SADF in the vicinity of electric pylons in the Kaoko area also continued to take their toll after independence. In October 1990 at Omomakuara along the Ruacana/Kamanjab road it was reported that some thirty sheep, two goats and two cattle belonging to a Kaoka businessman were killed when straying into a minefield, the fourth such incident in four months. Earlier in 1990 two cattle were killed in a similar incident in which local people also discovered a human leg where an explosion occurred.[228]

Mines also pose an ecological threat. Mine explosions are thought to have been responsible for huge veld fires that swept through the area, causing serious damage to grazing lands. The minefields were "cleared" in 1991.[229]

Continued landmine incidents are concentrated in the north of the country, specifically in Kaokoland and Ovamboland provinces. There are also concentrations along the Angola border. Some of these northern regions are heavily populated. Namibian authorities claimed in November 1996 that ninety-six people have been killed and over 216 injured in explosions, many of landmines, in

---

[227] *The New Era* (Windhoek), March 28 to April 3, 1996.

[228] *The Namibian* (Windhoek), October 26, 1990.

[229] Ibid.

Namibia's northern regions since 1989.[230] More than half of the casualties were children. In 1995 nine people were killed and twenty-five injured in landmine explosions, a further reminder of the indiscriminate lethal legacy of these weapons retain.

A recent news report stated that, according to government statistics, more than one hundred people have died through landmine explosions since independence seven years ago.[231] The same account said that recently five children, ages ten to nineteen, were seriously injured in the Ohangwena region when they apparently picked up a mine and threw it into a fire out of curiosity.

**Mine Clearance and Awareness Initiatives**

The Namibian Police has the responsibility for destroying any ordnance (including landmines) not associated with an active military base or activity since independence. Limited resources and personnel have precluded systematic mine clearance by its Explosive Disposal Unit, but despite such limitations Nampol reported having cleared 163 antitank mines and 555 antipersonnel mines between 1989 and December 1994.[232]

Technically mine clearance is not the sole responsibility of Nampol and the police have over the past five years pushed for the military to take over some responsibility. In February 1991 the permanent secretary of the Ministry of Home Affairs, Ndali Che Kamati, communicated that his ministry had ruled that police explosive experts and the Namibian Defence Force (NDF) should come together urgently to plan for a joint campaign to clear the minefields. This has not happened, partly because of a history of antipathy between the police and army, and partly due to disarray in the NDF. A liaison committee between the Namibian police and the NDF has been ineffective.

Between 1991 and 1994 the NDF received training from the British Military Assistance Training Team (BMATT), including Explosive Ordnance Disposal (EOD) techniques. Former BMATT trainers refused to tell Human Rights Watch in London whether this EOD training dealt with landmines.

---

[230] SAPA news agency, November 12, 1996.

[231] Tabby Moyo/AIA, "Namibia sets to wipe out mines by the end of the year," Windhoek, February 27, 1997.

[232]Figures provided by Nampol to Human Rights Watch, April 1996.

Continued civilian casualties from landmines resulted in further questions in the National Council of parliament about the lack of mine clearance operations. On November 24, 1993 Mr. Hisikushitja told the Council:

> The region is littered with undetonated mines. To give an example, among the four regions, namely Ohangwena, Omusati, Oshikoto and Oshana, around sixty-seven persons and a number of animals have been killed since independence. So the Council requests the Ministry of Defence to clear up these mines, especially around the former military bases.[233]

In 1994 the Namibian government invited a U.S. Department of Defense Demining Assessment Team to visit Namibia from September 2-10, 1994 to provide it with mine clearance training assistance. A Memorandum of Cooperation between the U.S. government and the Namibian government over mine clearance training was subsequently signed in February 1995.

In March 1995 a team of U.S. military explosive experts from the Army Special Forces arrived in Oshakati to start a mine clearance training project. These U.S. experts spent eights weeks instructing a group of Namibian military personnel on how to train others in mine clearance operations. These Namibian military, with U.S. assistance, then conducted a five-to-seven week course training a Namibian demining team. The U.S. team withdrew in September 1995, with a small number of U.S. military trainers remaining to evaluate how the national demining efforts developed. The primary objective of the project was to encourage the NDF to professionally engage in national mine clearance programs rather than leave it to Nampol.[234]

A total of twenty-three NDF personnel and one Namibian police officer received training from the U.S. Army Special Forces soldiers. These NDF trainers in turn trained an additional fifty-three personnel. In late 1995 these Namibians began mine clearance operations in northern Namibia or were assigned to the Namibian contingent of UNAVEM III in Angola.[235]

---

[233] Republic of Namibia, *Debates of the National Council*, Seventh Session, First Parliament, October 12 to November 30, 1993, vol.4, p.294.

[234] Information provided by U.S. Embassy, Windhoek, April 1996.

[235] Ibid.

The U.S. also donated $1.2 million of demining equipment, including an armored caterpillar tractor and roller system designed to detonate mines, hand-held metal detectors, and explosives to blow mines in-place.

In July 1996 the NDF reported that it had cleared 475 antipersonnel mines. According to a recent news article, over 1,000 antipersonnel mines and explosive devices have been destroyed. Defence Deputy Permanent Secretary Hopelong Ipinge said an area of more than 76,000 square meters had been cleared in the Omusati and Kunene regions.[236]

The clearance operations have not been without controversy. At Ruacana township the NDF cleared 102 mines (fifty-nine by bulldozer, forty-eight by hand).; at Hurricane base 192 mines (ninety-nine by bulldozer and ninety-three by hand). But South African data indicated that 648 mines were unaccounted for at Ruacana and 209 at Hurricane base.[237]

Still, in December 1995 the NDF announced that the minefield at Ruacana was now safe. The NDF removed the fence around the 2,329 meter long and thirty meter wide minefield on the instruction of the Governor of Kunene region. Tragedy struck on December 22, 1995. Absalom Luuwa, age twelve, lost his left leg when he stepped on an antipersonnel mine (a South African R1 M2 mine) in the "cleared" minefield surrounding Ruacana township. Absalom's family is devastated. He cannot walk to school any longer and has been sent eighty miles away to a hostel. His family cannot pay for his medical treatment.

The whole community is frightened by the threat of landmines and has moved the local school several miles away, making children lose more study time. The councillor of Ruacana, Absalom's uncle, told Human Rights Watch on April 15, 1996:

> This minefield has been cleared twice, by the South Africans and now by the Namibian Defence Force with U.S. military help. But these mines still kill and maim. We don't trust anybody now about these mines--Americans, South Africans and our own government. The solution is to ban these mines, and those who make these killers should pay for their legacy... Ruacana cries because of mines. Our families want them eradicated. If you can do it for small-pox, you can do it for landmines.

---

[236] Tabby Moyo/AIA, "Namibia sets to wipe out mines by the end of the year," Windhoek, February 27, 1997.

[237] Infomation provided by Nampol, Windhoek, April 1996.

The community also demanded that fencing be re-erected around the field. When Human Rights Watch visited the site in April 1996 this had still not happened.

Accidents in so-called "cleared" fields continued in 1996. On February 10, 1996 a cow belonging to Lt. Moses Nashenga detonated an antipersonnel mine in the minefield around Ruacana Military base. This minefield had been demined a few weeks previously by the NDF.[238]

The urgency of proper humanitarian clearance was demonstrated when another boy, fifteen year-old Frederick Nanjedi, was injured on February 23, 1996, when he tampered with an antipersonnel mine which he found in the Etale minefield. He apparently found it, picked it up, and cut it open with a knife. It exploded when he then hit it with a stick. He would have been killed had he not removed the main explosive charge prior to the explosion.[239]

In March 1996 the NDF suspended its clearance operations because of accidents. In February two deminers fortunately escaped injury when they accidentally cut off the top part of a mine they were clearing.[240] Human Rights Watch asked the Deputy Defence Minister about the recent accidents but was told, "The NDF is a professional force. We suspect someone has maybe laid new mines to undermine confidence in it."[241] There is little evidence to support this claim.

Clearance of Namibia's minefields today has been complicated by the nature of the SADF's clearance efforts in 1989, which pushed some mines deep into the ground without detonating them. The U.S. trainers did not seem to take this into account, in advocating the bulldozer and roller method, for example, which had already been shown by the Namibian Blasting Agents experience in 1991 to be unsatisfactory for humanitarian clearance standards. Even basic issues such as the size of the mesh of the roller were overlooked by the U.S. team; the mesh was larger than the horizontal and vertical measurements of the South African mines in the fields. When Human Rights Watch tried to raise these issues with the U.S.

---

[238] Human Rights Watch interview with NDF soldier at Ruacana, April 15, 1996.

[239] Information provided by Nampol, April 1996.

[240] Information provided by NDF, Oshakati, April 15, 1996.

[241] Human Rights Watch interview with Deputy Defence Minister Erkki Nghimtina, Windhoek, April 12, 1996.

Embassy in Windhoek, the ambassador and his staff refused to discuss the topic, describing it as a military issue.

A U.S. Embassy cable sent in July 1996 stated:

> Namibia has seen a dramatic decrease in the number of civilian mine casualties since the initiation of its humanitarian demining program in the summer of 1995. Pre-demining program civilian casualties averaged approximately 47 killed or injured per year. Post-demining program civilian casualties numbered 3 killed and 2 injured from September 1995 to the present [July 1996].[242]

The cable does not mention the importance of heightened awareness of landmines by civilian populations, especially after accidents following demining operations. As already mentioned, between December 1995 and March 1996 there had been two civilians injured and four cattle injured in minefields described as "clear."

Civilian education about the danger of landmines is also important. In November 1990 Nampol embarked upon a landmines public awareness program in conjunction with the Ministries of Information and Broadcasting and Education and Culture. This worthy initiative soon ground to a halt due to the lack of properly trained personnel, equipment shortages and a lack of funding.

On April 26, 1995, the government launched a second mine awareness campaign, which included the distribution of T-shirts and pamphlets warning the public about the dangers of explosives. The campaign was supported by $1.5 million from the U.S. The U.S. is also assisting the newly established National Demining Liaison Committee in conjunction with the Ministries of Defence, Home Affairs and Information and Broadcasting.[243]

Through this project ten Ministry of Information and Broadcasting personnel have been trained to provide mine awareness programs and education. Public awareness programs were broadcast in 1996 on the radio in five different national languages in addition to Afrikaans and English. There have also been television commercials and regional mobile video shows and a mine awareness poster and pamphlet campaign.

The National Demining Liaison Committee was established in late 1995 to coordinate the national program, collect data, set priorities, and monitor all mine

---

[242] U.S. Embassy cable, Windhoek, No. 260051Z, July 1996.

[243] Ibid.

related issues. The Liaison Committee has one Police Liaison Coordinator and one NDF Liaison Coordinator attached to it. Radio and television have taken the lead in the campaign, overseeing all mines awareness programs, while Nampol assists and supports the development of the campaign throughout the regions.

Civic education about landmines is especially important in northern Namibia because local people are not only at risk to step on mines, but are purchasing weapons, including landmines, from Angolan traders in the belief they can make quick money from extracting "red mercury" from the devices. Many people along the border are under the impression that certain weapons contain "red mercury", that this "red mercury" can be used in nuclear weapons, and can be sold for $300 per kilogram. Some seventy-eight people have been killed and 300 injured since 1990 due to explosions from attempts to dismantle weapons bought from Angolans, according to Police Deputy Commissioner Koos Theyse.[244]

**Continued Laying of Mines**

A number of landmines have been planted in Namibia since independence. On December 12, 1992, a Toyota Land Cruiser being driven along the fence on the Namibian side of the Namibian/Angolan border struck a landmine, killing the driver, Joseph Chant, and injuring three others, including a two-month-old baby. A police examination concluded that the mine was probably a recently laid Russian TM-57.[245]

In 1996 there were a few reports of newly laid landmines, some of them almost certainly laid by poachers. It appears that several of the mines were laid only days before local people walked or rode over them. Although police have intimated that the mines may have been laid as part of local animosities, there is little evidence of this. Claims that rebel UNITA troops from Angola may have been responsible also appear unfounded. But, poachers, among them ex-combatants who know how to use landmines, are active in these areas and can easily obtain landmines from Angola.

**The Disabled**

An estimated 600 former PLAN fighters and 500 from the SWATF are war disabled; there are over 2,000 disabled in total including civilians. Rehabilitation of South African troops took place in Windhoek, although officers went to Pretoria for treatment. PLAN soldiers did not enjoy such good treatment

---

[244] *The Arizona Republic* (Phoenix), November 3, 1994.

[245] Information provided by Nampol, Windhoek, April 1996.

but did receive medical support in Lubango (Angola). According to social workers in Oshakati, the number of war disabled in the north increases the closer to the border you get because of landmines. Medical rehabilitation has historically been based in the main hospital in Windhoek. For people in need of prostheses or other equipment there is a modern, well-equipped national orthopedic workshop in Windhoek. There is no other source of artificial limbs in Namibia. In 1991 the workshop made 361 artificial lower limbs, mainly for war disabled. The workshop runs an outreach program to three northern centers—Oshakati, Katimo and Rundu.

Landmine victims find it particularly difficult to survive in an economy with 45 percent unemployment. Despite training programs, as little as 5 percent of war disabled have found employment, often because employers discriminate against their disability. War disabled, especially former PLAN soldiers, have been vocal in their feeling that government officials are enjoying the good life, while they and their disabilities have been forgotten.[246]

**Antipersonnel Mine Ban Position**

While putting increased emphasis on the need for mine clearance in the past two years, the government of Namibia has shown little interest in the international effort to ban antipersonnel mines. Namibia has not announced any unilateral steps regarding the continued use and stockpiling of antipersonnel mines. The government has not participated in any of the important governmental landmines conferences in Geneva, Ottawa, and Vienna in 1995, 1996 and 1997, and did not send a representative to the NGO conference in Maputo in February 1997. Namibia did, however, vote for the December 10, 1996 U.N. General Assembly resolution calling for the conclusion of a comprehensive ban treaty "as soon as possible."

In March 1997 the Namibian government made its first statement in support of a global ban on antipersonnel mines. According to *The Namibian* newspaper, Foreign Affairs Minister Theo-Ben Gurirab told the National Assembly that Namibia had joined the worldwide crusade for an immediate and total ban on antipersonnel landmines. Gurirab said, "Namibia encourages all other on-going initiatives aimed at banning antipersonnel landmines."[247]

---

[246] Pam Zinkin, "The War, disability and rehabilitation in Namibia," in Rosemary Preston (ed.), *The Effects of War in Namibia* (Windhoek: Namibian Institute for Economic and Social Research, 1993), pp. 7-1 to 7-29.

[247] *The Namibian* (Windhoek), March 26, 1997.

## VII. SOUTH AFRICA

South Africa obtained majority rule in mid-1994 following its first ever multiparty elections. The African National Congress (ANC) is the main partner in a transitional government.[248] For some two decades, South Africa was the only significant producer or exporter of antipersonnel mines in sub-Saharan Africa. In March 1994 South Africa placed a formal moratorium on the export of antipersonnel mines, and in February 1997 the government made the dramatic announcement that it was permanently banning the use, production and trade of antipersonnel mines and would destroy its stockpile of such mines.

### Landmine Warfare in South Africa

Landmines have not been used extensively inside South Africa. South African security forces sometimes placed antipersonnel mines on suspected ANC infiltration routes in northern and eastern Transvaal. The ANC also occasionally used mines on border tracks and maintained substantial supplies of mines in its Angolan bases. Umkonto we Sizwe (MK), the armed wing of the ANC, favored using limpet mines—explosives attached to specific targets, which do not pose the same dangers to civilians as antipersonnel mines, unless directly targeted against them.

The first reported landmines were found by security forces in arms caches in 1983. The first recorded landmine incident on South African soil was on November 26, 1985, in the Soutpansberg Mountains, killing one man and injuring eight others, including four soldiers. Within the following five days four other antitank mines injured four people on farm tracks close to South Africa's northern border with Zimbabwe. The first fatalities were in December 1985; four children and two adults were killed and two children and three adults injured when their vehicle detonated a landmine on the farm Chatsworth, forty-five kilometers west of Messina.[249] In early January 1986 two whites were killed and two injured when their vehicle struck an antitank mine at Stockpoort, Ellisras, near the Botswana border. Two black men were killed and eight injured in a landmine incident near Davel on May 25, 1986. There were two further landmine incidents near Nelspruit

---

[248] Africa Watch, *The Killings in South Africa: the Role of the Security Forces and the Response of the State* (New York: Human Rights Watch, 1991); and Africa Watch, *Half-hearted Reform: The Official Response to the Rising Tide of Violence* (New York: Human Rights Watch, 1993).

[249] Information provided by Ian Phillips Member of Parliament, May 5, 1996.

125

on July 17, 1986.[250] A further reported landmine incident was in 1989 in the north Transvaal near the Zimbabwe border, an incident which former SADF officials described as an "anomaly." The most recent incident was on April 7, 1997 and involved an antipersonnel mine. Seven Zimbabwean farm workers were injured, one seriously, when the mine was triggered off by a pick while they were clearing bushes for the construction of a new road.[251] Ephert Chari's hands were severely injured when he struck the mine with a pick. He also suffered a deep chest wound and injuries to his head and right eye. The explosion occured on Tom Argyle's farm Waterplaas at Weipe about 30 kilometers north of Messina near the South African-Zimbabwe border. Northern Province policespokesperson Ronel Otto told the press that experts were convinced that the mine had been planted by insurgents at the height of the anti-apartheid struggle in the 1980s. In 1988 a landmine was defused about 100 meters from the spot of the April 7 incident. Otto said a number of antipersonnel mines were often planted around an anti-vehicle mine during insurgent activity in the 1980s.[252]

Landmine use by the ANC was mainly limited to roads and tracks of isolated border farms, aimed at inducing white farmers to abandon their property. Mines were also targeted at the security force's border patrols. MK's use of landmines was justified as a response to the Soutpansurg region being declared an area defense region in November 1983. The ANC's then leader Oliver Tambo in 1986 in his annual January 8 address justified the mine attacks saying:

> The use of landmines in the white farming areas does not constitute a change in policy. These areas have long been proclaimed and treated by the Pretoria regime as military zones. There are laws on the South African statute book which oblige the white farmers in these areas to be part of South Africa's so-called security system. When the apartheid regime instituted these measures, we were among the few people who warned against its dangers. It puzzles us that we are, today, being

[250] Peter Swift, pp.118-119.

[251] *The Herald* (Harare), April 8, 1997.

[252] South African Press Association, "Explosion in North Prov was an Anti-Personnel Mine: Police," Pretoria, April 8, 1997.

criticized for carrying out armed action in these areas that have
been turned into military zones by the racist regime.[253]

During the Truth and Reconciliation Commission hearings in Nelspruit in
September 1996 two victims of anti-vehicle landmine incidents in South Africa
described their ordeal and the legacy of these incidents ten years later. Johannes
Frederick van Ec described how he lost his wife, son and daughter when a
landmine exploded while they were spending the December holidays with friends
on a farm in Northern Province in 1986.[254]

Taliya Annie Segage also described how her daughter and granddaughter
were blown up in a landmine explosion on a farm road at Carino outside Nelspruit
in 1986. "When we got there, the families of the victims had to gather all the
pieces of their children. There was nothing left," she said. She also told the
commission that her daughter was the only income earner and that her death had
never been investigated. She asked the commission for help in raising her
daughter's two remaining children, now aged fourteen and fifteen, and to
investigate her daughter's death. The commission deputy chairman, Alex Boraine,
acknowledged at the hearing that landmines were indiscriminate, and that many
innocent people, including blacks, had been killed by them. "Landmines don't have
names on themselves," he said.[255]

On October 29, at another hearing of the Truth and Reconciliation
Commission, the public heard how a landmine was used in 1987 to blow up the
bodies of three anti-apartheid activists who had been tortured and murdered,
apparently in a bid by the apartheid security forces to destroy evidence.[256]

The ongoing conflict in KwaZulu Natal has not yet seen the use of
landmines, although Inkatha Freedom Party (IFP) recruits reportedly were trained
by security force officials in the planting of landmines in 1990-1992. According
to the testimony of Warrant Officer Wille Nortje before the Goldstone

---

[253] *Radio Freedom*, broadcast in English from Lusaka, January 8, 1986.

[254]The ANC submission to the commission justified the attacks claiming Messina,
Louis Trichardt, Piet Retief, Zeerust and Amsterdam were key towns in the apartheid
government's strategy against liberation forces.

[255] South African Press Association, "Landmine Explosions Feature Prominently
at Mpuma TRC," Nelspruit, September 3, 1996.

[256] *The Star* (Johannesburg), October 30, 1996.

Commission, at training camps in northern Zululand, particularly Mlaba and Umfolozi camp, "about 500 IFP recruits on a two-week course had been trained in the use of SADF-issue rifles, AK-47s, RPG-7s, explosives and the planting of landmines."[257] During the murder and fraud trial of ex-police colonel Eugene de Kock (former commander of the "hit squad" headquarters Vlakplaas), evidence was also submitted that de Kock received two truck loads of weaponry from Mechem's Wallmansthal arsenal in October 1993, six months after he had left the police. The list includes RPG-7 rockets, 700 antitank mines, 1,300 hand grenades, thousands of rounds of ammunition for AK-47 and R1 rifles, ninety-eight antipersonnel mines and 200 shrapnel mines. It seems these weapons went to Ulundi for use by IFP.[258]

In a bizarre twist, a Cape Town-based man who described himself as a "commodities dealer" advertised for sale M-18 Claymore, PMN and PMD-2 antipersonnel landmines in *The Star* newspaper's "Under R200" classified section on November 5, 1996. He recommended the mines, which he said were "surplus stock," be planted in gardens as do-it-yourself protection for South African homeowners. He claimed to have sold more than 200 landmines "to white South Africans," and said, "one or two [clients] said they would be placing them in strategic places in their gardens near high security walls." The Arms and Ammunition Act prohibits possession of such weapons. It is also an offense under the terms of the Defence Act.[259] A few landmines reach South Africa as part of the much more lucrative illegal trade in light weapons. According to official Police figures, they seized in 1992 eleven landmines and in 1993, one, during their operations.[260] The numbers seized remain tiny, suggesting that as yet there is little market demand.

**Production and Trade of Landmines**

South Africa began producing landmines in the 1970s, if not earlier. As early as 1968 some basic tests by the Research Defence Unit were carried out on

---

[257] *The Sunday Times* (Johannesburg), October 15, 1995.

[258] Ceasefire, *Anti-War News*, no. 3, March 1996.

[259] *The Star* (Johannesburg), November 5, 1996.

[260] Jacklyn Cock, "A Sociological Account of Light Weapons Proliferation in Southern Africa," in Jasjit Singh (ed), *Light Weapons and International Security* (Delhi: Indian Pugwash Society and British American Security Information Council, 1995), p.119.

counter-mine techniques. However only in 1972, with a rising number of mine related incidents against the police in the Caprivi strip, did serious research begin. By 1982, the South African government claimed it had self-sufficiency in a wide range of landmine-related products, including antipersonnel and antitank mines, mine detectors and mine resistant vehicles.

Mines have been produced by Naschem, a subsidiary of the Denel (Pty) Ltd. Group, at its factory in Potchefstroom. Another subsidiary, Swartklip Products in Cape Town, produced a wide range of fuzes. Denel was formally launched on April 1, 1992, as the nominally privatized successor to the Armaments Corporation of South Africa Ltd (Armscor), the state company under which South Africa's weapons production had been centralized since 1968. In practice, Denel remained a state company, with all shares owned by the government. Naschem was founded in 1968, through the transfer of a plant run by African Explosives and Chemical Industries (a joint venture of South Africa's De Beers group and Britain's Imperial Chemical Industries) to the newly created Armscor. It has produced at least two antipersonnel landmine types, according to trade publications. Though Naschem appears to have originally operated the manufacturing facilities, a Naschem executive said in 1989 that the company was subcontracting all component manufacturing to private contractors. Naschem's own facilities, officials said, were used for filling and assembly, product testing and research and development.[261]

Mechem is also part of the Denel family and has in the past been involved in the research and design of landmines, although in recent years its greatest efforts have been in counter-mine equipment and mine clearance. Mechem also exports weapons, especially special force equipment. In 1995, according to Mechem, these weapons sales to Gulf clients made R218,000 profit.[262]

South African-made mines have been widely used against neighboring southern African people and governments. South Africa's mines have been found in Angola, Mozambique, Namibia, Zambia, and Zimbabwe. They have also been discovered farther afield, in Rwanda, Somalia, Iraq and Cambodia. South Africa in the past advertised a number of landmine-related products for export, but very

---

[261] Human Rights Watch and Physicians for Human Rights, *Landmines: a Deadly Legacy* (New York: Human Rights Watch, 1993).

[262] "South African Mine-Clearance," note by V.P. Joynt, June 1995.

little is known about the quantity or destination of exports.[263] In March 1995 at the Idex95 Arms Expo in Abu Dhabi, Denel's spokesperson Paul Holzhausen denied that many landmines in Mozambique were of South African origin and said that because Eastern Bloc countries could produce mines at very low prices, "It was not really a worthwhile market for us, and I think more than ten or fifteen years ago South Africa stopped manufacturing those."[264]

Deputy Minister of Defense Ronnie Kasrils in July 1994 stated that, "[t]he new MOD has been surprised to learn that only about 3,900 mines were exported prior to this moratorium [March 1994]. Of course this is a commercial figure and does not include mines supplied to UNITA and RENAMO by the former Defense Force in the past. That supply, too, has long ceased."[265] Vernon Joynt of Mechem has said that, "A total of only 17,000 landmines were sold to other groupings" besides the SADF and its allies.[266]

Little past trade details are available because virtually all South African weapons trade was conducted covertly during the U.N. arms embargo between 1963 and 1994.[267] However, weapons trade documents leaked to journalists in 1991 reveal that at least one South African company, Nimrod International, included mines (type not specified) in a 1985 shipment of $600,000 worth of weaponry to Iraq. Mines were probably only a small part of the shipment to Iraq which also included "bombs, grenades, torpedoes...guided weapons, and missiles and similar munitions of war and parts thereof."[268]

By 1985, Armscor's export offerings included at least one non-metallic mine. In 1991, Naschem and Mechem displayed a range of sophisticated mine

---

[263] In 1993 Arsmcor refused to issue Denel any further export permits to Rwanda and it had to dishonor an order worth US$45 million. This order included 5,000 Antipersonnel mines. Early in 1994 an order from Burundi requesting weapons including 1,000 Antipersonnel mines was also turned down. See, Jacklyn Cock, "A Sociological Account of Light Weapons Proliferationin Southern Africa," footnote eight, p.123.

[264] *Monthly Review Bulletin* (London), April 1995.

[265] "Statement by Deputy Minister of Defence," July 29, 1994.

[266] Jacklyn Cock, "A Sociological Account of Light Weapons Proliferation in Southern Africa," p. 123.

[267] "Statement by Deputy Minister of Defence," July 29, 1994.

[268] Human Rights Watch, *Landmines: A Deadly Legacy*, p. 97.

products for trade show audiences. These included a mine scattering system and an electronically automated off-route antitank mine. South African producers have also advertised their mine clearing line charge system, the Plofadder, as a low-cost alternative to similar British and American products. South Africa has also sold mine-resistant Buffel armored personnel carriers to Sri Lanka and leased mine-resistant armored personnel carriers to United Nations Transition Assistance Group (UNTAG) forces during the Namibian transition to independence.

South Africa in the 1990s has invested in the research and design of a new generation of "smart" landmines. In 1996, Spescom, under contract for Denel Division Naschem, was developing three separate electronic mechanisms to self-destruct or self-deactivate landmines after a pre-set period of time. The technology is believed to be applicable to both hand-placed and air or artillery delivered mines. Work is also reportedly being undertaken on remote disarming mechanisms which would allow the mines to be rendered "safe" and handled for redeployment.

A related development believed to be taking place at Spescom is the integration of micro-computers and sophisticated sensors into anti-vehicle mines. The new anti-vehicle mines are thought to use an array of sensors, including seismic sensors, which are designed to determine the type, speed and direction of a vehicle to enable greater target discrimination. Also believed to be under development at Spescom are offset or standoff mines comprising a rocket and sensor which are to be placed some distance from a road. The sensor is intended to aim and fire the rocket at vehicles passing across its field of vision.[269] Naschem has already advertised its Intelligent Horizontal Mine and Somchem its ATR Autonomous Antitank Mine on the market.[270]

Taken together, these products demonstrate South Africa's ability to field advanced landmine-related products which have the potential to compete with some modern American and Western European designs.

**Types and Sources of Mines**

On February 19, 1997, South Africa announced a comprehensive ban on antipersonnel mines, including its intention to destroy its existing stockpile of such mines. The government stated that it would retain "a very limited and verifiable number of antipersonnel landmines, solely for training specific military personnel

---

[269] *Engineering News* (Pretoria), November 17, 1995.

[270] Christopher Foss and Terry Gander (eds.), *Jane's Military Vehicles and Logistics 1995-96* (Coulsdon: Jane's Information Group, 1995), pp.230-231.

in demining techniques and for research into assisting the demining process."[271]

South Africa's landmine stockpile consists of domestically manufactured mines, mines captured during its Angolan operations, and mines purchased illegally in contravention of U.N. sanctions. In his February 1997 announcement, the minister of defence said South Africa had 160,000 antipersonnel mines in its inventory. Yet, in response to a question in parliament on May 15, 1996, the minister of defence said that the SANDF had a total of "311,179 landmines in stock. Of these 261,423 are of the antipersonnel type and 49,756 antitank." He indicated that "No stocks are being held by other organizations for the National Defence Force." Human Rights Watch asked Col. B. Roussouw, a SANDF mine specialist why there was a discrepency in the figures. He explained that the 1996 figure included antipersonnel mines that were needed to activate South African antitank mines and these had been excluded.[272]

Antipersonnel mines types in stock in South Africa are:[273]

- Belgium: PRB M409; PRB M966; PRB M966B/Type 1
- Italy: Valmara 69
- South Africa: No.69 Mk1; R1M2; R2M1; Shrapnel No.2; S.A. non-metallic; Mini-MS 803.
- Soviet Union: MON-50; MON-100; OZM-4; OZM-72; PMN; PMND-6; POMZ-2; POMZ-2M.
- Portugal: M-969
- Yugoslavia: PMA-1; PMA-2; PMA-3; PMR-1; PMR-2A; PROM-1
- Czechoslovakia: PP-MI-BA; PP-MI-D; PP-MI-SR.

Twenty-three types of antitank mines are recorded in South Africa, three of them manufactured in the Republic: Intelligent horizontal mine; No.8; SA non-metallic. The others are: MK-7 (UK); PRB M3 (Belgium); PT-MI-BA II, PT-MI-BA III, PT-MI-D, PT-MI-D, PT-MI-K (Czechoslovakia); TMA-2, TMA-3, TMA-4, TMA-5,

---

[271] Press Statement by the Minister of Defence, the Hon. Mr. J. Modise, "South African Government Policy on Antipersonnel Landmines," February 20, 1997.

[272] Human Rights Watch interview with Col. B. Roussouw, Harare, April 20, 1997.

[273] U.S. Army Foreign Science and Technology Center, Intelligence Report, "Landmine Warfare - Mines and Engineer Munitions in Southern Africa (U)."

TMA-46 (Yugoslavia); TM-46, TMN-46, TM-57, TM-62B, TM-62D, TM-62M, TM-62P, TMD-44, TMD-B, TMK-2 (Soviet Union); UKA-63 (Hungary).

**Antipersonnel Mine Ban Position**
    South Africa was one of the few African governments to participate in the more than two year process (March 1994-May 1996) for the Review Conference of the 1980 Convention on Conventional Weapons (CCW)and its Landmines Protocol. In July 1994 the Department of Foreign Affairs recommended to the cabinet that South Africa become a State Party to the CCW Convention. Cabinet approval for the accession was obtained in August 1994, the South African parliament ratified accession to the CCW on in August 1995, South Africa acceded to the CCW in September 1995, and formally became a State Party in March 1996.[274] The CCW Landmines Protocol is a weak instrument that places minimal restrictions on certain uses of antipersonnel mines. South Africa's policy during this period from 1994 to 1996 was to promote "smart" landmines that are supposed to self-destruct after a short period of time as the solution to the humanitarian crisis caused by antipersonnel mines.
    In March 1994, South Africa, largely in response to a U.N. General Assembly resolution of December 1993, officially imposed an immediate moratorium on the export of all types of landmines. On July 29, 1994 this moratorium was announced in the *Government Gazette*.[275] In September 1995 South Africa announced a permanent ban on the export of all long-life "dumb" anti-personnel mines, but maintained that short-life, "smart" landmines should be developed for Defense.[276]
    In March 1996 it became apparent that the cabinet was split on whether to ban landmines and that the "hawks" carried the day. But as international and domestic momentum grew, so the numbers in the cabinet against a ban declined. In April the cabinet ordered a revision of South Africa's policies regarding landmines. One reason was increasing Western support of a ban, but also members

---

[274] "Position on Landmines: Department of Foreign Affairs," IDASA Conference, Pretoria, August 28, 1995.

[275] *Government Gazette* no.15891, July 29, 1994.

[276] "Statement by Mr. Abdul Minty, Head of the South African Delegation at the First Review Conference of the States Parties to the Convention on Prohibitions or Restrictions on Certain Conventional Weapons which May be Deemed to be Excessively Injurious or to have Indiscriminate Effects," Vienna, September 26, 1995.

of the cabinet, particularly those in the ANC, felt South Africa should demonstrate that it did not fear conventional attacks from across its borders, and a ban on landmines would reinforce this perception.[277]

On May 3, 1996, at the end of the CCW Review Conference in Geneva, South Africa announced a permanent ban on the export of all antipersonnel mines and a suspension of the use of antipersonnel mines by the South African Defence Force, pending a study of their military utility.[278]

In October 1996 South Africa joined forty-nine other nations in the first government-sponsored conference for "pro-ban" nations, held in Ottawa, Canada. In a final declaration these nations committed themselves to work towards the rapid completion of a complete ban on the production, stockpiling, transfer and use of antipersonnel landmines. South Africa played a prominent role in the conference and began to emerge as a leader in the ban movement.

Deputy Defence Minister Ronnie Kasrils told Human Rights Watch in late October that the military utility study would be completed in a month.[279] This failed to happen. Meanwhile, senior serving and retired South African military soldiers began arguing publicly that there is little military utility for landmines. On October 15, 1996 high-ranking military veterans appealed to President Mandela in an open letter to implement an immediate and total ban of antipersonnel landmines, stating that such a move would be both "humane" and "militarily responsible." Retired soldiers Kwedie Mkalipi of the Azanian People's Liberation Army (APLA) Veterans Association, Lietenant-General Raymond Holzhausen of the Council of Military Veterans' Organization and Wilson Ngcayiya of Umkhonto we Sizwe (MK) read the open letter to Mandela saying that the banning of antipersonnel mines "would not undermine South Africa's military effectiveness, nor the safety of..forces."[280]

---

[277] *The Cape Times* (Cape Town), April 11, 1996.

[278] "Review of Land-Mine Policy and a Suspension of the Operational Use of Anti-personnel Land-mines," Geneva, May 3, 1996.

[279] Human Rights Watch interview with Deputy Defense Minister Ronnie Kasrils, Cape Town, October 29, 1996.

[280] "Open Letter to President Mandela," October 20, 1996, signed by: Azanian People's Liberation Army (APLA); Veterans Association; Ex-servicewomen's League; Ex-South African Military Nursing; Service Association; Gunners Association; Memorable Order of Tin Hats (MOTH); Naval Officers Association of Southern Africa; Sappers

In February 1996 one of South Africa's leading military landmine experts, Colonel A.J. Roussouw, the Senior Staff Officer, Combat Engineers, South African National Defence Force, endorsed in his personnel capacity an ICRC study which concluded that, "[t]he material which is available on the use of AP landmines does not substantiate claims that AP mines are indispensable weapons of high military value."[281]

In early 1997 it was apparent the Department of Foreign Affairs and the majority of cabinet members supported a total ban, but any policy change was seemingly being deferred until the completion of the Ministry of Defence landmine utility study. Pressure for a decision mounted, however, both domestically from the South African Campaign to Ban Landmines and internationally from NGOs and other governments leading the pro-ban movement.

Austria hosted an international conference February 12-14, 1997 to discuss the elements of a total antipersonnel mine ban treaty. Of the 111 governments present, South Africa was the first to speak, after the host, and made one of the strongest statements in favor of concluding a total ban treaty, without compromises or exceptions, very rapidly.

Spurred by the approach of the 4th International NGO Conference on Landmines, South African Minister of Defence Joe Modise announced the new policy decision on February 20, 1997:

> I am pleased to inform you that, on my recommendation and motivation, Cabinet decided, on the 19th of February 1997, to ban the use, development, production and stockpiling of antipersonnel landmines -- with immediate effect.... In terms of this decision, we will be preparing to destroy our stockpile of existing antipersonnel mines, which amounts to 160,000. We will

---

Association; South African Air Force Association; South African Scottish Regiments Association; South African Jewish Ex-Service League; South African Infantry Association; South African Medical Services Veterans Association; Special Forces League; St Dunstan's Association for South African War Blinded Veterans; The Naval Association of South Africa; The SA Armour Association; The Royal Air Forces Association; The Royal Naval Association; Umkhonto we Sizwe (MK) Military Veterans Association.

[281]International Committee of the Red Cross, *Anti-personnel Landmines: Friend or Foe? a study of the military use and effectiveness of anti-personnel mines* (Geneva: ICRC, 1996), pp.71-73. Colonel Roussouw was also a former commander of field squadrons, mine warfare and clearance operations in Angola and Namibia.

be retaining a very limited and verifiable number of antipersonnel landmines, solely for training specific military personnel in demining techniques and for research into assisting the demining process."[282]

Acknowledging that the limited military utility of antipersonnel mines is far outweighed by the appalling humanitarian consequences, Modise said:

[I]n adopting this position, the South African Government, through our Ministry of Foreign Affairs, is reinforcing efforts to bring about a universal ban on these mines and their complete elimination. We will resolutely pursue this objective, and do everything possible to encourage and influence governments and international institutions to adopt this position.

In April 1997 Col. Roussouw reported on how the South African National Defense Force re-evaluated the utility of landmines for the army. He said that while antipersonnel landmines can have an important role in war, as a defensive weapon and to push the enemy into a suitable killing area, these benefits are seriously compromised by the humanitarian after-effects.[283] Roussouw stated that, for South Africa, the lack of a military threat against the country meant that humanitarian considerations could be the determining factor and its policy could exclude the use of antipersonnel mines. He said the the SANDF (and ultimately, the RSA government) came to the conclusion that a ban on long-lasting "dumb" mines, but with continued use of so called "smart mines" (that would self destruct), could reduce the humanitarian problem after a conflict, but such an arrangement would be very difficult to control and impossible to enforce internationally. He said that in the absence of any serious threat against the RSA, presently or in the immediate future, there could be no motivation whatsoever not to support a worldwide ban on antipersonnel mines.

---

[282] Press Statement by the Minister of Defence, the Hon. Mr. J. Modise, "South African Government Policy on Antipersonnel Landmines," February 20, 1997.

[283] Col. A.J. Rossouw, "Report on the Re-evaluation of the Military Utility of Landmines by the South African National Defence Force," paper presented at "Antipersonnel Landmines: What future for Southern Africa?," ICRC Regional Seminar for States of the Southern Africa Development Community, Harare, Zimbabwe, April 20 to 23, 1997.

South Africa has emerged as one of the key governments pushing the diplomatic initiative known as the Ottawa Process, which is aimed at the signing of a comprehensive antipersonnel mine ban treaty in December 1997. South Africa will host an important OAU conference on landmines in Johannesburg from May 19 to 21, 1997.

The South African Campaign to Ban Landmines (SACBL), officially launched on July 24, 1995, was influential in pushing the government toward a ban. The SACBL is a coalition of more than one hundred NGOs, community-based organizations, religious groups, and others in South Africa. It has circulated a petition for the ban of landmines which over 20,000 people have signed. Since its launch the South African Campaign has become increasingly active, organizing a high-profile trip to Mozambique in May 1996 of South African politicians—including ANC MP Tony Yengani and the deputy secretary general of the ANC, Cheryl Carolu—to visit demining sites and tour a hospital where landmine victims are treated. It has also lobbied the Ministries of Foreign Affairs and Defence and made presentations in December 1995 and in March 1996 to the Parliamentary Portfolio Committee on Foreign Affairs and the Parliamentary Portfolio Committee on Defence, respectively.  It played an important role in preparing for the February 1997 Fourth International NGO Conference to Ban Landmines in Maputo. The SACBL engaged in extensive discussions with officials in Foreign Affairs and Defence prior to the February 20 ban announcement.

# VIII. SWAZILAND

Swaziland obtained formal independence from Britain on September 6, 1968. Longstanding Swazi political stability was rocked by the death of King Subhuza in August 1982. There followed a prolonged power struggle the results of which are still felt today, although a new monarch, King Mswati III, was sworn in on April 25, 1986. Since mid-1989, opposition parties have been growing more vocal in their demands for greater political pluralism in the kingdom.

Despite Swaziland's professed neutrality in international affairs the country has been distinctly pro-western, and has also been involved in regional politics. In the 1980s, Mozambique's Renamo rebels launched attacks from bases inside Swaziland, and until 1989 relations with the Mozambican government were poor. Swaziland maintained a complex relationship with South Africa and signed a secret non-aggression pact with South Africa in February 1982, in part hoping to regain 'lost lands' and reunite the 'Swazi' people, many of whom live in South Africa. However, in the late 1980s Swaziland also remained an important infiltration route for the armed wing of the ANC.

Swaziland does not have a serious mine problem, although there has been a limited spill-over from Mozambican border minefields. In late December 1988 Swazi authorities blamed Renamo rebels for planting some sixty mines in Swazi soil following cross-border operations. However, in the 1990s the Swazi authorities have blamed the Mozambican government for planting them. A number of Swazi nationals were injured by these mines.[284] In 1997, a Swazi diplomat noted that several Swazi citizens have been killed or maimed by mines along the Mozambique border, including Army officers patrolling the border and Ministry of Agriculture officials rehabilitating the fence which controls the spread of foot-and-mouth disease. He stated, "To date, ten known antipersonnel mines have not been demined in this area."[285]

---

[284] Economist Intelligence Unit, *Namibia, Botswana, Lesotho Swaziland*, EIU Quarterly Country Report, February 1989.

[285] "Swaziland's Policy Position on Antipersonnel Landmines," statement made by H.E. Mr. J.M. Dube, High Commissioner of Swaziland to Mozambique, to the 4th International NGO Conference on Landmines, Maputo, Mozambique, February 27, 1997.

In 1995, the Royal Swaziland Police seized three landmines, along with rifles and other light weapons, that were apparently being smuggled from Mozambique across Swaziland and into South Africa.[286]

The government of Swaziland had been largely silent on the issue of an international ban on antipersonnel mines until the February 1997 4th International NGO Conference on Landmines, held in Maputo, Mozambique. At that conference, Mr. J.M. Dube, Swaziland's high commissioner to Mozambique, stated that Swaziland "is convinced that the use, development, production, and stockpiling of antipersonnel landmines should be banned with immediate effect." Noting that landmines "are an illegal weapon," he said, "This weapon must be eradicated from the face of the earth as soon as possible." Moreover, he said, Swaziland "fully supports the fast track diplomatic initiative aimed at the signing of a ban treaty in Ottawa, Canada in December 1997."

Although the Umbutfo Swaziland Defence Force is believed to maintain a small stockpile of landmines, Mr. Dube stated, "Swaziland does not use, buy or manufacture landmines."[287]

---

[286] Glenn Oosthnysen, *Small Arms Proliferation and Control in Southern Africa* (Johannesburg: South African Institute of International Affairs,1996), p. 68.

[287] "Swaziland's Policy Position on Antipersonnel Landmines," statement made by H.E. Mr. J.M. Dube, February 27, 1997.

## IX. TANZANIA

Tanganyika, a United Nations Trust Territory under British trusteeship, was granted internal self-government in May 1961 and achieved independence on December 9, 1961. In October 1964 the name of the country was changed to the United Republic of Tanzania after its merger with Zanzibar. After more than thirty years of single party rule the constitution was amended in 1992 to allow a multiparty state and in October and November 1995 the first multiparty parliamentary and presidential elections were held. Benjamin Mkapa won a four-way race with 62 percent of the vote.

Tanzania experienced a limited number of landmine incidents on its soil in the 1960s. In April 1966 a woman and a man in the village of Kilambo, about five miles from Mahurunga, stepped on landmines; security forces subsequently found and destroyed another mine. In November 1966 four Tanzanians died from mine explosions in the village of Mahurunga, about thirty miles from the port of Mtwara. Six mines had been laid according to the police.[288] The OAU Standing Committee on Defence condemned these landmine incidents and blamed the Portuguese.[289] A Ministry of Foreign Affairs spokesperson in Lisbon denied that their forces were responsible, claiming, "It is not one of our methods to place mines on trails used by peaceful populations, and even less so in a foreign country. In Mozambique we are fighting foreign-based rebels." [290] According to Major-General John Walden of the Tanzanian army, there have been no other landmine incidents since the 1960s.[291]

Tanzanian armed forces used landmines in their operations in Uganda in 1979 and in Mozambique in 1986-1988.

The Tanzanian government has said little about the international effort to ban antipersonnel mines. However, in a November 1996 letter to the NGO ban campaigns in Zimbabwe, Mozambique and South Africa, Minister for Foreign Affairs Jakaya M. Kikwete wrote: "We therefore have no hesitation in supporting your proposals...to develop greater cooperation and coordination among NGOs,

---

[288] *The East African Standard* (Dar-es-Salaam), April 14, 1967.

[289] *Radio Dar-es-Salaam*, in English, April 18, 1967.

[290] *The East African Standard* (Dar-es-Salaam), April 20, 1967.

[291] Human Rights Watch interview with Major-General Walden, London, January 6, 1997.

IOs [International Organizations] and governments aimed at a comprehensive antipersonnel mine ban...[and to] urge other SADC members to sign a protocol prohibiting the use, production, trade and stockpiling of antipersonnel landmines."[292]

[292] Letter from Minister for Foreign Affairs and International Cooperation Jakaya M. Kikwete to the Zimbabwe Campaign to Ban Landmines, Mozambican Campaign Against Landmines, and South African Campaign to Ban Landmines, November 26, 1996.

## X. ZAMBIA

**Background**
Zambia gained independence from Britain on October 24, 1964, and Kenneth Kaunda became Zambia's first president. Soon after independence Zambia began supporting independence guerrilla groups from Angola, Mozambique, Namibia, Rhodesia and South Africa. This support increasingly made Zambia a target for counter-subversion. Violent incidents, including the use of landmines, occurred in Western Province border areas and along the Rhodesian and Mozambique frontiers.

Due to the military operations, including the laying of mines, of guerrilla forces infiltrating into Rhodesia from Zambia, the Rhodesian administration in January 1973 closed the border along the Zambezi River for everything except Zambia's copper exports. For their part, Rhodesian forces planted mines in Zambia during cross-border raids against varied targets, including two raids on Lusaka in 1979. Only in late December 1979 following a lasting ceasefire in Zimbabwe did the situation improve.

Following growing domestic pressure for reform, multi-party presidential and legislative elections were held in October 1991 which brought an end to Kaunda's three decades in power. The chairman of the Movement for Multi-party Democracy (MMD), Frederick Chiluba, won with 76 percent of the vote to Kaunda's 24 percent. On November 18, 1996 Zambians voted again in controversial parliamentary and presidential elections in which President Chiluba and his MMD party were returned for a second term.[293]

**Western Province**
The part of Western Province most affected by South African military actions was the area around Sesheke, close to the Namibian border, stretching northwest to the Senanga sector. This had been an area of tension since the start of SWAPO nationalist activity in Namibia in the early 1970s.

The first documented landmine incident on Zambian soil occurred on November 12, 1970, when a Zambian Government Mechanized Services Branch vehicle detonated a landmine in Western province. The driver survived but had to

---

[293] See Human Rights Watch/Africa, "Zambia: Elections and Human Rights in the Third Republic," *a Human Rights Watch/Africa Report*, vol.8, no.4 (a), December 1996.

have his leg amputated. A Zambian police investigation identified the mine as being of British origin.[294]

Following a mine incident in mid-1971 in Caprivi (Namibia), South African forces engaged in more frequent cross-border raids against SWAPO targets, often using landmines. Between May 1971 and February 1973 antitank mines on roads near the border killed ten and injured twenty-two persons. Civilian traffic particularly suffered, an indication of the indiscriminate nature of the laying of these mines. On May 16, 1971 a United Bus of Zambia (UBZ) bus detonated a mine while traveling on the Ikelenge-Mwinilungu road, injuring eighteen people.[295]

South African forces also planted mines near the Angolan border in the 1970s, as did Portuguese forces in an attempt to curtail MPLA infiltration. In November 1971 an antitank mine killed two Zambian soldiers near the Angolan border, after army personnel had defused one of three such mines on the road they were patrolling. They had been told about the mines by a school girl who had triggered an antipersonnel mine but escaped unharmed.[296] In September 1972 a mine killed a woman in Mwinilunga, on the Zambian side of the Angolan border.

The conflict escalated seriously in 1978 and 1979. The South Africans stepped up clandestine operations in Western Province against PLAN hideouts and bases, which were also protected by mines. On August 23, 1978 SWAPO/PLAN and the Zambian army shelled the small South African garrison town Katimo Mulilo in eastern Caprivi (Namibia). In March 1979 the South Africans embarked upon an overt cross-border assault, "Operation Safraan," in retaliation for the shelling of Katimo Mulilo. Following this raid President Kaunda was forced to deny PLAN rear base facilities in Zambia, resulting in a marked decline in PLAN attacks in eastern Caprivi. South Africa forces in Operation Safraan occupied the border area for five weeks in 1979 before withdrawing.

The following four years saw a limited number of South African incursions into this one hundred kilometer-wide strip of Zambia between the Zambezi river and the Angolan border. The South Africans engaged in widespread mining of roads and the burning of some villages. It appears that South Africa was trying to make a depopulated area west of the Zambezi river aimed at preventing future potential SWAPO incursions. The South Africans also mined roads across the Zambezi. The road between Imusho and Sesheke was mined by the South

[294] Zambia Police, *Annual Report*, 1970, p.6,

[295] Zambia Police, *Annual Report, 1971*, pp.4-6.

[296] *The Zambia Daily Mail* (Lusaka), December 8, 1971.

Africans on several occasions. In 1980 the Zambian army laid minefields along the Caprivi border in anticipation of further South African cross-border raids.

By April 1981 the Zambian Red Cross reported that thousands of villages were suffering from famine brought about by the South African raids and that hundreds of people had died. Relief agencies dropped food from helicopters and drove four-wheel drive vehicles through the bush to avoid the mined roads. The threat of further conflict in the zone, and particularly the risk of stepping on landmines, seriously disrupted local life. Even today villagers still regard some areas as "no go" zones, fearing the continued presence of landmines. In April 1989 two people were injured and one killed when their vehicle hit a mine on a farm road joining the Livingstone and Kazungula border road.[297]

The Zambian Defence Forces (ZDF) laid a few small minefields along the Angolan border in the mid-1980s in an apparent attempt to show solidarity with the Angolan government (Zambia had in the mid-1970s supported UNITA). From February 1986 to October 1988, the Zambian Ministry of Defence recorded fifteen border incidents with UNITA in which at least one Zambian was killed. UNITA was particularly active in the border areas in late 1987 and early 1988 during the siege of Cuito Cuanavale in south-eastern Angola, when Zambian security forces were deployed in Western Province to try and prevent Zambia from being used as a supply route.

### Recent Trade in Mines in Western Province

The flow of weapons from Angola into western Zambia continued to be a concern to the Zambian police in the 1990s. In February 1995 police seized weapons, including antiaircraft guns and landmines, during a sweep along the border, where members of the Lozi ethnic group have demanded self-rule. Authorities fear that weapons could be used by Lozi militants to stage an armed insurrection in the border area, formerly known as the British protectorate of Barotseland. Since the protectorate was incorporated into Zambia at independence in 1964, Lozi leaders have repeatedly demanded autonomy from the government in Lusaka. Police estimated that at least 500 weapons, including landmines, could be in the hands of pro-secession villages.[298]

---

[297] *The Times of Zambia* (Lusaka), April 12, 1989.

[298] *Monthly Review Bulletin*, April 1995.

**Eastern Province**

Rhodesian forces were responsible for the covert laying of a small number of mines on Zambian soil in Eastern Province in the early 1970s, although at the time Portuguese forces were blamed. These mines were intended to disrupt Zimbabwe Africa National Liberation Army (ZANLA) infiltration routes into northeastern Rhodesia. The first incident reported in Zambian police records was on November 18, 1970 when six antitank mines were unearthed along the Feira road. A few days later a man was killed by a mine while walking along the Luangwa river. Up to 1974 there were occasional landmine incidents along this part of the Zambian-Mozambican border. In June 1973 two Zambian villagers were charged with planting landmines on the Feira road near the Mozambican border in order to assist Portuguese agents trying to stop the construction of a border road. In all probability these mines were planted by Rhodesian forces.[299]

Rhodesian laying of mines in Zambian border areas to disrupt nationalist infiltration routes became more regular in the mid-1970s and peaked in 1979. On November 19, 1973 a group of school children found a mine along the Zambian shore of Lake Kariba. From mid-1977 Zambia became the target of a growing number of cross-border Rhodesian raids ostensibly aimed at Zimbabwean nationalist targets. These raids included the planting of landmines in ambush operations. A member of a Rhodesian SAS unit described the laying of a landmine in Zambia in June 1978, saying, "The road was made up of sand, stone and rock...and it took them two-and-a-half hours to dig a hole deep enough to take the landmines. Then, just for good measure, thirteen kilograms of plastic explosive was added, making a total of more than twenty kilograms."[300] Another member of the Rhodesian SAS wrote, "The Rhodesian SAS did a lot of mine operations on the north side of Lake Kariba, in Zambia" to dissuade the guerrillas from using infiltration routes. He described a typical Zambian operation:

> The road was not surfaced and our plan was to lay one mine every kilometer or so. The South African antitank mines we carried were nicknamed 'Chocolate Cakes' because they were round and painted a chocolate colour. They contained a charge of about thirteen pounds of Amatol and detonated under a pressure of only...twenty-six pounds. We also carried a special

---

[299] Zambia Police, *Annual Report*, 1970.

[300] Barbara Cole, *The Elite: The Rhodesian Special Air Service* (Transkei: Three Knights, 1984), p.208.

mining kit which consisted of digging tools, poncho, para-cord, a brush, and carpet over-boots to avoid leaving the spoor of the soles of our combat boots.[301]

The Rhodesian SAS reportedly lost eleven men laying mines in such operations.[302] Rhodesian operations intensified along the 450-mile border in 1978. Eleven Zambian soldiers were killed by landmines in January and February 1978 on the shores of Lake Kariba. In 1979 Rhodesia engaged in further dramatic cross-border raids into Zambia against ZIPRA targets. In June 1979 Rhodesian forces claimed to have destroyed more than 500 antitank and antipersonnel mines in a raid against a ZIPRA supply depot near Lusaka.[303] ZIPRA used landmines to protect its bases from attack. In October 1979 two Rhodesian SAS soldiers were injured by shrapnel from two POMZ-2 fragmentation antipersonnel mines attached to either side of a trip wire during an operation against a ZIPRA camp.[304]

Because of the Rhodesian incursions President Kaunda declared a nation-wide military mobilization in 1979. Some minefields were laid along what is now the Zimbabwe border, as well as around key bridges. Despite the mines the Rhodesians in 1979 destroyed all main bridges south to their border and mined roads in anticipation of an invasion of Rhodesia by ZIPRA forces. The invasion never came as a December 1979 ceasefire held.

**The Minefields**

Zambia has minefields along its Angolan border. In 1992, repatriation of Angolan refugees was suspended because of the danger of border minefields in both Zambia and Angola. Refugees from Angola have to travel in only three or four corridors into Zambia in order to avoid minefields. There are also minefields in Zambia along the Angolan border where the Zambezi river flows south into Zambia.

There is another minefield in Western Province along the Namibian border. This was laid in 1980 following a South African incursion. In the early

[301] Peter McAleese, *No Mean Soldier: The Story of the Ultimate Professional Soldier in the SAS and other Forces* (London: Orion, 1994), pp.152-153.

[302] Ibid.

[303] Barbara Cole, *The Elite*, p.325

[304] Ibid., p.392.

1980s the Zambian Defense Force (ZDF), with multinational assistance, conducted mine clearing operations in the southern region of Western Province, near the Caprivi strip, where both South African forces and the Zambia Defense Forces had laid mines. The U.S. military has reported that in 1990 Zambia and Namibia conducted a joint mine clearance exercise in the Katima Mulilo border area, although local Namibian and Zambian officials have told Human Rights Watch the exercise never occurred.[305] Whatever the case, this area is still not considered safe by local residents.

The mine-affected areas in Western Province are Sinembala, Imusho and Shangombo. The Sioma-Ngwezi national park off the Senanga roads and areas around Kaoma are also dangerous. Other locations are the lower Zambezi in Chirundu and other parts of Southern Province. Musiya and Kalomo, former ZIPRA bases, have also had landmine incidents.

**Landmines Found in Zambia**

The Zambia Defense Forces maintains stocks of antipersonnel mines, many of them provided to ZIPRA in 1979 by the former Soviet Union and former Yugoslavia. After Zimbabwean independence the Zambian government assumed control of the mines.

Nearly thirty types of antipersonel mines from ten nations have been found in Zambia. The following list of antipersonnel mines found in Zambia should not be considered comprehensive. It is likely that there are others.

- Belgium: PRB M409.
- China: Type 72.
- Italy: Valmara 50; VS Mk2.
- Portugal: M969.
- Rhodesia: RAP No.2; Shrap No.2; No.69 Mk1.
- Soviet: OZM-4; OZM-72; POMZ-2M; POMZ-2M; PMD-6; PMD-6M; PMD-7TS; PMN; MON-100; MON-50; OZM-160; OZM-3.
- East German: PPM-2.
- West German: DM-31.
- Czechoslovakia: PP-MI-SR; PP-MI-SR-II.
- USA: M14; M16; M18A1.

---

[305] U.S. Army Foreign Science and Technology Center, Intelligence Report, "Landmine Warfare - Mines and Engineer Munitions in Southern Africa (U),"; Namibian officials denied to Human Rights Watch in 1996 that any joint clearance operation had occurred.

Antitank mines found in Zambia include: M15, M19, M7A2 (U.S.); MAT-76 (Romania); MK-7 (UK); No.8 (South Africa); PRB M3 (Belgium); PT MI-BAIII (Czechoslovakia ex); TM-57 (Bulgaria); TM-46, TM-62M, TM-62P, TMD-B, (Soviet); TMA-2 (Yugoslavia ex); TMA-3, TMA-4, TMA-5 (Yugoslavia ex); TMN-46 (East Germany).

**Continued Human Cost**

Zambians continue to be victims of mines laid over fifteen years ago. According to government statistics over 200 Zambians have been killed or maimed since Zimbabwean independence in 1980, but many believe the figure is much higher.[306] In November 1991 Sylvia Maphosa, a twenty-seven-year-old pregnant Lusaka housewife, stepped on a ZIPRA landmine while collecting firewood on a Lusaka West farm. The explosion left Maphosa half paralyzed. She cannot walk and speaks with difficulty. She sustained severe head wounds and had her right limbs shattered. The farm served as ZIPRA headquarters, dubbed "Victory Camp," during the liberation war. Although the Zambian Army combed the area for mines in 1980 and 1981, Maphosa can attest that they failed to clear it of mines completely.[307]

In December 1991 Defense Minister Ben Mwila and Army Commander Major-General Nobby Simbeye refused to talk to the press about Zambia's landmines legacy and the Lusaka West accident. However, a Zambian Army official anonymously reported that its engineering squadron did not have adequate equipment to clear parts of Lusaka West infested by landmines and booby-traps left by Zimbabwean nationalist guerrillas ten years previously. Local residents also reported to the press that they had been told there was "no equipment," and there was nothing the army could do. The army official told the *Weekly Post* newspaper that "[p]robably the issue could have been forgotten by them (army) because nobody has been killed or injured until recently."[308]

In June 1994 Defence Secretary Brigadier-General Jack Mubanga confirmed that Zambia had a problem:

---

[306] Zarina Geloo/AIA, "Zambians Pay Heavy Price for Freedom of their Neighbors," Lusaka, February 26, 1997.

[307] *The Weekly Post* (Lusaka), November 29 to December 5, 1991.

[308] *The Weekly Post* (Lusaka), December 20 to December 26, 1991.

There are a lot of mines in Southern and Western provinces but it is too costly for the Government to embark on an exercise to have them removed. It is very expensive to carry out such an assignment.... We have educated the locals about the dangers of the mines in almost all the affected areas. The response has been good. No one would like to risk his or her life by passing through infested areas.[309]

According to the Zambia Red Cross there are a couple of landmine accidents a year. Johnson Sakala from the Zambia Red Cross visited Shangombo in 1989 and nearly stepped on an antipersonnel mine:

It was a very sandy area and our vehicle which we used to distribute the relief aid had got stuck. I went looking for wood and twigs to put under the vehicle when the driver screamed at me, "Stop!" Under the pile of branches I was going to lift was an antipersonnel mine. There are regularly landmine incidents in Shangombo, but the government is doing little about it.[310]

In 1996 a commercial firm began repairing the road to Shangombo by bulldozing and grading the soil. There has been no mine clearance on the road and several vehicles have been damaged by mines, although there has been no publicity of the incidents. The bulldozing is likely to simply push the mines to the verges, where they will become exposed by wind and rain erosion. When the road is opened, any such mines will claim their civilian victims.

Many mines were planted around small, now-abandoned guerrilla military bases. Human Rights Watch visited one former base, the Matondo farm in Lusaka West, and found that there continued to be landmine incidents there. The Sri Lankan farm manager told us that although the army cleared the area, he had mines explode on three occasions in 1993 when burning undergrowth along a stream. Although the explosions produced lots of shrapnel, nobody was injured. He also described how when he became farm manager in January 1991 he found the workers collected unexploded ordnance and children played with it. "We have

---

[309] *The Times of Zambia* (Lusaka), June 20, 1994.

[310] Human Rights Watch interview with Johnson Sakala of the Zambia Red Cross, Lusaka, September 18, 1996.

reported the matter to the police, but they don't want to leave town. They tell us that the army cleared the area in 1980 and 1981," he informed us.[311]

The fear of landmines around these former bases lingers. Around another former ZIPRA base in Lusaka West people were cautious, having bought the land cheaply because of the possible presence of mines.

*The Times of Zambia* concluded that although "the army has been noted as saying the jungle was demined, it remains doubtful that the job was thorough. Footpath traversers...face the frightening possibility of a crudely volatile portal to mortality."[312]

Public awareness of Zambia's landmine legacy is growing. In March 1997 member of parliament Jerry Muloji asked when the Ministry of Defense would send military experts to clear landmines along the border area with Angola in his district.   Deputy Defense Minister Mike Mulomgoti told parliament, "It's impossible to clear all landmines at the moment. They will only be cleared on an 'as is found' basis."[313]

**Antipersonnel Mine Ban Position**
In September 1996 a group of students and staff at Lusaka's University Training Hospital launched the Zambia Campaign to Ban Landmines in an effort to lobby the government and raise public awareness of Zambia's and southern Africa's landmine problem.   Members of the campaign include the Zambia Red Cross Society, medical students and various NGOs.

The Zambian government had been generally quiet on the landmines issue, saying it was not a priority. However, Zambia issued a statement on October 24, 1996 at the 51st session of the U.N. General Assembly expressing support for an international ban. Noting that "the widespread use of landmines is one of the most critical challenges facing the international community," Deputy Permanent U.N. Representative Kunda said, "[W]e call upon the international community to conclude an international agreement to ban the use, stockpiling, production, and

---

[311] Human Rights Watch interview with farm managei, Matondo farm, Lusaka West, September 12, 1996.

[312] *The Sunday Times of Zambia* (Lusaka), December 11, 1994.

[313] *The Post* (Lusaka), April 3, 1997.

transfer of antipersonnel landmines."[314] Zambia subsequently voted in favor of the December 10, 1996 U.N. General Assembly resolution calling for a ban "as soon as possible."

---

[314] Statement by Mr. Humphrey B. Kunda, Deputy Permanent Representative, to the First Committee of the 51st Regular Session of the U.N. General Assembly, New York, October 24, 1996.

## XI. ZIMBABWE

Zimbabwe, formerly Rhodesia, achieved self-rule and independence in 1980 following a fierce nationalist war in which at least 30,000 people died. Landmines were widely used by both Rhodesian and nationalist forces during the war. Rhodesian security forces constructed lengthy minefields along the borders with Zambia and Mozambique, boasting they constituted the second largest man-made barrier in the world, after the Great Wall of China. Current estimates of the number of mines in Zimbabwe range from one to three million. Mines still claim casualties today.

**Background**

Rhodesia (more properly the British colony of Southern Rhodesia) was founded upon an institutionalized form of racial discrimination not unlike the apartheid system in neighboring South Africa. Blacks, who made up the overwhelming majority of the population, were excluded from political power and were only allowed to farm land in designated areas.

Any attempt to challenge the status quo by nonviolent political methods was met with repression. In the early 1960s the opposition groups Zimbabwe African People's Union (ZAPU) and ZimbabweAfrican National Union (ZANU) were banned and their leaders, including Robert Mugabe and Joshua Nkomo, detained without trial. In November 1965 the government declared a State of Emergency, which gave it power to detain opponents without trial. Hundreds of Zimbabwean nationalists were imprisoned, many for years at a time. On November 11, 1965, a few days after introducing the state of emergency, the Rhodesian Front government led by Ian Smith made a Unilateral Declaration of Independence (UDI) from Britain, which signaled an increase in the repression of black nationalism and an end to any hope of peaceful constitutional reform. In the late 1960s the nationalist parties launched an armed struggle against the (technically illegal) Rhodesian regime, which from 1972 onwards developed into a major war.

The security forces responded to the bush war with brutal measures against the rural population. Three-quarters of a million rural Zimbabweans were moved into 220 protected villages (PVs). The strategy, practiced by the British in Malaya, the United States in Vietnam, and others elsewhere, was to isolate the civilian population from the guerrillas by forcing them to live in compounds. Villagers were forced to stay in the PVs by strict dusk-to-dawn curfews. Curfew-breakers were shot. By late 1977, a population of 580,832 from 203 villages country-wide were concentrated in PVs. Forced removals combined with the curfew meant that some people could not reach their fields to cultivate. In the first year of protected villages in one area, deaths increased by 37 percent. In tandem with the PV policy the military carried out "Operation Turkey," the army's ironic code name for a policy of destroying food in the rural areas. The ostensible aim was to allow only the barest minimum of food to reach the rural population so that they would have none to share with the guerrillas. The army burned down kraals and granaries, closed shops and grinding mills and shot cattle. The combined effect of the protected villages and Operation Turkey was to increase the demoralization and war weariness of the people, and arguably create pressure on the leaders of the nationalist parties to accept less favorable terms of independence.

The Rhodesian war can be divided into three phases. From UDI to 1972, the small Rhodesian security forces were engaged in a winning war. From 1972-76 the war was in a stalemate phase. From 1976-80 the Rhodesian security forces became engulfed in a losing war. If the Lancaster House talks had not intervened, the Rhodesian security forces would have faced military defeat. By December 1978, 75 percent of the country was under martial law. This figure reached over 90 percent in 1979.[315]

A ceasefire took effect on December 28, 1979, ending the war. By January 4, 1980 more than 18,000 guerrillas had entered the designated assembly points monitored by a British-led Commonwealth force of 1,300 men.

In February 1980 the first ever multiparty election attracted a 93 percent turnout. ZANU's Robert Mugabe won with fifty-seven of the 100 seats in the assembly to ZAPU leader Joshua Nkomo's twenty. Another twenty seats had been reserved for whites in a separate election. On April 18, 1980 Zimbabwe became independent with Robert Mugabe as Prime Minister, later to become President.

Although after his electoral victory Mugabe initially followed a strongly reconciliatory stance in governance, tensions continued between ZANU and ZAPU supporters resulting in violence in Matebeleland. By 1982 there were numerous reports of indiscriminate violence in the province by ZAPU-supporting dissidents and in 1983 serious allegations of indiscipline and atrocities against innocent civilians were made against the Fifth Brigade as it sought to crush the dissidents. Violence continued until 1987 when both parties signed a unity agreement, ending the violence.[316]

---

[315] Paul Moorcraft, *African Nemises*, p.124.

[316] See Africa Watch, *Zimbabwe, a Break with the Past?: Human Rights and Political Unity* (New York: Human Rights Watch, 1989).

## Landmine Warfare

As early as 1969 the possibility of nationalist use of landmine warfare within Rhodesia was discussed at length within Rhodesian military circles. The first mine incident targeted against the Rhodesian security forces was actually on Mozambican soil on April 27, 1971 at Mukumbura, killing one Rhodesian soldier. Fifteen months later the second recorded incident happened in the same area.[317]

The Rhodesian security forces anticipated that it was only a matter of time before mines were used by nationalists forces on Rhodesian soil. In July 1971 Rhodesian police uncovered a number of crates of weapons in Salisbury, including six antipersonnel mines. These crates were part of a consignment which had been brought by road from Zambia since November 1970. The weapons were, according to one author, to have been redistributed to secret caches across the country in preparation for increased nationalist operations.[318]

The first incident reported on Rhodesian soil followed soon afterwards, in August 1972, when a white farmer and his family were injured when their car struck a mine in the Mana Pools game reserve in the Zambezi valley. This was followed in October by an incident in Chete Game Reserve, west of Lake Kariba. On December 21, 1972 a Rhodesian Security Force vehicle triggered a landmine when coming to assist an isolated farm at Altena under nationalist attack. Not all the Altena mines found a target. The security forces recovered a Chinese TM-46 mine reinforced with sixteen kilograms of high explosive.[319] This marked the start of mine warfare in Rhodesia and in late 1972 a South African/Rhodesian Joint Mine Warfare Committee was formed to exchange information and ideas on how to counter the threat. By January 1973 the Rhodesians reported that one white soldier and nine others had been injured in landmine incidents in the Centenary area, 150 kilometers north of Salisbury (now Harare).

ZANLA guerrillas favored using Chinese-made TM57, unmarked TM46 and TMH46 (with an anti-handling device) and wooden TMD-B mines. POMZ antipersonnel mines were also used. ZANLA's strategy was to restrict mobility by

---

[317] Michael Morris, *Armed Conflict in Southern Africa* (Cape Town: Jeremy Spence, 1974), p.52.

[318] Ibid.

[319] Peter Swift, *Taming the Landmine*, p.45

liberally mining roads and protecting approaches to bases. In the late 1970s both sides used captured landmines extensively.[320]

The Protected Villagers were also a target for landmines laid by nationalist forces. In some cases the residents would tell the Rhodesian authorities, but in many cases they did not. One Rhodesian Special Branch official wrote about the dangers of lifting mines:

> ZANLA had done a beautiful job! They had taken a Chinese POMZ-2 stick grenade and buried it in the ground just under the gate leaving a fragment of the top visible. This was the fuse, which they had attached with a string to the bottom of the gate. Open the gate, pull the fuse, and bang. It all looked very straightforward, but it was a little bit obvious and I was instantly suspicious...I approached the bomb, knelt down and begun brushing away the earth around it with my fingers. I worked very carefully indeed because these Chinese fuses only need a two pound weight to set them off. Soon I revealed some of the pineapple body of the grenade and saw that the fuse was a MUV-2 with a three-second delay. Still suspicious, I worked deeper and saw the real danger. Underneath the first grenade was second. This had an instant pull-type MUV fuse tied to the first grenade. If you fell for their booby trap and lifted the first grenade thinking that was all there was to it, you set off the second beneath it and died.[321]

By 1974 the Rhodesian security forces admitted that insurgent landmine warfare was exacting "a heavy toll on vehicles and lives" and that fifty-seven civilians had been killed, thirty-four of them Africans.[322]

From December 1972 until January 1980, when the war ended, there would be 2,405 incidents involving vehicles detonating nationalist planted

---

[320] H. Ellert, *The Rhodesian Front War: Counter Insurgency and Guerrilla Warfare 1962-1980* (Gweru: Mambo Press, 1989), pp.183-186.

[321] Peter McAleese, *No Mean Soldier*, pp.181-82.

[322] Peter Swift, *Taming the Landmine*, pp.46-47.

landmines, resulting in 632 dead and 4,410 injured. By 1979 landmine incidents increased dramatically, a reflection of the spread of the war.[323]

### Landmine Incidents (1978-79)

| Year | Detonated | Recovered | Total | Average per Day |
|------|-----------|-----------|-------|-----------------|
| 1978 | 578 | 316 | 894 | 2.44 |
| 1979 | 1178 | 911 | 2089 | 5.72 |

The number of landmine incidents increased in 1979 by 234 percent. Many of these mine incidents did not involve the security forces. Fifty-nine buses carrying Africans were reportedly destroyed by mines during the conflict, killing 345 Africans.[324]

## Minefields

The Rhodesians boasted that by 1979 their border minefields were the "Second Largest Man-Made Obstacle in the World," after the Great Wall of China. Whatever the truth of this claim, these border minefields still contain from one to three million mines and continue to claim human, livestock and game victims even though the war ended over fifteen years ago.

The first Rhodesian minefield to be laid was a hectare of 3,000 homemade PMN box mines around the Kariba Power Station. It was completed on November 11, 1963, a few weeks prior to the formal distribution of federal assets at the Victoria Falls Butler Conference in December 1963. The minefield was aimed at hindering any Zambian post-Federal efforts towards gaining control of the jointly owned installations, in addition to thwarting sabotage attempts by guerrilla units.[325] When the Kariba Power Station was not also protected by observation and direct

---

[323] Ibid.

[324] Peter Swift, *Taming the Landmine*, p.84.

[325] Martin Rupiah, "A Historical Study of Land-Mines in Zimbabwe, 1963-1995," *Zambezia*, vol.22, no.1, 1995.

fire, however, saboteurs simply shoveled their way across the minefield, did their damage and left.[326]

Only in 1973 with increasing nationalist infiltration did the Rhodesian authorities consider building new minefields. Other options were also considered including the planting of sisal or regular aerial and vehicle patrols. The decision was finally made in 1974 to build a minefield along the northeastern border, coupled with the creation of a "no-go area." Villagers residing in the area were to be relocated and any living creature remaining in the zone was to be shot on sight.

A "Cordon Sanitaire" (Corsan) Committee, chaired by the deputy prime minister was appointed to coordinate the civil-military aspects of mine warfare. Under this committee, senior representatives from the Army, Air Force, Police, Treasury, Internal Affairs and the Department of Tsetse and Trypanosomiasis Control were coopted to assist in the planning of the minefields for the Musengezi, Mukumbura, and Nyampanda to Ruenya border areas. The committee also looked at the western border from Kanyemba as a potential zone for a mine field. The area between Kazangula and Chirundu was not thought to require a minefield because it was flanked by the Zambezi river and was to be covered by a radar system, buttressed by minefields on those sections which could be crossed by foot or vehicle. Some anti-vehicle mines were laid by the Rhodesians in addition to antipersonnel mines.[327]

Ironically, the first border minefield was an eight kilometer stretch inside Mozambique, at Mukumbura in Tete province, laid in 1974 as a joint project with the Portuguese colonial authorities in an attempt to stop ZANLA infiltration.[328]

Several types of minefields were examined by the Joint Planning Services, before an Israeli model was chosen. However, the Israeli system proved too costly for the Rhodesians, who were already burdened by international sanctions, and a downgraded Israeli system was adopted in its place, which was "expected to serve as a killing barrier without necessarily being covered by fire at all times." Some Rh$10 million was approved for the minefields, which would include thousands of mostly Portuguese type-M969 antipersonnel mines. The planned density of the minefield was three blast mines per meter or 5,500 per kilometer. Later, other

---

[326] International Committee of the Red Cross, *Anti-personnel Landmines: Friend or Foe? a Study of the military use and effectiveness of anti-personnel mines* (Geneva: ICRC, 1986), p.48.

[327] Martin Rupiah, "A Historical Study of Land-Mines in Zimbabwe," p.67.

[328] Ibid.

mines were put into the fields, including South African R2M1 and R2M2 and Italian VS50 antipersonnel mines.[329]

With South African technical assistance the Rhodesians developed their own landmine production capacity and began using the Rhodesia RAP No.1 (nicknamed Carrot Mine) and RAP No.2 (nicknamed Adams Grenade). These Rhodesian mines were more dangerous to handle and equally hazardous to produce. Carrot Mines were produced by Cobrine Engineering, which was run by a United States citizen. Local production of these mines reduced costs from R$57 for imported mines to R$2.60 of which R$2.40 was local content. The production process was so dangerous that following a spate of accidents the Rhodesians closed the operation down and relied mainly on supplies of landmines from South Africa in the last years of the war.[330]The production of a Claymore type mine, the PloughShear was more successful. The concave disk of extruded plastic used in PloughShear mines was made in Bulawayo by Saltrama Plastex and the mines were filled at Nkomo Barracks.[331] In order to keep up with domestic demand the Rhodesian Engineer Corp took over responsibility for filling these mines.[332]

Handling Rhodesian mines in the field was risky. Up to the end of November 1979, the Rhodesian Engineer Corp suffered the loss of twenty-five men killed and ninety-one injured, the majority from the laying of crude locally made mines. In one incident RAP No.1 mines exploded in an Army Engineers' base at Victoria Falls, killing seven soldiers and wounding many others.[333]

Laying mines in these fields began in May 1974 and continued to November 1979. With Mozambican independence in 1975, ZANLA was able to expand its operations from Tete province to the Limpopo river in the south. ZANLA opened up seven new sectors in addition to the four existing sectors.

---

[329] Ibid.

[330] Human Rights Watch interview with Vernon Joynt, director of Mechem, Pretoria, April, 1997.

[331] Col T. J. Dube, "4th International NGO Conference on Landmines: Toward a Mine Free Southern Africa," Maputo, February 26, 1997.

[332] Martin Rupiah, "A Review of Mine-Warfare during Zimbabwe's War of Independence: November 1963 - April 1980," ICRC/OAU Regional Seminar, "Anti-personnel Land-Mines: What Future for Southern Africa," Harare, April 20 to 23, 1997, p.9.

[333] Peter Swift, *Taming the Landmine*, p.84.

With increasing infiltration, the effectiveness of the frontier minefields was reviewed. The initial review revealed that guerrillas were "using small spades to scoop out safe footsteps through the danger zone." The result was a recommendation that the minefield be extended from twenty-five meters to 300 because the field was being breached in only two hours. In January 1977 a strip of land between Cecil Kop and the Forbes border post along the Eastern highlands was declared a "no-go" zone and fenced and mined. In March the strip was expanded from the border post up to Vumba. During this phase the minefield was modified further because of the cost of road clearing along the minefield had reached Rh$30,000 per kilometer. New construction was done next to existing roads. Game fencing was also replaced by simple five strand cattle fencing. In November 1979 a "Reinforced Minefield" was constructed in Chicualacuala in the far southeast of the country.[334]

The early border minefields were constructed in the conventional manner, demarcated on both sides by security fencing with prominently displayed warning signs. Later the fence on the hostile side was taken down. By 1977 the Rhodesians had not only stopped demarcating the minefields on the "hostile" side but had also stopped clearing the area of bush and grass around it and had planted mines among the bush and in trees. Maintenance and care of the minefields declined as the war progressed. Mine laying became uncontrolled and unrecorded and booby trapping flourished.

Each Army Engineer Squadron developed its own peculiar mine warfare methods, which meant that one squadron could not safely enter another's minefield. The growth of barbed wire-like vegetation, such as Jesse, fish-hooked wag-'n-bietjie thorn and Mauritian thorn was encouraged along the minefields.[335]

Without fencing, there was considerable triggering of mines in remote areas by game animals. Many hundreds of elephants were killed toward the end of the Rhodesian war by mines. An elephant would wander into the minefield and initiate an explosion, and once wounded it would stagger into other mines, setting off further explosions. A dead animal in the minefield would result in additional mine incidents from scavenging animals attempting to feed on its body.

---

[334] Martin Rupiah, "A Historical Study of Land-Mines in Zimbabwe," p.67.

[335] Ibid., p.84.

These minefields failed to stop infiltration, a fact the Rhodesian security forces admitted in 1978.[336] The nationalist forces advertised their breaching of the minefields in their propaganda: ZANLA showed their forces breaching the minefields in a 1978 edition of its *Zimbabwe News* .[337]

The military utility of the Rhodesian Cordon Sanitaire minefield was dismissed by a former member of the Rhodesian SAS, Peter McAleese. He wrote that it was:

> an extraordinary feat of military engineering, a barrier of mines 830 miles long to prevent guerrilla infiltration across the Mozambique border. This was the second biggest minefield in the world after the U.S. minefields across the DMZ between North and South Vietnam and I believe it was a total waste of time and money. It ignored the fundamental military principle that an obstacle is not an obstacle unless covered by fire, i.e., unless observed by soldiers, which CORSAN wasn't. The enemy just ignored it or removed it. Quite often, rains washed away the fragile African soil and revealed the mines standing out of the ground.[338]

Rhodesian forces also suffered injuries when they tried to breach their own Corsan after operations in Mozambique. McAleese writes that:

> We waited on the Mozambique side and watched as Rhodesian Army Engineers cleared a breach for our trucks. They had just finished when I saw a major walk forward. His foot hardly

---

[336] The ninety-three kilometer Modified, Modified Corsan, laid in 1977-78 to protect Umtali (now Mutare), recorded sixty-nine killed and fifty-seven captured. Ninety percent of kills were by PloughShears. Martin Rupiah, "A Review of Mine Warfare during Zimbabwe's War of Independence," p.9.

[337] *The Zimbabwe News*, vol.10, no.5, September to October 1978 (Maputo: Department of Information and Publicity, ZANU Headquarters), p.15,17.

[338] Peter McAleese, *No Mean Soldier: The Story of the Ultimate Professional Soldier in the SAS and Other Forces* (London: Orion, 1994), pp.142-143.

brushed the ground at the side of the breach but the earth erupted and his leg disappeared in a cloud of red spray.[339]

Following the December 21, 1979 Lancaster House ceasefire, the laying of landmines did not stop. Antipersonnel and antitank mines were laid on likely approaches leading to some of the thirteen assembly points as a precaution against any Rhodesian hostile action.[340]The Rhodesian Engineer squadron responsible for laying and maintaining the Victoria Falls to Mlibizi stretch of the border minefield also continued for several weeks after independence to lay mines, believing that the country might return to war.[341]

## Landmine Warfare Since Independence

### *Matebeleland*

There is only one account of a landmine having been used during the 1983-1987 conflict in Matebeleland. However, according to Phyllis Johnson and David Martin, ZAPU dissidents received from South African-linked sources forty-seven TM57 Russian anti-vehicle mines between April and November 1983; at least one was laid in Western Matebeleland that year. When captured, the individual allegedly responsible for laying the mine is reported to have taken the security forces to the site, where the mine was deactivated.[342] In December 1983 Zimbabwean military officials, with intelligence gleaned from ZAPU dissidents handed over to them by Botswana security authorities, retrieved several ZAPU dissident arms caches hidden in Botswana including "a variety of mines." [343] For the rest of the Matebeleland crisis the dissident groups were poorly armed, mostly restricted to using AK-47s, but they did also use improvised mine-like devices in

---

[339] Ibid., p.143.

[340] Martin Rupiah, *opcit.*

[341] Martin Rupiah, "A Review of Mine Warfare during Zimbabwe's war of Independence," p. 7.

[342] Phyllis Johnson and David Martin, "Zimbabwe: Apartheid's Dilemma," in P. Johnson and D. Martin (eds.), *Destructive Engagement: Southern Africa at War* (Harare: Zimbabwe Publishing House, 1986), pp.58-60.

[343] Ibid.

some of their operations. Edward Moyo (his nom de guerre) was a ZIPRA engineer, who had for a while served in Nkomo's body guard. He told Oxford University academic Joclyn Alexander, "We were now able to manufacture our own landmines for destroying all that moved on the roads. I personally was responsible for manufacturing them."[344]

## Eastern Highlands

Incursions into Zimbabwe along the Eastern Highlands by Mozambique's Renamo rebels saw the renewed use of landmines on Zimbabwean soil. Incursions began in June 1987 and continued until the partial Rome agreement in December 1990 when Renamo privately agreed to cease its cross-border raids. From June 1987 to April 1989, government sources reported 335 Zimbabweans were killed and some 280 injured in Renamo raids. An additional 667 Zimbaweans were reported abducted in this period.[345] Several mine incidents in this period were probably due to Renamo action. The only one to attract international attention was the maiming and killing of a British tourist, David Pearson, in 1989 while on a family holiday at the Chimanimani National Park on the Zimbabwe-Mozambique border. Although the Zimbabwean authorities described this as a "freak accident," there were other mine incidents in the area before, including one in which one person had been killed.[346] Information about mine incidents during this period was suppressed by the local residents, who were fearful of reprisals by the security forces. The Zimbabwean authorities also downplayed this incident because of fear that it would discourage tourism to Zimbabwe, a lucrative source of foreign exchange.

Landmines also claimed victims in other places. In the first six months of 1994 alone, the Mount Darwin hospital, 110 kilometers north of Harare, dealt with half a dozen cases of people seriously injured after stepping on mines. There

---

[344] Interview by Joclyn Alexander with Edward Moyo, Matebeleland, September 18, 1995.

[345] Phyllis Johnson and David Martin, *Apartheid Terrorism*, p.67.

[346] *The Daily Telegraph* (London), May 10, 1995. Pearson died after an eighteen hour delay in treating him; the Zimbabwean authorities refused to send a helicopter, fearing the presence of other antipersonnel mines.

continued to be incidents in this area.[347] On November 20, 1996 a fourteen-year-old boy, Muyaradzi Karidza, was sitting on an ox-drawn cart when one of the oxen triggered a landmine on a gravel main road in Mukumbura in Zambezi; he was injured and both his animals died instantly. Police suspected that the mine was newly laid because the road had been used daily by buses and trucks and had been resurfaced several times with heavy earthmoving machinery over the previous sixteen years.[348] Nine days later Zhuwawo Aghshuto, a seventy-four year old man, stepped on an antipersonnel mine while working in his fields in nearby Muzarabani. He lost his left foot and sustained serious injuries to his other leg.[349]

In October 1995 police also detained William Nhamakonha in connection with an alleged conspiracy to assassinate President Robert Mugabe. According to police, Nhamakonha was a member of a shadowy Zimbabwean dissident group, the "Chimwenjes," and was found to be in possession of weapons including a landmine.[350]

## The Landmines

Some of the Rhodesian mines were from stocks inherited from the pre-independence government and some were locally manufactured. In addition, the South African military and arms dealers from several other countries clandestinely supplied antipersonnel mines to the Rhodesian regime. The white Rhodesian Special Police forces designed and manufactured two antipersonnel landmines: RAP No.1 and RAP No. 2. A third locally manufactured mine was the Rhodesian Antipersonnel Mine-Shrapnel (RAPS), better known as the "PloughShear." Early production of landmines was very hazardous and without safeguards and very much a cottage industry. Initially a shack behind 2 Engineers Squadron at Cranborne served as a makeshift filling plant, but a Canadian who specialized in this work had to be closed down after several accidents. By the late 1970s the Rhodesians had constructed a more sophisticated filling plant at the Central Ammunition Depot at Nkomo Barracks. Here they continued to produce the PloughShear mines but stopped production of the unstable RAP No. 1 and RAP

---

[347] Simon Baynham, "Landmines in Africa: Indiscriminate warfare," *Africa Insight*, vol. 24, no. 4, 1994.

[348] *The Herald* (Harare), November 21, 1996.

[349] *African Topics* (London), no.17, April to May 1997.

[350] AIM (Maputo), October 9, 1995.

No. 2, preferring to purchase South African mines or use captured mines.[351] After independence Zimbabwe continued to produce the RAPS, redesignated ZAPS, at the Toolmaking and Engineering factory in Bulawayo, and perhaps the RAPS No. 1, redesignated ZAP No. 1, as well.[352] Fragments of both these mines have been found in clearance operations in Mozambique and ZAP No. 1s have also been found in northern Namibia. At Zimbabwe's annual International Trade Fair in 1994 in Bulawayo, landmines featured prominently among the products exhibited by the state-owned Zimbabwe Defence Industries (ZDI).[353] A 1996 study of landmines by the Centre for Defence Studies, King's College, University of London reports that landmines have been exported from Zimbabwe to the SPLA rebels in Sudan.[354]

Zimbabwe's status as a producer became a contentious issue in Harare as a result of Zimbabwe's alleged inclusion on a list of landmine producers which government officials claim the UNHCR and UNICEF have used to stop buying goods from any listed country.[355]

In February 1997, a Zimbabwean official said that while Rhodesia made three types of mines, it stopped production in 1977, and "at independence in 1980, Zimbabwe did not adopt the programme to manufacture the antipersonnel

---

[351] Human Rights Watch interview with Vernon Joynt, director of Mechem, Pretoria, April 18, 1996.

[352] In the post-independence period, a mine known as the ZAP No. 1 has been identified in the Zimbabwe arsenal, and has been found in other countries also. It is not clear if these are new mines produced and exported by the Zimbabwe government, or older Rhodesian mines that have been renamed. When Human Rights Watch raised this ambiguity at the ICRC/OAU regional seminar, "Anti-personnel Landmines: What Future for Southern Africa?," in Harare, April 20 to 23, 1997, Col. Nyikayaramba made an official announcement that this was a reclassification of the Rhodesian label, and that the production facility for the RAP No.1 was destroyed when Nkomo barracks was sabotaged in 1980.

[353] Fernando Gonçalves, "Landmines: Seeds of Death," *Southern Africa Political and Economic Monthly* (Harare), February 1996.

[354] Chris Smith (Ed.) *The Military Utility of Landmines...?* (London: Centre for Defence Studies, King's College, University of London, 1996), p.13.

[355] UNHCR and UNICEF have stated that they do not intend to award contracts to companies involved in antipersonnel landmine production, but Human Rights Watch is unaware of any commitment to stop buying goods from countries where mines are produced.

mines."[356] Yet, in March 1995, a senior government official acknowledged to Human Rights Watch that Zimbabwe had produced ZAP PloughShear ("Claymore" type) mines until October 1992, and had recently made a decision not to produce further antipersonnel mines.[357]

Zimbabwe Defense Industries has also acknowledged manufacturing the PloughShears, while maintaining that "a Claymore mine is not a land mine." On March 5, 1996 retired Colonel Tshinga Dube, general manager of ZDI held a press conference in Harare to try and dispel reports that ZDI produced landmines.

"Our defense industries have never acquired any landmine technology. No country can ever witness any purchases of landmines from Zimbabwe," said Col. Dube, adding that there might be confusion between a landmine and a Claymore mine. According to him ZDI stopped making Claymore mines in 1992 following an order from the Ministry of Defence to stop production of anything called a mine. ZDI opposed this but, "In spite of the argument that we put against classifying a landmine together with the Claymore mine the order [to stop production] stood. As a result ZDI was forced to destroy stocks of Claymore mines. Our defense industries have never been a secret even to some diplomats accredited to this country. We are small and transparent. We welcome any U.N. agencies to come and inspect our industries," Col. Dube offered.[358]

More recently, Col. Dube stated, "The tools [to make mines] that were owned by the Rhodesian Forces were blown up in an ammunition stores sabotage soon after independence and nothing was left of it. Zimbabwe Defence Industries, however, did acquire technology to manufacture mini claymores from individual people.... This production was only carried out between 1990-91."[359]

On March 25, 1997, the Zimbabwe Campaign to Ban Landmines toured the ZDI factory in Domboshawa at the invitation of Col. Dube, who told them that

---

[356] Statement by representative of the Zimbabwe Delegation to the Expert Meeting on the Convention on the Prohibition of Antipersonnel Mines, Vienna, Austria, February 12, 1997.

[357] Another official told Human Rights Watch that production stopped in 1993 after the Zimbabwean military withdrawal from Mozambique.

[358] *The Herald* (Harare), May 7, 1996.

[359] Paper presented by Col. (rtd) T.J. Dube, General Manager of Zimbabwe Defence Industries, to the 4th International NGO Conference on Landmines, Maputo, Mozambique, February 27, 1997.

ZDI produced Claymore mines at the Toolmaking and Engineering factory in Bulawayo until 1991, but not anymore. The campaign pointed out that even after production stops, stockpiles remain, and called for a total ban on production, trade, stockpiling and use.[360]

On February 12, 1997, at an international landmines conference in Austria, Zimbabwe's representative said, "My delegation would like to take this opportunity to state clearly and categorically that Zimbabwe does not [nor] intends to produce or manufacture any antipersonnel mines, nor does it export or sell such weapons."[361] Human Rights Watch warmly welcomes this commitment by the government of Zimbabwe not to produce or export antipersonnel mines in the future.

**Mine Types and Sources**

Below is a list of antipersonnel mines found in Zimbabwe. This list has been compiled from the U.S. Department of Defense data base, interviews by Human Rights Watch and information provided by the Zimbabwe Defence Forces Army Headquarters. The Zimbabwe National Army maintains a stock of mines, including antipersonnel mines. Human Rights Watch was told in April 1997 that the antipersonnel mine stock is small, about 1,000 mines.[362]

- Soviet Union: POMZ-2; POMZ-2M
- Rhodesia: POMZ-10 (a blast mine manufactured by the Rhodesians in the early 1970s); RAP No.1; RAP No.2
- South Africa: R2M1; R2M2; No.2
- Italy: VS 50
- Portugal: M969
- Zimbabwe: ZAP No.1; ZAPS (PloughShear).

---

[360] Press Release, Zimbabwe Campaign to Ban Landmines, March 25, 1997.

[361] Statement by representative of the Zimbabwe Delegation to the Expert Meeting on the Convention on the Prohibition of Antipersonnel Mines, Vienna, Austria, February 12, 1997.

[362] Col. Nyikayaramba of the the Zimbabwe National Army, Harare, April 23, 1997.

## Landmine Records

Good minefield records are not available. Additionally, in Zimbabwe's sandy soil, mines tend to drift and change location over time. As a result effective demining in Zimbabwe is dependent on extensive survey work. However the general location of minefields is known. Their total length is approximately 700 kilometers. The border minefield is not continuous and can be divided into the following sectors.[363]

| Minefield | Distance | Numbers Remaining | |
|---|---|---|---|
| | | Aps | PS |
| Victoria Falls to Mlibizi | (143km) | 19,800 | 1,100 |
| Cabora Bassa to Ruenya River | (335km) | 1,005872 | 5,385 |
| Sheba Forest to Leakon Hill | (50km) | 246,000 | 250 |
| Burma Valley | (3km) | 60 | 20 |
| Rusitu (Junction Gate)-Muzite | (75km) | 12,960 | 720 |
| Malvernia (Songo) to Crooks Cnr | (50km) | 19800 | 1100 |
| Kariba Power Station | (1 km) | 3000 | |

A survey of the minefields—funded by the European Union—was completed by the private Zimbabwean mine clearance firm, Mine-Tech, in December 1994.[364] The survey concluded that the density of mines in these fields was far higher than previously expected, and they number over a million. The survey estimated, however, that it could take as little as two years full-time work to clear the fields if sufficient resources were available.

The survey established that five distinct types of minefields were created by the Rhodesians:

a. Cordon-Sanitaire (Corsan) Mine Field: Kanyemba/Musengezi to Ruenya. This is a twenty-five meter wide strip, treated with defoliants on either side. Mines in the field were laid in patterns according to pre-selected rope markers. But survey work now indicates that the rope markers were rarely used in fixed order, reflecting the change in the laying teams or a few days break in laying.

---

[363] The following section is drawn from, Mine-Tech (Private Limited), *Zimbabwe Minefields Survey Report*, Harare, December 1994 and from information provided by the Zimbabwe National Army.

[364]Ibid.

b. PloughShear Mine Field (PSF): Mukumbura, Burma Valley, Junction Gete to Jersey Tea Estate and Victoria Falls to Mlibizi. These fields have three rows of tripwire, above ground, directional antipersonnel blast mines. Fields vary in depth from 500 meters to twenty-three kilometers. The three lanes of PloughShear devices are on pickets some one meter above the ground and are protected by clusters of three mines to discourage disarming.

c. Reinforced PloughShear Mine Field (RPSF): Stapleford Forest to Mutare/Vumba Mountains and Malvernia (Songo) to Crooks Corner. A minefield in which the standard three lanes of PloughShears are reinforced with a row of antipersonnel mines placed three to five meters forward of each PloughShear row.

d. Antipersonnel (AP) Mine Field: Kariba power station. Three lanes of antipersonnel mines in defensive clusters.

e. Dummy Mine Fields (DF): Junction Gate to Jersey Estate; Malvernia/Songo. Dummy fields with pickets and tripwires but no mines. Sometimes a few antipersonnel mines were put in these fields especially after 1978, when Rhodesian derivatives became widely available.

**The Human, Ecological and Economic Cost**

The Zimbabwe government estimates that there are one to three million mines in Zimbabwe.[365] These mines not only pose a danger to innocent civilians but are an environmental and economic hazard. The Mine-Tech survey claims that an estimated 35,000 peasant farmers who settled on the communal lands along the Mozambican border after 1980 have been barred from access to thousands of hectares of arable and pasture land.

For those living in the border areas, *"bakoni"* (the nickname for landmines) pose a daily threat even though fifteen years have passed since the war ended. Official statistics for mine casualties in post-independence Zimbabwe are low: forty-six deaths and over 200 injuries.[366] Mine-Tech puts the figures higher: sixty-six people killed and 402 maimed. The true figure is probably much higher, many hundreds according to local accounts. The director of the Catholic

---

[365] More recent estimates are as high as two to three million mines. See, Paper presented by Col. (rtd) T.J. Dube, General Manager of Zimbabwe Defence Industries, to the 4th International NGO Conference on Landmines, Maputo, Mozambique, February 27, 1997.

[366] Zimbabwe Defence Forces Headquarters, "Information on the problem of mines in Zimbabwe." Paper prepared for the International Seminar on Landmines and the 1980 Weapons Convention, Harare.

Commission for Justice and Peace, Mike Auriet, told Human Rights Watch in Harare in March 1995, "We hear of new civilian casualties every week." One recent news report cites unspecified Ministry of Defence figures in stating that, "Over 200 people are killed by landmine explosions annually in Zimbabwe."[367]

One reason for the low estimates is apparently that comprehensive official statistics of mine accidents are not kept. The police reportedly keep no records and the Ministry of Health does not note on its files how injuries or violent deaths are caused. Only the Ministry of Defence records landmine deaths and injuries, and only a small percentage are reported to them.

Simply reporting landmine incidents to the authorities was until recently problematic for people living in the border areas. Ernest Katoma from Dendera village, a few hundred meters from the Mozambican border, told a Zimbabwean magazine in 1994:

> People are afraid they will be locked up if they report a landmine incident to the Police. During the war in Mozambique, villagers would be interrogated by the Zimbabwean security forces if we reported such incidents to them because they were afraid people were collaborating with Renamo.[368]

Since the war ended in Mozambique in October 1992, villagers living on the border remain ambivalent about reporting landmine incidents. They fear that the police will suspect them of being, or helping, border-jumpers from Mozambique, BJs as they are commonly known.

The majority of the BJs are not economic migrants from Mozambique but market women from Harare avoiding customs formalities. They often hire guides to take them through the minefields on safe paths. Guides charge between $120 and $200 per trip. A police official told Human Rights Watch that dry river beds are a favorite route.[369]

Although many of minefields had been demarcated by fences, concrete beacons and warning signs, 90 percent of the fencing is now gone, removed by local people and converted for their own use, leaving only concrete posts in place.

---

[367] Angus Gova/AIA, "Zimbabwe: Demining--A Costly Business," Harare, Zimbabwe, February 25, 1997.

[368] George Mangwiro, "The Killing Fields of Mudzi," *Horizon*, August 1994.

[369] Human Rights Watch interview with police officer, Mutare, November 6, 1995.

Although these posts act as a warning to humans, they do not stop livestock and game from entering the minefields, and thousands of animals have been killed or injured. Since 1980, 9,084 cattle have been reported killed in minefields, representing a loss of income of some Z$15 million. Many people have been injured trying to save or retrieve livestock which has strayed into minefields. Cattle are not just food for these people, they play a critical social and economic function. A cow represents family wealth, insurance against periods of hardship and a form of payment for rituals, such as marriages. The loss of cattle is therefore very significant.[370]

The Hwange and Gonarezhou national game parks have also reported many mine incidents involving wildlife and there have been several cases of Buffalo wounded by landmines attacking people living near the game parks. Landmines have also threatened the development of Zimbabwe's premier tourist attraction, Victoria Falls. Minefields that start in Kazungula encircle the resort town and continue due east for some six kilometers to the western shore of Lake Kariba. These minefields have some 66,00 antipersonnel mines placed in them, including 22,000 PloughShears. Tourists who are hiking, kayaking or bungee jumping pass through cleared paths in these minefields. But the fields are poorly fenced and there is the danger that a tourist may stray off the cleared paths, or that mines could be washed into the cleared areas. Further expansion of Victoria Falls is also hampered by the minefields and the town's sewage system can not be expanded to cope with increased tourist demand, resulting in frequent spillages and raw affluent flowing into the Zabezi river.[371]

Clearance of border minefields has also become an urgent priority for the tsetse fly and foot-and-mouth disease control programs, as the minefields act as potential havens of these livestock and game diseases. On October 31, 1996, Jerry Grant of the Zimbabwean Commercial Farmers Union (also the regional coordinator of the campaign to eradicate tsetse fly from southern Africa), claimed that landmines, especially along the Zimbabwe-Mozambique border, hampered efforts to eradicate the fly.[372]

---

[370] Martin Rupiah, *Deadly Legacy: Landmines in Zimbabwe* (Harare: Southern Africa Political and Economic Series, forthcoming).

[371] Ibid.

[372] *Noticias* (Maputo), November 2, 1996.

**Mine Clearance Initiatives**
In August 1980 then Prime Minister Robert Mugabe announced in parliament that minefields covered an area of 2,500 square kilometers along 750 kilometers of Zimbabwe's border and that a group of soldiers had been assigned to remove the mines as a matter of urgency.[373] In 1981 as part of resettlement and reconstruction program, the ZIM-Cord Conference Documentation described mine clearance initiatives:

> Clearing of the minefields has to be done by military engineers with specialized expertise using special equipment. It will be done over a space of three years by bulldozers and bobcat flails, which are devices for locating mines without danger to the operator. They will clear first the areas where the danger is greatest and where productive activities are inhibited by the presence of mines. In areas not scheduled for immediate clearance it will be necessary to replace the lost protective fencing to prevent accidents. The fencing will be recoverable on completion of the exercise and can later be used on resettlement schemes.[374]

Britain provided Z$461,000 and the United States Z$850,000 for mine clearance. The then Federal Republic of Germany donated clearance equipment and by late 1982 Zimbabwe National Army (ZNA) Engineers began official clearance operations. Earlier, following the elections, ex-combatants from both sides had started to clear mines from around the assembly areas and elsewhere in an ad-hoc fashion. Army operations have since continued with funding from the government. By 1995 the areas cleared were:[375]

•       Batorka Gorge near Victoria Falls, for a proposed hydro electric scheme.
•       Penhalonga near Mutare, for mining activities by Lonrho.

---

[373] *Zimbabwe Broadcasting Co.*, "The Week in Parliament," 0410 gmt, August 16, 1980.

[374] *Zimcord Conference Documentation, March 23-27, 1981* (Salisbury: Government Printer, 1981), pp.31-32.

[375] Zimbabwe Defence Forces Headquarters, "Information on the problem of Mines in Zimbabwe."

- Burma valley, south of Mutare, for commercial farms.
- Zona/Jersey tea estates south of Mutare (commercial farmland).
- Victoria Falls, for maintenance of electricity pylons by the Zimbabwe Electricity Supply Authority (ZESA).
- Gaps opened in Mukumbura for movement of rural people. (communal lands).
- Various areas along the northern border for tsetse control projects of the Ministry of Agriculture.
- Areas near Nyamapanda, for mineral claims at the Chera Mine and a microwave tower for the Posts and Telecommunications Corporation.
- Forbes border post, near Mutare, for maintenance of electricity pylons and the oil pipeline from Beira to Mutare.
- Sango communal lands near the Limpopo River, for the safe movement of the local population and management of wildlife.
- Kariba dam, for the extension of hydroelectric power facilities.
- Tamandai communal lands, for the safe movement of the local community and their livestock.
- Nyamapanda, Mukumbura, Chipinge and Sango border posts for repatriation of Mozambican refugees. This was done in conjunction with the office of the United Nations High Commissioner For Refugees (UNHCR), which provided demarcation materials.

As the above list shows, initial mine clearance priorities were primarily areas of economic and infrastructural interest. The border minefields have generally not been a government priority due to scarce resources and political commitments elsewhere, the conflict in Matebeleland, and later the Army's involvement in Mozambique. Although attempts began in 1983 to clear the ninety-seven kilometer minefield beginning at Victoria Falls and proceeding eastward along Zimbabwe's border with Zambia, this is still far from completion.

Since 1983, the Army's National Army Corp of Engineers has cleared only some 10 percent of Zimbabwe's minefields. They have destroyed only about 12,500 mines.[376]

During initial mine clearing efforts in 1983 Zimbabwe converted British commercial tractors and bulldozers for the mechanized clearance of the minefields. Although Zimbabwe produces a mine detector, the NMD-78, most of its equipment dates from pre-independence. Hand-held clearance techniques have also been used by the Army.

---

[376] Panafrican News Agency, Harare, April 10, 1997.

By the early 1990s only "economic priority zones" were being cleared, with financial assistance from the U.S. government. Much of the heavy mine clearing equipment given to Zimbabwe shortly after independence was no longer working because of a lack of spare parts and maintenance problems. In 1996 the U.S. military provided funding for the training of Zimbabwe National Army personnel in mine clearance techniques and for the rehabilitation of some mechanical clearance equipment.

Following the end of the Mozambican civil war in 1992, the Zimbabwean government has became increasingly interested in seeing its border minefields properly cleared. This commitment was expressed in international forums, notably during the 1995 SADC Consultative Conference in Lilongwe, and through the ACP-EU Joint Assembly resolution on landmines on February 2, 1995. On May 16, 1996, Defence Minister Moven Mahachi said in a written response to parliament that Zimbabwe needed more than 83 million Zimbabwe dollars over five years to clear an estimated two million antipersonnel mines.[377]

The European Union in January 1996 agreed to fund an Ecu 10 million program to clear the Mukumbura minefield, the Cahorra-Bassa to Twenya river minefield, a length of 335 kilometers. Mukumbura has been made a priority by the Zimbabwean government because of the need of the local population to gain access to water resouces and reclaim land in the area, but also because the Rhodesian minefield did not follow the border, making a new defacto border.[378] There is also illegal gold prospecting in the area.

The program is to last two years and will also clear the way for another E.U.-funded program for the erection of border fences extending 359 kilometers, mainly to control animal movements. In late February 1996 the government said that the project was soon to be put to open tender and that work was expected to start in 1997. In 1997 the tenders had yet to be agreed and it is likely that work will only start in 1998. A second contract is also being drawn up for quality assessment of the operation. There are reports that several Zimbabwean military officials are interested in the contract and that even the nephew of President Mugabe, Leo Mugabe, might be competing for the contract.[379]

---

[377] SAPA news agency, Johannesburg, in English 1854 gmt, May 16, 1996.

[378]Col. T.J. Dube "4th International NGO Conference on Landmines," Maputo, February 26, 1997.

[379] Interview with Patrick Blagden, the E.U. consultant responsible for drawing up the terms of contract for the Zimbabwean government, Harare, April 23, 1997.

A front-runner for the contract is Mine-Tech. Founded in 1992, Mine-Tech is a division of Strongman Engineering Ltd, based in Harare. The company is directed by Col. (Rtd) Lionel Dyck, a former commander of Zimbabwe Special Forces who retired from the army in 1992, and employs demobilized ZNA military personnel. Mine-Tech conducted an E.U.-financed study of the border minefields in 1994 and 1995 with the objective of defining the precise location and nature of the minefields, assessing their socio-economic impact and preparing a costed and prioritized proposal for their clearance. In 1995 and 1996 Mine-Tech engaged in several mine clearance contracts for local commercial firms. Mine-Tech also conducted mine survey, awareness and clearance in Mozambique.

In 1996 a second mine-clearance firm, Special Clearance Services, became operational in Zimbabwe. It, like Mine-Tech, used Zimbabwean demining personnel.[380]

## Antipersonnel Mine Ban Position

On October 3, 1996 a group of concerned individuals, NGO workers, academics and journalists formed the Zimbabwean Campaign to Ban Landmines. It has lobbied government officials, held a press conference at its launch and pushed for greater media attention.[381]

Since 1996, the government of Zimbabwe has shown interest in the international effort to ban antipersonnel mines. Zimbabwe attended the meeting of pro-ban governments in Ottawa, Canada in October 1996, voted for the U.N. General Assembly resolution calling for a ban "as soon as possible" in December 1996, and both attended and made a statement at the international landmines meeting in Austria in February 1997.

As noted above, at that meeting in Austria a Zimbabwean official stated that Zimbabwe did not now and would not in the future produce or export antipersonnel mines. He also said, "Zimbabwe subscribes to the...contents of the Austrian draft convention on the banning of antipersonnel landmines. Zimbabwe

---

[380] A small Harare-based firm, Rom-Tech, published an interim report in February 1996 claiming to have designed a detector for non-metallic mines. A Zimbabwe-based trust called Margef, headed by former President Banana, has also advertised mine clearance services.

[381] *The Herald* (Harare), October 7, 1996.

is fully behind all efforts to ban the manufacture, stockpiling, transportation, and the use of antipersonnel mines."[382]

In light of these encouraging statements, it was hoped that Zimbabwe would join South Africa and Mozambique in announcing a ban on use of antipersonnel landmines at the time of the 4th International NGO Conference on Landmines, held in Maputo, Mozambique at the end of February 1997. In a speech to the conference, Zimbabwean representative Col. T. J. Dube, came close to such an announcement. Saying he was speaking on behalf of the minister of defence, Col. Dube stated that the minister "assured me about the commitment of our government on the ban of landmines, and that he will soon be signing the moratorium on the use of all kinds of landmines like our neighbor, South Africa, did last week."[383]

One month later, *The Namibian* newspaper reported that Col. Dube had restated Zimbabwe's support for a ban on use, manufacture and trade in landmines, and would "soon sign the treaty." He was quoted saying, "We are still finalizing the papers for signing the treaty. We will do so in our own time. We don't want to be rushed or pressured into signing it."[384]

Col. Dube was more specific during the ICRC/OAU regional seminar on landmines for SADC states in Harare on April 21, 1997. Col Dube stated that,

We are finalizing the documents for our minister of defence and foreign affairs to announce the complete ban on landmines. This must be done properly. We do not cheat. Announcing the moratorium only to find out that we do not tell you what will happen to the antipersonnel landmines that are held in our ZDF stocks will be cheating. Those of our fellow campaigners who visited our factory a month ago, will witness that they actually

---

[382] Statement by representative of the Zimbabwe Delegation to the Expert Meeting on the Convention on the Prohibition of Antipersonnel Mines, Vienna, Austria, February 12, 1997.

[383] Paper presented by Col. (rtd) T.J. Dube, General Manager of Zimbabwe Defence Industries, to the 4th International NGO Conference on Landmines, Maputo, Mozambique, February 27, 1997.

[384] *The Namibian*, (Windhoek), March 26, 1997.

observed some technicians dismantling some landmines which will now be only good for training purposes.[385]

---

[385] Col. (Rtd) Dube, "Anti-personnel Landmines: What Future for Southern Africa?," paper presented at ICRC/OAU regional seminar on antipersonnel mines for SADC states, Harare, April 21, 1997.

# XII. TOWARD A REGIONAL AND GLOBAL BAN ON ANTIPERSONNEL MINES

As the most mine affected region in the world, southern Africa should be at the forefront of the global effort to ban antipersonnel landmines. In 1997 that has emerged as a very real possibility. However, until recent months, the governments of southern Africa—and all of Africa—have been most notable for their silence on the issue of a comprehensive ban on antipersonnel landmines.

This chapter will look at the history, current status and future prospects of the international movement to ban antipersonnel mines, and particularly the role of the nations of southern Africa.

## The International Campaign to Ban Landmines

Nongovernmental organizations brought the global landmines crisis to the attention of the public and governments in the early 1990s, and have been the driving force in the international ban effort. Six NGOs launched the International Campaign to Ban Landmines (ICBL) in 1992 and it has grown into one of the most diverse and successful NGO coalitions ever. The ICBL now consists of more than 900 NGOs in more than fifty nations. It includes organizations involved in demining, victim assistance, rehabilitation, human rights, arms control, humanitarian relief, medical, veterans, religious issues and more. A senior UNICEF official has said that the ICBL is "the single most effective exercise of civil society since World War II."[386] The ICBL has two calls: for a comprehensive ban on the use, production, stockpiling and export of antipersonnel mines, and for increased resources for humanitarian mine clearance and victim assistance programs.

In southern Africa, various coalitions of NGOs or concerned people have formed national campaigns to ban landmines as part of the ICBL. The oldest is the South African Campaign to Ban Landmines, which began in July 1995. The Mozambique Campaign to Ban Landmines was formally launched in November 1995. The planning and networking in preparation for the ICBL's 4th NGO Conference on Landmines, held in Maputo, Mozambique in February 1997, stimulated the formation of four new campaigns in Africa: Zambia in September 1996, Zimbabwe in October 1996, Angola in November 1996, and Somalia in February 1997.

---

[386] Stephen Lewis, Deputy Director of UNICEF, Statement in Ottawa, Canada, October 4, 1996.

The movement quickly grew beyond just NGOs, and has been endorsed by the ICRC, UNICEF, UNHCR, DHA, and influential media, such as the *New York Times* and *The Economist*. Under pressure, governments began coming on board. Belgium became the first nation formally to legislate a total ban in March 1995, and Norway followed suit in June 1995. Also under pressure, governments agreed to review and revise the Landmines Protocol of the 1980 Convention on Conventional Weapons (CCW), the international treaty governing use of landmines.

## Landmines in International Law

Human Rights Watch believes that any use of antipersonnel mines is a violation of international humanitarian law.[387] The weapon is inherently indiscriminate, and its use clearly fails to meet the proportionality test of humanitarian law: the short-term military benefits are far outweighed by the long-term human and socio-economic costs.

Customary international humanitarian law states that parties to a conflict must always distinguish between civilians and combatants. Civilians may not be directly attacked, and indiscriminate attacks and the use of indiscriminate weapons are prohibited. Human Rights Watch views any use of antipersonnel landmines as an indiscriminate attack within the meaning of customary humanitarian law, as codified by Article 51 of 1977 Additional Protocol I to the Geneva Conventions of 1949. This conclusion arises from the delayed action nature of the weapon. By their nature, mines cannot distinguish military objects and civilians, their temporal effects cannot be controlled, and a mine explosion cannot be directed at a specific military objective.

Customary law also requires that the military value deriving from the use of a weapon outweigh its humanitarian costs. This proportionality principle is codified in Article 35(1) and (2), and Article 51(4) of Protocol I. With respect to any particular use of mines, the weapon's inherent time delay renders it impossible for a field commander to make the proportionality calculation in any meaningful way. When the proportionality rule is applied to mines as a whole weapon system, the humanitarian cost is so enormous that it undeniably outweighs any military utility of mines.

In southern Africa, in every war since 1961, every group has used landmines in contravention of international humanitarian law. The Portuguese colonial military forces, minority rule South African units, Rhodesian forces,

---

[387] For a comprehensive legal analysis of landmines, see Human Rights Watch, *Landmines: A Deadly Legacy*, pp. 261-318.

Movimento Popular de Libertação de Angola (MPLA), Frente Nacional de Libertação de Angola (FNLA) and UNITA in Angola, People's Liberation Army of Namibia (PLAN),  Umkhonto we Sizwe (MK) in South Africa, Comité Revolucionário Moçambicana (Coremo) and Frelimo in Mozambique and the Zimbabwe African National Liberation Army (ZANLA) and Zimbabwe People's Revolutionary Army (ZIPRA) in the Rhodesian war are all guilty of this. The same is true in the post-colonial wars in Angola and Mozambique, where the governments, forces supporting them (such as Cubans, Tanzanians, and Zimbabweans), and rebel groups (such as UNITA, Renamo and Angola's Cabindan Frente Nacional de Libertação de Cabinda) and their foreign sponsors (noteably Rhodesia, the United States and South Africa) have used landmines in a manner in which civilians were the greatest victims.

### The Landmines Protocol

The Landmines Protocol of the 1980 Convention on Conventional Weapons, an international treaty intended to diminish the impact on civilians of landmine use, has proved utterly ineffective in stemming the landmines crisis in southern Africa or elsewhere. South Africa became the first southern African nation to ratify the CCW in September 1995.[388]

Complex rules, discretionary language, and broad exceptions and qualifications have undermined the utility of the Landmines Protocol. Moreover, even its limited rules have been rarely followed. Government armies and rebel groups have both regularly used mines deliberately against noncombatants and failed to take even minimal precautions to safeguard against collateral harm to civilians.

The Landmines Protocol was amended in a more than two year review process ending in Geneva in May 1996. South Africa took part as a State Party, while Angola, Mozambique, Tanzania, Zambia and Zimbabwe attended the negotiating sessions as observers. The revised protocol that emerged continued to be weak, the result of the lowest common denominator being agreed upon in the search for consensus. Military considerations dominated the discussion to the almost complete exclusion of humanitarian concerns. Nations concentrated on negotiating loopholes to restrictions on use, while giving no attention to negotiating the elimination of the weapon. Rather than stigmatizing the use of antipersonnel mines as an indiscriminate killer of civilians, the protocol encourages nations to use

---

[388] Other African states that have acceded to the CCW include Tunisia (1987) Benin (1989), Niger (1992), Uganda (1995), Togo (1995), Djibouti (1996), and Mauritius (1996).

a certain kind of mine that is promoted as having less impact on civilian populations: those that self-destruct and self-deactivate, and are detectable--"smart mines" as they are often called.

But the "smart mine" technological answer to the problem is no lasting solution. The southern Africa experience shows that landmines are rarely used responsibly, and that even just one mine accident can terrorize a community for years. Smart mines too are indiscriminate, will have a failure rate, and will cause civilian casualties. Moreover, given the magnitude of the crisis, the only way to significantly affect use is to attach to antipersonnel landmines the same stigma attached to chemical and biological weapons, and such a stigma cannot come about if some mines are legal and others illegal.

When the negotiations finally concluded on May 3, 1996 the results were sharply criticized by the ICBL as unlikely to make a significant difference in the humanitarian crisis. Still, it was clear that an ever-growing number of governments recognized the insufficiency of an approach based on complicated restrictions and technical fixes, and that a comprehensive ban was the only answer.

At the first formal negotiating session of the Review Conference, in Vienna in September 1995, the ICBL could only count fourteen governments that had publicly called for an immediate ban on antipersonnel landmines. By May 3, 1996 that number had grown to forty-one, with many announcing their support during the final two weeks of CCW negotiations—including Angola and South Africa on May 3.

**Momentum for a Ban**

Internationally, the move toward a total ban on antipersonnel mines has clearly overtaken the limited CCW approach to controlling mines. Many dozens of governments have publicly stated their support for an immediate and total ban. Mozambique was the first in southern Africa to do so, in October 1995. Angola and South Africa made statements in May 1996, Zambia in October 1996, Tanzania in November 1996, Zimbabwe, Malawi and Swaziland in February 1997, and Namibia in March 1997.[389] However, for many pro-ban nations, their actions have not matched their rhetoric.

Still, the U.N. General Assembly passed a resolution on December 10, 1996 by a vote of 156-0, with ten abstentions, urging nations to "pursue

---

[389] Elsewhere in Africa, pro-ban statements have been made by Burkina Faso (October 1995), Congo (April 1996), and Nigeria (October 1996). Burundi, Cameroon, Cote D'Ivoire, Guinea, Kenya, Mauritania, Mauritius, and Senegal have also expressed interest in a ban.

vigorously" an international ban and recognizing the need to conclude a ban agreement "as soon as possible." Clearly, a new international norm is emerging. No southern African states were among the abstentions. Of the twenty-five African governments co-sponsoring the resolution, ten were from SADC: Angola, Botswana, Lesotho, Malawi, Mauritius, Mozambique, Namibia, South Africa, Zambia and Zimbabwe.

In addition, some thirty nations have already unilaterally suspended or banned use of antipersonnel mines, including South Africa, Mozambique, Germany, France, Canada, Australia, Belgium, Norway, Portugal, and the Philippines. At least sixteen former mine manufacturers have prohibited the production of antipersonnel mines, including South Africa, Zimbabwe, Germany, France, Italy and Portugal. More than fifty governments have prohibited export of antipersonnel mines, including South Africa and Zimbabwe, the only two southern African nations known to have exported mines. U.S. military sources indicate that there have been no significant antipersonnel mine exports globally in over two years. Lesotho and Mauritius have declared that they have no stockpiles of antipersonnel mines.[390]

The Organization of African Unity (OAU) has endorsed a total ban, first with a Resolution of the 62nd Council of Ministers in June 1995 and again in 1996. The Organization of American States adopted a resolution in June 1996 calling for the establishment of a hemispheric mine free zone. The six Central American states declared themselves the first mine free zone in September 1996, and the CARICOM (Caribbean)states followed suit in December.

A key event was the Canadian government-sponsored conference held in Ottawa October 3-5, 1996 which brought together fifty pro-ban governments, as well as twenty-four observer states, dozens of nongovernmental organizations with the ICBL, the International Committee of the Red Cross and other international groups. Present in Ottawa were Angola, Mozambique, South Africa, and Zimbabwe.

In Ottawa, states agreed to a Final Declaration committing themselves to "seek the earliest possible conclusion of a legally-binding agreement to ban the production, stockpiling, transfer and use of antipersonnel mines and to increase support for mine awareness programs, mine clearance operations and victim assistance." Perhaps more importantly, the participants developed a Chairman's Agenda for Action, which laid out concrete steps at the international, regional and national levels for achieving a ban rapidly. And in a dramatic announcement at the

---

[390] Human Rights Watch interview with government officials, ICRC Seminar, Harare, April 21-23, 1997.

end of the conference, Canada's Foreign Minister Lloyd Axworthy stated that Canada would host a ban treaty signing conference in December 1997. The conference also featured perhaps unprecedented cooperation between governments and NGOs, which has continued in the wake of the Ottawa conference.

There has been great enthusiasm for what is often called the Ottawa Process. Austria hosted a preparatory meeting from February 12-14, 1997 to begin discussions of the elements of a ban treaty. One hundred and eleven governments participated, though many of them were not prepared to commit to a December 1997 time frame. Present in Vienna were Angola, Botswana, Mozambique, Namibia, South Africa, and Zimbabwe. South Africa, the first nation to speak, made a particularly strong statement in support of the Ottawa process. Zimbabwe also made a statement of support. Austria circulated a draft ban treaty prior to the conference that served as the basis for discussion.

The Ottawa process is now well established. As of April 1997, some sixty nations had indicated to Canada their intention to participate in a December 1997 ban treaty signing. Among them were South Africa, Mozambique, Malawi and Swaziland. South Africa has been especially active in this diplomatic initiative and is part of the "core group" of nine nations taking responsiblity for moving the process forward. Austria's draft ban treaty is being revised for further discussion in a meeting to be held in Belgium June 24-27, 1997. Norway will then host formal treaty language negotiating sessions in September 1997. The treaty is to be concluded and signed in Ottawa in December.

A key event in the region was the International Campaign to Ban Landmines 4th NGO Conference on Landmines, "Toward a Mine-Free Southern Africa," held in Maputo, Mozambique from February 25-28, 1997. The conference was jointly hosted by the ICBL and the Mozambican Campaign to Ban Landmines. More than 450 delegates from sixty countries attended. The organizers considered the conference an unqualified success, meeting its goals of expanding the campaign network throughout the region and the continent, of moving southern Africa toward becoming a mine-free zone, and increasing support for the Ottawa Process. In the months preceeding Maputo, extensive preparatory work for the conference throughout the region helped to generate new national ban campaigns in Angola, Zambia, Zimbabwe, and Somalia. Widespread coverage by national and regional press, in the months leading up to and then during the conference, heightened public awareness of both the landmine problem and the international movement to ban the weapon.

Attention generated by the conference, along with extensive work by their national campaigns, resulted in the decisions by South Africa the week before the conference and Mozambique during the conference to unilaterally ban antipersonnel mines. Government interest in the conference was such that seventeen governments addressed the meeting. Malawi and Swaziland used the occasion to announce their support for the Ottawa Process and their intention to sign the ban treaty in December.

After four days of strategy sessions and informational workshops, the conference ended with a final declaration which stated that "the Ottawa Process is the most clear expression of the will of the international community as stated in the 10 December 1996 United Nations General Assembly resolution calling for the conclusion of an international ban treaty 'as soon as possible'." The Final Declaration called upon all governments to commit publicly to the objective of signing an international treaty banning all antipersonnel landmines in December 1997 and to participate actively in the treaty negotiating process as well as taking unilateral and regional steps to ban antipersonnel mines. Additionally, the conference called for greatly increased resources for mine clearance for all mine contaminated countries, and particularly in those nations and regions that have banned the weapon, and for more resources for victim assistance for all mine-contaminated countries.

At an ICRC seminar held in Harare April 21 to 23, 1997, military and foreign affairs officials from all twelve SADC nations called on southern African governments to establish a regional antipersonnel mine free zone, to immediately end all new deployments of antipersonnel mines, and to enact comprehensive national bans on the weapon. Participants also called upon governments to announce their commitment to sign a ban treaty in December 1997. Joint training for mine clearance, the creation of an antipersonnel mines data bank, the promotion of technological cooperation between SADC nations, and expanded programs for assistance to mine victims were proposed as urgent priorities for the region. The meeting was held in cooperation with the OAU and the government of Zimbabwe.[391]

A region-wide ban on use, production, stockpiling, and transfer of antipersonnel mines in southern Africa is an achievable goal. Two important events are on the horizon as this report goes to press that are expected to advance the cause of a regional ban: an OAU meeting hosted by South Africa in Johannesburg from May 19 to 21, 1997 devoted to a ban, mine clearance, and victim assistance issues and the OAU summit meeting on May 26, 1997, which is also expected to address the matter of a regional mine ban.

---

[391] Final Declaration of Participants, ICRC Seminar "Antipersonnel Mines: What Future for Southern Africa?," Harare, April 21-23, 1997; ICRC Press Release, "Experts from throughout Southern Africa call for regional Mine-Free Zone," Harare, no date.

International and regional momentum is growing rapidly. The southern African nations should follow the example of the Central American and Caribbean states to become the world's third mine-free zone. This is what their citizens seek. Afonso Lumbala, a thirty-two-year-old farmer from Caxito in Angola has first hand experience with landmines. He stepped on an antipersonnel mine in April 1995. His view is:

> All soldiers lay these mines. They don't care about us, the people. We suffer for them. They never warn us about mines. We find out by losing our limbs. We want them to clear the mine mess and leave us alone. The leaders and their soldiers are responsible for this. So are the people who make these evil weapons.

## APPENDIX
## Antipersonnel Mines Reported in Southern Africa

**Austria**

APM-1
Manufacturer: Hirtenberger/Sudsteirische Mettallindustrie Gmbh (SMI)
Type: Antipersonnel fragmentation
Initiation: tripwire
Reported in: Angola

A small mine, not dissimilar to the U.S. M18A1 Claymore mine, which sprays 290 steel balls 5mm in diameter.

APM-2
Manufacturer: Hirtenberger/Sudsteirische Mettal-industrie Gmbh (SMI)
Type: Antipersonnel fragmentation
Initiation: tripwire
Reported in: Angola

The APM-2 contains 1,450 steel balls, with an effective range of 50 meters.

**Belgium**

PRB M35
Manufacturer:
Type: Antipersonnel blast
Ignition: Pressure
Reported in: Angola

When 5-15 kg of pressure is applied to this mine the fuze membrane is moved, allowing the aperatures to expose the percussion caps. When the striker pins are released there is an ignition. The mine is 63mm in diameter.

PRB M409
Manufacturer: Poudres Reunie de Belgue (PRB SA)
Type: Antipersonnel blast
Initiation: Pressure
Reported in: Angola; Mozambique; Namibia; South Africa; Zambia

185

This is a small mine, approximately 80mm in diameter and 28mm high. It contains 80 grams of RDX/TNT. It comes with the detonator sealed in position and is totally waterproof. Operating pressure is approximately 10 kg. It has very low metallic content and is thus difficult to detect.

## China

Type 59
Manufacturer: China North Industries, Beijing
Type: Antipersonnel bounding fragmentation
Initiation: Pressure or tripwire
Reported in: Mozambique

This mine is similar to the Soviet POMZ-2M and can be set to explode by pressure or tripwire. On detonation it bounds to 1.5 meters before exploding, discharging approximately 250 metal fragments over a lethal radius of more than ten meters.

Type 69
Manufacturer: China North Industries, Beijing
Type: Antipersonnel fragmentation
Initiation: Pressure or tripwire
Reported in: Angola; Mozambique

This mine on detonation bounds to 1.5 meters before exploding and discharging 200 fragments of metal of one gram or more in weight over a lethal radius of 7.5 meters.

Type 72 and 72B
Manufacturer: China North Industries, Beijing
Type: Antipersonnel blast
Initiation: Pressure or anti-disturbance
Reported in: Angola; Mozambique (Type 72); Zambia (Type 72)

These small, green, plastic antipersonnel mines are among those most frequently encountered in southern Africa. Because of its low metal content, it is very difficult to detect. The 34-gram explosive charge is small, but is sufficient to produce severe injuries. The Type 72 and 72B are externally identical, but whereas the Type 72 operates only by pressure, the Type 72B also has an anti-disturbance mechanism, making it extremely unstable, so that the mine will explode when it is handled or disturbed in any way.

**Czechoslovakia (former)**

PP-MI-BA
Manufacturer:
Type: Blast
Initiation: Pressure
Reported in: Namibia; South Africa

This mine is a manually placed, non-metallic blast mine with bakelite upper and lower body components, a raised pressure plate, an internal fuze, and the explosive components. The two sections are threaded together after the fuze is installed. The pressure plate is pre-weakened so that it will shear if 25 kg of force is applied.

PP-MI-D
Manufacturer:
Type: Blast
Initiation: Pressure
Reported in: South Africa, Namibia

This is a wooden version of the box mine with a two-piece case that is based on the former Soviet PMD-6. The lower section is a rectangular wooden box that houses the main TNT charge, the MUV-type fuze and detonator assembly. The lid section is hinged to the lower box at one end and is designed to close over the lower box. In the armed position, the lid rests on a striker retaining pin at the end of the fuze. When pressure is applied, the lid removes the pin, beginning the initiation process. Probing for small box type mines with their low pressure thresholds is a very hazardous operation.

PP-MI-SR and PP-MI-SR II
Manufacturer: Czechoslovak State Factories
Type: Antipersonnel bounding fragmentation
Initiation: Pull or pressure
Reported in: Angola (PP-MI-SR); Mozambique (PP-MI-SR II); Namibia (PP-MI-SR); South Africa (PP-MI-SR); Zambia

Initial activation of this metallic-cased bounding mine may be by pull-fuze using a tripwire or by pressure-fuze. These fuzes set off the propellant charge, which, after a three second delay, causes the mine to leap upwards to a tethered height of one meter before detonation. The casing of the mine then acts as fragments.

**France**

MAPDV 59 (Mi AP DV 59) (nicknamed "inkstand")
Manufacturer: Societe d'Armement et d'Etudes Alsetex
Type: Antipersonnel blast
Initiation: Pressure
Reported in: Mozambique

This mine replaced the MODEL 1951 AP mine. The case is made of plastic with the undetectable Ai-PR-ID-59 pressure fuze inserted in the top of the mine. The mine has a removable metal detector plate, which is normally removed prior to emplacing the mine.

**Germany (former GDR)**

PPM-2
Manufacturer: Former East German state factories
Type: Antipersonnel blast
Initiation: Pressure, electric charge
Reported in: Angola; Mozambique; Namibia; South Africa; Zambia

Black, plastic-cased mine consisting of a two-piece threaded mine case with rubber gasket. The integral fuze is delay-armed, pressure initiated and electrically fired and utilizes a central spring-loaded "snap column" to transmit pressure on the pressure plate to the piezocrystal.

**Germany (former FRG)**

DM-11
Manufacturer: DIEHL Ordnance Division, Rothenbach
Type: Antipersonnel blast
Initiation: Pressure
Reported in: Angola and Zambia

This mine is 33.5mm high by 82mm diameter with a 122 gram RDX/TNT main charge. It requires direct pressure of between 5-10kg for detonation.

DM-31
Manufacturer:
Type: Bounding Fragmentation
Initiation: Pressure
Reported in: Angola; Zambia

Upon initiation this device bursts, showering the surrounding area with small fragments of chopped steel rod. The mine consists of a fuze, an outer steel case, a pyrotechnic delay and propelling charge, and an inner case containing a bursting charge and about 1.18 kg of fragments. The DM-56 initiates an approximate two-second pyrotechnic delay. The expelling charge propels the inner case upward to about 1.2 meters. At this point a pull wire to the still-buried outer case releases a pin from the ball-release firing device, allowing the spring-loaded firing pin to strike the detonator and initiate the bursting charge.

**Hungary**

Gyata 64
Manufacturer:
Type: Blast
Initiation: Pressure
Reported in: Angola; South Africa

This mine consists of a plastic lower body component, a plastic pressure plate, a black rubber pressure plate cover, a spring-loaded firing device, and the explosive components. The rubber cover is secured to the lower case component so that the mine is waterproofed. Opposing openings on the side of the mine allow the user to insert the booster and detonator on one side and the cocked striker mechanism on the other. Both holes have thread plugs and gaskets. The cocked striker is delay-armed by a lead strip. A thin wire on the tail of the spring-loaded striker must be pulled through the lead strip.

**Israel**

No. 4
Manufacturer:

Type: Antipersonnel blast mine
Initiation: Pressure
Reported in: Angola

This is an updated plastic version of the wooden No. 3 mine. There are 188 grams of TNT in the mine, which is 135mm in length and 50mm in height.

**Italy**

Valmara V-69
Manufacturer: Valsella Meccanotecnica SpA, Brescia
Type: Antipersonnel bounding fragmentation
Initiation: Pressure or tripwire
Reported in: Angola; Mozambique; South Africa; Zambia

This bounding mine is filled with either 650 6mm steel ball bearings or 1,200 4mm steel cubes which act as shrapnel. It can be initiated by either ten kg of direct pressure on the fuze prongs or six kg exerted on a tripwire. Upon initiation, the mine is fired to approximately 1.2 meters vertically on a tether wire before exploding; it has a killing zone of twenty seven meters throughout and an arc of 360 degrees.

VS-Mk2
Manufacturer:
Type: Blast
Initiation: Pressure
Reported in: Angola; Zambia

This is a small, round mine. Although it was designed to be scattered from helicopters, it is most often encountered having been emplaced by hand, usually buried. The mine is blast resistant and will defeat most explosive countermeasures, including explosive line charges.

AUPS
Manufacturer:
Type: Antipersonnel blast fragmentation
Initiation: Pressure
Reported in: Mozambique

AUPS mines can be used for sabotage and demolition and in water against swimmers. Because the only metal components are the firing pin tip and a small spring, detection by an electronic mine detector is difficult. A stake and serrated fragmentation jacket converts this mine into an antipersonnel fragmentation mine with a ten-meter lethal radius. This mine can be scattered from a low-flying aircraft.

VS-50
Manufacturer:
Type: Blast
Initiation: Pressure
Reported in: Angola; Zambia; Zimbabwe

This is a small, round plastic-cased mine. Although it is designed for scattering from helicopters, it is most often encountered having been emplaced by hand, usually buried. The mine is blast resistant and will defeat most explosive countermeasures, including explosive line charges and fuel air explosives.

VAR-40
Manufacturer:Tecnovar Italiana, Bari
Type: Antipersonnel blast
Initiation: Pressure
Reported in: Mozambique

This mine is compact enough to be carried in a pocket or knapsack. It is buried with a button head jutting out. Twelve kilograms of pressure produces an explosion powerful enough to damage light vehicles.

VAR-100
Manufacturer: Valsella Meccanotecnica SpA, Brescia
Type: Antipersonnel blast
Initiation: Pressure
Reported in: Mozambique

This plastic-cased mine, like the VAR-40, can be carried in a pocket or knapsack, but has a larger blast. It can severely damage light vehicles. a 12 to 13 kg force on the button head activates the mine.

**Portugal**

M966
Manufacturer: Explosivos da Trafaria
Type: Antipersonnel bounding fragmentation
Initiation: Pressure or tripwire
Reported in: Namibia; South Africa

This is a copy of the U.S.-designed M2A4 bounding fragmentation mine. The dual action fuze can operate either by pressure or tripwire. When the fuze is activated, a charge at the bottom of the mine projects a 60mm mortar shell into the air and starts a delay burn element. The delay ignites the main charge of the warhead, bursting the shell.

M969 (also known as MAPS)
Manufacturer: Explosivos da Trafaria
Type: Antipersonnel blast
Initiation: Pressure
Reported in: Mozambique; Namibia; South Africa; Zambia; Zimbabwe

The Portuguese M969 is a copy of the Belgian NR409. It is sometimes called Mina Anti-pessoal de Plastico (MAPS) because it is almost entirely non-metallic. The mine body color is normally olive green but may be sand colored dependent on customer requirements. The mine comes with a safety cap which is removed when the mine is laid.

PRB M411
Manufacturer:
Type: Blast
Initiation: Pressure
Reported in: Namibia

This is a plastic-bodied, circular mine. During transportation, the pressure membrane is protected by a safety plate with raised ridges. The fuze is a double percussion type with two opposing steel firing pins. The strikers are held apart by a sliding bolt attached to the pressure plate. The bolt has an aperture holding two percussion caps. When the bolt is displaced, the strikers are released and detonate the percussion caps. The only metal components are firing pins and two aluminum primer caps. This is a copy of the Belgium PRB M409.

## Romania

MAI 75
Manufacturer:
Type: Blast
Initiation: Pressure
Reported in: Angola

The MAI 75 is a simple, pressure initiated, blast mine. The plastic body limits the total metal content to fuze components.

MAIGR 1
Manufacturer:
Type: Blast
Initiation: Pressure
Reported in: Angola

This mine can be either emplaced or scattered using a helicopter mounted mine scattering system. The mine is detonated when pressure is applied to the top of the mine. The plastic limits the total metal content to fuze components.

## South Africa

M2A2
Manufacturer: Denel Ltd
Type: Antipersonnel
Initiation: Pressure
Reported in: Angola; Mozambique; Namibia; South Africa; Zimbabwe

This small pressure-operated blast antipersonnel mine was known as the R2M1 before 1984. The mine body is made of plastic. The overall body color is brown. It requires approximately ten kg of pressure to cause it to function and contains approximately fifty grams of RDX/TNT. Its dimensions are approximately sixty mm in diameter and fifty mm in height. The metallic content is minimal. This mine was sometimes placed on top of a one lb (commercial) Pentolite explosive booster to increase its lethality.

R2M2

Manufacturer: Denel Ltd (Successor to Armscor)
Type: Antipersonnel
Initiation: Pressure
Reported in: Angola; Mozambique; South Africa; Zimbabwe

R2M2 is a high explosive antipersonnel mine. Its waterproof features allow it the versatility for employment in streams and rivers up to one meter deep. The functioning of the R2M2 is essentially the same as the R2M1. The metallic content of the R2M2 is minimal with only the striker pin, three locking balls, and firing pin made of metal. This greatly reduces the success of detection by metallic mine detectors.

No.69 Mk1.
Manufacturer: Denel Ltd (Successor to Armscor)
Type: Antipersonnel bounding fragmentation
Initiation: Pressure or tripwire
Reported in: Mozambique; South Africa; Zambia

This bounding mine is a copy of the Valmara 69 but is distinguishable by its brown color. (The South Africans use a standard color for vehicles, equipment and mines, which is known as Nutria brown—middle brown).

Shrapnel Mine No.2
Manufacturer: Denel Ltd. (Successor to Armscor)
Type: Antipersonnel directional, fixed fragmentation
Initiation: Remote or tripwire
Reported in: Angola; Mozambique; South Africa; Zambia; Zimbabwe

This is a copy of the U.S.-manufactured M18A1 Claymore and is called the No.2 mine. It is also identifiable by its brown body color.

SA Non-Metallic AP
Manufacturer: Denel Ltd
Type: Blast
Initiation: Pressure
Reported in: Angola; Mozambique; South Africa

The South African Non-Metallic AP mine is a direct copy of the Chinese Type 72.

MIM MS-803
Manufacturer: Denel Ltd (Successor to Armscor)
Type: Antipersonnel directional, fixed fragmentation
Initiation: Remote or tripwire
Reported in: Angola; Mozambique; South Africa

This is a smaller version of an American M18A1 Claymore, designed to be used either singly or stacked in twos or threes.

**Soviet Union (former)**

PMN
Manufacturer: Soviet State Arsenals
Type: Antipersonnel blast
Initiation: Pressure
Reported in: Angola; Mozambique; Namibia; South Africa; Zambia

The PMN, a very common mine, may be responsible for more mine-related deaths and amputations throughout the world than any other mine. Although easily detected, this mine device has a large explosive content (240 grams of TNT) and requires as little as 0.25kg of direct pressure to initiate an explosion. Injuries from this mine can often be fatal.

PMN-2
Manufacturer: Soviet State Arsenals
Type: Antipersonnel blast
Initiation: Pressure
Reported in: Angola; Mozambique

The PMN-2 differs from the PMN most notably in that the delay arming mechanism is irreversible and there is no known neutralization technique.

PMD-6(M) (nicknamed "box" mine)
Manufacturer: Soviet State Arsenals
Type: Antipersonnel blast
Initiation: Pressure
Reported in: Angola; Mozambique; Namibia; Zambia

This mine employs a wooden box body with a block of cast TNT initiated when one to ten kg of downward pressure on the box forces the pin out of a MUV-2 fuze. The design has been widely copied. After having been buried for some time, this mine becomes unstable and finally ineffective once the wood rots. There is a high metallic content in the fuze, aiding detection. The U.S. Dept. of Defense records in its 1996 CD-Rom, *MineFacts,* that this mine was also manufactured in Namibia. However, Human Rights Watch was unable to confirm this report during its field mission to Namibia in 1996.

PMD-7
Manufacturer: Soviet State Arsenals
Type: Antipersonnel blast
Initiation: Pressure
Reported in: Angola; Zambia

This box mine consists of a two-piece wooden case. The lower section is a rectangular wooden box that houses the main TNT charge and fuze-detonator assembly. The lid section is hinged to the lower box at one end and is designed to close over the lower box. In the armed position, the lid rests on the winged striker retaining pin of the MUV fuze. Some of these mines are equipped with a metal rod, which, when inserted into the lower wooden box, prevents the lid from contacting the striker retaining pin.

POMZ-2 and POMZ-2M
Manufacturer: Soviet State Arsenals
Type: Antipersonnel fragmentation
Initiation: Tripwire
Reported in: Angola; Mozambique; Namibia; South Africa; Zambia; Zimbabwe

Both types consist of a cast iron fragmentation casing mounted on a wooden stake. The casing contains a seventy-five gram charge of TNT and a fuze (normally an MUV fuze) which protrudes from the top of the casing. This mine is normally placed within vegetation with the top of the mine approximately thirty cm above ground with the tripwire attached to a fixed object. More than one mine can be attached to several tripwires, or several tripwires may be attached to one mine. A tripwire is connected to a striker-retaining pin in the fuze. A pull of approximately one kg on the trip wire will release the striker and initiate an explosion. The POMZ-2 has six rows of fragmentation; the POMZ-2M has only five. Both mines have an effective killing range of up to twenty-five meters.

OZM-3
Manufacturer: Soviet State Arsenals
Type: Antipersonnel bounding fragmentation
Initiation: Remote, pressure, pull or tension-release
Reported in: Angola

This mine can be initiated by electrical or other remote control, or, depending on fuzing, by pressure, pull, or tension release. Following initiation, the mine explodes, expelling the main charge to a height of 1.5 to 2.4 meters before it explodes. Height is determined by a tether wire. The charge throws metal, from an inner fragmentation shell, with an effective radius of up to ten meters.

OZM-4
Manufacturer: Soviet State Arsenals
Type: Antipersonnel bounding fragmentation
Initiation: Pull or pressure
Reported in: Angola; Mozambique; Namibia; South Africa; Zambia

A larger derivative of OZM-3 (above), but cannot be fired electrically. The lethal range on fragmentation is fifteen meters.

OZM-72
Manufacturer: Soviet State Arsenals
Type: Antipersonnel bounding fragmentation
Initiation: Pull, pressure, or remote
Reported in: Angola; Mozambique; South Africa; Zambia

This mine is fired by either electrical remote control or a pull or pressure fuze. As the mine is fired a propellant charge blows it upwards until a tethering wire is drawn taut which detonates the fuze at about one meter above the surface. The main charge explodes, sending the steel shrapnel in all directions. It has a lethal radius of twenty-five to thirty meters. When an electric detonator is used the mine will explode immediately. In this role the mine will normally therefore be placed above the ground.

OZM-160
Manufacturer: Soviet State Arsenals
Type: Bounding fragmentation
Initiation: Pull

Reported in: Angola, Zambia

The OZM-160 is one of the original OZM bounding fragmentation mines. a subsequent development, the OZM with UVK-1, utilized any of a variety of artillery or mortar sheels as the main charge. The OZM-160 mine is a complete package with a standard charge, an integral fuze, and a munition that is contained in a cylinder for simplified logistics and employment.

MON-50
Manufacturer: Soviet State Arsenals
Type: Antipersonnel directional fragmentation
Initiation: Remote or tripwire.
Reported in: Angola; Mozambique; South Africa; Zambia

The MON-50 is a copy of the U.S. M18A1 Claymore, with a lethal range of fifty meters. This mine has a plastic body with rows of imbedded fragments on the side facing the target. Two variants exist, one with steel ball bearing fragments, and the other with cylindrical chopped steel wire fragments. The height of the fragmentation pattern can be adjusted.

MON-100; MON-200
Manufacturer: Soviet State Arsenals
Type: Antipersonnel directional fragmentation
Initiation: Remote or tripwire
Reported in: Angola; Mozambique (MON-100); South Africa (MON-100); Zambia

This mine has cylindrical casing and has a face diameter of 220mm; it contains 450 pieces of steel fragmentation mounted in five kg of plastic explosive. The killing area is reported to be one hundred meters and the manufacturers boast that 50 percent of its steel fragments will strike within five meters of the mine's aiming point.

The MON-200 is a larger version of the MON-100. It consists of a metallic case, containing the explosive charge and 900 steel fragments. Like the MON-100 the cylindrical steel fragments are embedded in the plastic matrix in front of the explosive.

## Spain

PS-1
Manufacturer: Explosivos SA
Type: Fragmentation Bounding
Initiation: Pressure or tripwire
Reported in: Angola

This mine is buried in the ground with the end of the tripwire out of the ground. When the mine is activated, the internal bounding portion of the mine bounds upwards to an altitude of 1.2 meters. The internal bounding portion's main charge of cast TNT then detonates, projecting steel fragments in a 360 degree direction.

## Sweden

FFV 013
Manufacturer:
Type: Directed fragmentation
Initiation: Command detonated
Reported in: Angola

This is a large claymore-style mine. The prefragmented hardened steel plate disintegrates on detonation to form approximately 1200 fragments with a hexagonal cross section. The explosive content and fragment size create an effective target sector out to 150 meters across a four-meter-high one hundred-meter width. This weapon is intended for area denial uses such as defense against airborne/heliborne assault landings, airfield defense, ambushes, defense against vulnerable areas, or perimeter defense.

## United Kingdom

No.6
Manufacturer: Royal Ordnance, Chorley; Forpearch Ltd.
Type: Antipersonnel blast
Initiation: Pressure or tripwire
Reported in: Mozambique; Zimbabwe

At independence, the Rhodesians inherited stocks of this mine from the Southern Rhodesian colonial authorities, which also became the model for a Rhodesian imitation. The spring-loaded striker is retained by a plastic shear ring. A load acting upon the pressure prongs breaks the ring releasing the striker. The striker fires the built-in detonator which fires the charge. The mine ceased to be manufactured in the 1980s.

**United States**

M16A1 and M16A2
Manufacturer:
Type: Antipersonnel bounding fragmentation
Initiation: pressure or tripwire
Reported in: Angola; Malawi; Zambia

The M16 series employ the M605 fuse and can be initiated by 3.6-20kg direct pressure or between 1.6-3.8kg pull on a tripwire. They are bounding fragmentation mines with a cast-iron fragmentation sleeve inside a sheet steel outer casing. When the fuze functions, the cast-iron sleeve is propelled into the air by a black powder charge. At the same time, two delay charges are ignited. The delay charges ignite the main charge when the mine is approximately one meter in the air, exploding at waist or chest height and ripping apart the torso of anyone within twenty meters. The main charge expels cast-iron fragments in all directions, with an effective range of approximately thirty meters.

M18A1 Claymore
Manufacturer: Mohawk Electrical Systems, Inc.
Type: Antipersonnel directional, fixed fragmentation
Initiation: Remote or tripwire
Reported in: Angola; Malawi; Mozambique; Zambia

When exploded, usually by a pull wire or remote electric firing device, 700 steel ball bearings are projected in a 60-degree arc for more than 50 meters to a height of six feet.

M-14
Manufacturer:
Type: Antipersonnel, non-metallic, blast
Initiation: Pressure
Reported in: Angola; Malawi; Mozambique; Zambia

An extremely compact plastic pressure mine, measuring only 56mm in diameter and 40mm in height, and weighing less than one hundred grams. It requires 9-16kg of direct pressure to initiate an explosion. Metallic content is limited to the tip of the firing pin, making the mine difficult to detect using mine detectors.

**Yugoslavia**

PROM-1
Manufacturer: Federal Directorate of Supply Procurement
Type: Antipersonnel bounding fragmentation.
Initiation: Pressure
Reported in: Mozambique; Namibia; South Africa;

Pressure pushes the cylinder down, freeing the retaining balls which allows the striker to hit percussion cap. This ignites the delay element high burns for approximately 1.5 seconds and then ignites the bounding charge, which in turn ejects the mine 0.7 to 1.5 meters above the surface of the ground (as limited by a tether wire). The main charge then explodes, causing fragmentation which is lethal to a radius of fifty meters and dangerous to a radius of one hundred meters.

PMA-1
Manufacturer:
Type: Blast
Initiation:Pressure, mechanical
Reported in: Angola; Namibia; South Africa

This mine is a wooden version of a box mine with a two-piece case. The lower section is a rectangular wooden box that houses the main TNT charge and the MUV-type fuze and detonator assembly. The lid section is hinged to the lower box at one end and is designed to close over the lower box. In the armed position, the lid rests on a striker retaining pin at the end of the fuze. When pressure is applied, the lid removes the pin, beginning the initiation process. Probing for small box type mines with low pressure thresholds is a very hazardous operation.

PMA-2
Manufacturer:
Type: Blast
Initiation: Pressure
Reported in: Angola; Namibia; South Africa

This mine is small with a cylindrical body and a top-mounted UPMAH-2 chemical action pressure fuze. The surface area of the UPMAH-2 which is exposed to pressure is limited to a small pressure spider with six legs. As a result, the PMA-2 is considered hardened or blast resistant. He UPMAH-2 pressure fuze begins the firing train, which consists of a detonator, a Hexogen booster and a TNT main explosive charge. The sole metallic content in this mine and fuze is an aluminum disk (8.6mm in diameter and 0.05 mm in thickness). The small size and extremely small metallic content makes this mine hard to detect.

PMA-3
Manufacturer:
Type: Blast
Initiation: Pressure
Reported in: Namibia; South Africa

This is a small mine, which consists of a flat cylindrical body and a base-mounted UPMAH-3 chemical action pressure fuze. The PMA-3 is designed to function only when the upper pressure plate rotates with the lower assembly containing the UPMAH-3 fuze The design of a non-axial load means that the necessary pressure to function the mine decreases as the load is placed closer to the edge. The normal pressure necessary for the mine to function is described as a range of from 8.0 to 20.0 kg. However, it is possible that, when applied at the very edge, as little as three kg could activate the mine. The sole metallic content in the PMA-3 mine and fuze is the aluminum covering on the M-17 P2 detonator cap. This minimal metallic content makes the PMA-3 difficult to detect.

PMR-1
Manufacturer:
Type: Fragmentation
Initiation: Tripwire
Reported in: Namibia; South Africa

This stake mine consists of a serrated cylindrical cast-iron fragment sleeve, a seventy-five-gram TNT charge, a MUV-type fuze tripwire, and wooden stakes. The mine is normally placed in covering vegetation with the top of the mine approximately thirty cm above ground and the tripwire attached to a fixed object. More than one mine can be attached to several tripwires, or several tripwires attached to one mine.

PMR-2A
Manufacturer:
Type: Fragmentation
Initiation: Tripwire
Reported in: Namibia; South Africa

This is a stake-mounted fragmentation mine with nine rows of external serrations. The mine consists of a cast-iron fragment sleeve, a one hundred gram TNT charge, a MUV-type fuze tripwire, and wooden stakes. The mine is normally employed in covering vegetation with the top of the mine approximately thirty cm above the ground with the tripwire attached to a fixed object.

**Zimbabwe**

ZAP-1

Manufacturer: Zimbabwe Defence Industries, Harare
Type: Antipersonnel blast
Initiation: Pressure
Reported in: Botswana; Mozambique; Namibia; Zambia; Zimbabwe

The ZAP No.1 antipersonnel mine was originally known as the RAP (Rhodesian Antipersonnel Mine) No.1. Its name was changed at independence in 1980. This mine was originally designed and produced in the former Rhodesia, based on the British No.6 antipersonnel mine. These mines were also known as "carrot mines," due to their shape as well as the method of emplacement. It is unclear if new ZAP No. 1 mines have been produced by Zimbabwe or if older RAP No. 1 mines have simply been renamed.

ZAP No. 2
Manufacturer: Zimbabwe Defence Industries, Harare
Type: Antipersonnel blast
Initiation: Pressure
Reported in: Mozambique; Namibia; Zambia; Zimbabwe

These mines were originally produced in small numbers during the Rhodesian period. They appear to be modifications of Portuguese M969s. Production may have continued for a limited period after independence.

ZAPS (PloughShear)
Manufacturer: Zimbabwe Defence Industries, Harare
Type: Antipersonnel directional fragmentation
Initiation: Tripwire
Reported in: Botswana; Malawi; Mozambique; Namibia; Zimbabwe

Originally developed by the Rhodesians for border minefields (known as RAPS). This is a dish shaped directional fragmentation mine designed to be operated by tripwire. The fuzing mechanism is a standard U.K. pattern No.4 pull switch (a booby-trap switch) which is located in the middle of the dish. The Ploughshear differs from other directional fragmentation mines such as the Claymore (U.S. M18A1) in that the fragmentation portion (consisting of about 350 pieces of 6mm chopped steel bar) is on the concave rather than the convex surface, thus keeping the fragments in a fairly concentrated pattern rather than spreading them in an increasing arc. This is likely to increase the lethal range and hit probability. The stand provided with the mine is designed to allow the mine to swivel oncetension is put upon the tripwire so that it will always point along the line of the wire and thus directly at the object or person hitting the wire. The mine is approximately 250mm in diameter. The explosive filling is 150 grams of Pentolite (PETN/TNT).

Clusters of the PloughShear mine have been strung together in groups of four or more for use against rail lines in Mozambique. These mines have the capability to completely destroy rail segments and were probably taken from former Rhodesian minefields by Renamo for secondary use. The Zimbabwean government claims it ceased production of ZAPS in 1992.

Sources: U.S. Department of Defense *Mine Facts* CD-ROM Database; *Jane's Military Vehicles and Logistics: 1995-96.*